# THE FATE OF "CULTURE"

D0568694

# REPRESENTATIONS BOOKS

# The Fate of "Culture"

*Geertz and Beyond*

Edited by Sherry B. Ortner

University of California Press
BERKELEY    LOS ANGELES    LONDON

The essays in this book were originally published as a special issue of
*Representations* (summer 1997, no. 59)

University of California Press
Berkeley and Los Angeles, California

University of California Press, Ltd.
London, England

© 1999 by
The Regents of the University of California

Library of Congress Cataloging-in-Publication Data

The fate of "culture" : Geertz and beyond / edited by Sherry B.
    Ortner.
        p.   cm. — (Representations books ; 8)
    "The essays in this book were originally published as a special
issue of Representations (summer 1997, no. 59)"—T.p. verso.
    Includes bibliographical references and index.
    ISBN 0-520-21600-8 (alk. paper). — ISBN 0-520-21601-6 (pbk. :
alk. paper)
    1. Culture—Philosophy.   2. Geertz, Clifford.   I. Ortner, Sherry B.,
1941–   .   II. Representations (Berkeley, Calif.)   III. Series.
GN357.F37   1999
306′.01—dc21                                                    99-12900
                                                                        CIP

Printed in the United States of America
9  8  7  6  5  4  3  2  1

The paper used in this publication meets the minimum requirements of
American National Standard for Information Sciences—Permanence of
Paper for Printed Library Materials, ANSI Z39.48-1984.

# Contents

# Acknowledgments

This book is a slightly revised version of a special issue of the journal *Representations* (summer 1997, no. 59). I wish to thank Stephen Greenblatt and Carla Hesse, the co-chairs of the editorial board of the journal at that time, for encouraging me to put together that special issue, and Jean Day, Associate Editor of the journal, for her careful editorial work on the issue. I also wish to thank the other members of the board for their kind support during my brief sojourn at the University of California, Berkeley, and as a board member. The collective brainpower and knowledge of that group was nothing short of awesome.

As always I thank my family—my daughter, Gwen Kelly, and my husband, Tim Taylor—for all the little things, emotional and practical, of everyday life that have made this project possible.

# SHERRY B. ORTNER

## Introduction

CLIFFORD GEERTZ IS ONE OF THE FOREMOST figures in the reconfiguration of the boundary between the social sciences and the humanities for the second half of the twentieth century. Drawing on his own background in philosophy and literary studies, Geertz both revived and transformed the anthropological concept of culture in such a way as to make evident its relevance to a range of humanistic disciplines. At the same time, in insisting that human social life is a matter of meaningful activity only very imperfectly studied through the objectifying methods of (certain kinds of) science, he constructed an important alternative to the then-ascendant scientism of the social sciences, an alternative that continues to grow in influence in virtually every social science discipline to this day. As a result of all this—making visible the shared ways of thinking between anthropology and the humanities, on the one hand, and offering the social sciences a powerful alternative to the seemingly irresistible juggernaut of (a certain kind of) science on the other—Geertz's work in turn had the effect of radically repositioning the field of anthropology itself, moving it from a rather exotic and specialized corner of intellectual life to a much more central location.

At the same time, and unsurprisingly in the case of work as ambitious and important as Geertz's, his theoretical position has drawn a great deal of criticism almost from the outset. Attacked by the positivists for being too interpretive, by the critical studies scholars as being too politically and ethically neutral, and finally by the interpretivists (themselves products of the Geertzian revolution) as being too invested in a certain concept of culture, Geertz has frequently gotten it from all sides.

There were several motivations for producing this special issue of *Representations*, and for the particular form it has taken. I knew that Geertz was beginning to think about retirement from his professorship at the Institute for Advanced Study, and it seemed to me that the occasion could not be allowed to pass without some sort of celebration, something in the manner of the classic *Festschrift*. At the same time it seemed more interesting to bring together scholars whose work showed the range of impact (and transformation) of Geertz's work than to yield to the classic *Festschrift* impulse toward genealogical completeness (which often produces rather chaotic results in any event).[1] The inspiration for the particular form the project took came when I joined the editorial board of *Representations*, a journal founded by Stephen Greenblatt and colleagues who were developing the form of literary interpretation that came to be known as the New Historicism.[2] As

Greenblatt remarks in this volume, his work was influenced by Geertz's writings, not so much by the turn to "interpretation," which was after all not so radical in literary criticism, as by the ways in which Geertz's ("literary") approach to ethnography provided a way of opening up other cultural worlds that would work for a literary critic as well.

*Representations* thus seemed the perfect forum in which to reappraise Geertz's work across disciplines and across the work of a subset of anthropologists actively engaged, pro and con, with questions of "culture." The issue thus includes work by four anthropologists (myself, Lila Abu-Lughod, George E. Marcus, and Renato I. Rosaldo Jr.), as well as a literary critic (Stephen Greenblatt), a historian (Natalie Zemon Davis), and a historian-turned-sociologist-turned-political scientist (William H. Sewell Jr.).[3]

Before going on, a few words are in order about the absence from the volume of work from the interdisciplinary arena of "cultural studies." Cultural studies is notoriously difficult to define, in part because it is so broad in intellectual scope, and in part because it underwent fairly radical transformation as it crossed the Atlantic from Great Britain to the United States. My own interest would have been in the early (1970s) British form, where cultural work was embedded in both social history—for example, the work of E. P. Thompson and Raymond Williams—and a concern for social and political developments in the contemporary world—for example, Paul Willis's already classic *Learning to Labor*, or the work of Stuart Hall.[4] More recent, and mostly American, versions of cultural studies have been largely focused on media or "public culture" analysis and, despite some partially answered calls for ethnographic work on "reception," have tended to maintain a primarily textual focus. Moreover, almost none of this work sees itself as engaging with the Geertzian revolution or with cultural anthropology, which also tended to disqualify it for present purposes. At the same time, Lila Abu-Lughod, in her paper on women and television in Egypt, provides a valuable critical overview of some of this literature and, more important, offers a model of how to do work on public culture in an ethnographically deep and complex way.[5]

Cultural studies aside, however, the papers collected here present quite a powerful array of commentary on the significance of Geertz as a cultural theorist, an ethnographer, and a moral philosopher, and at the same time they construct a set of openings toward the future. In this brief introduction I will address a few of what seem to me the most significant issues as these appear in variously clustering subgroups of the papers. First, I consider how one or another of the papers speaks to two broad sets of criticism of Geertz's work: the positivist critique and the political critique. Second, I consider how they address the question posed by the title of this book: The Fate of "Culture." Although all of these are live issues, the sequence of discussion in this introduction also roughly represents the chronological sequence of criticism over the past thirty-five or so years.[6]

## Geertz as Realist and Scientist

Geertz argued that "culture" must be seen as the "webs of meaning" within which people live, meaning encoded in symbolic forms (language, artifacts, etiquette, rituals, calendars, and so on) that must be understood through acts of interpretation analogous to the work of literary critics.[7] He explicitly posed this interpretive, humanistic approach against a variety of kinds of reductionist and objectivist work that had become dominant in the 1940s and especially the 1950s in anthropology and the other social sciences. Not surprisingly, then, the first (and still continuing in many quarters) attack on Geertz came from positivists of various stripes, who viewed him as carrying anthropology into some abyss of uncontrolled subjectivism, nominalism, and constructionism.

Without reviewing these discussions here (see the essay by William Sewell in this volume for a valuable overview of these and other critiques), what is worth remarking in the present collection is the surprising degree to which Geertz comes across as committed to some form of recognizably "scientific" endeavor. Of course, "science" means many things, but here are a few examples. Against the claim that Geertz's cultural constructionism represents a repudiation of a commitment to the materiality of the world, Sewell calls attention to Geertz's careful laying out of an objective, materialist, evolutionary grounding of his entire theory of culture in the little-read paper "The Growth of Culture and the Evolution of Mind."[8] Coming from a very different direction, George Marcus argues that Geertz's commitment to a certain kind of ethnographic objectivism, despite his interpretive methods that may seem so counterscientific to some, played a major role in limiting the effect of certain insights in his work. Marcus demonstrates that Geertz had all the ingredients for making the reflexive critique that came together (and in which Marcus himself was a major player) in the 1980s but pulled back from this critique because of his commitment to the "historic anthropological project . . . in the line, for example, of Johann Gottfried von Herder, Franz Boas, Margaret Mead, and Ruth Benedict." Although Marcus, perhaps intentionally, never specifies this project, it is clear that objectivism—the externality of the anthropologist vis-à-vis the culture studied and the claims of objectivity of the ethnographic account—is central to it.

Stephen Greenblatt also addresses the issue of objectivity, discussing at length the importance of the ethnographically "real" in Geertz's work. As Greenblatt puts it, Geertz's "insistence on narrative and on textuality helps to justify the appeal to techniques of literary analysis, but it is not quite the same as an insistence that 'there is nothing outside the text.'" The fact that Geertz as ethnographer made truth claims about the real world was for Greenblatt central to the attraction of his work: "It is a tribute to Geertz that it was not his method that seemed powerful to me . . . but rather the lived life that he managed so well to narrate, describe, and clarify. That lived life, at once raw and subtle, coarse and complex, was the thing that had been progressively refined out of the most sophisticated literary studies."

Whether or not Geertz appears relatively objectivist, even scientific in a certain sense, is no doubt related to the larger intellectual context. Against the growing scientism of the fifties, Geertz, with his literary style, references, and method, looked terribly "soft." But against certain trends in contemporary intellectual life (one thinks particularly of the work of Jean Baudrillard) that have gone much further in, as Greenblatt says, refining the real out of theory, Geertz begins to appear very much committed to the reality of the world, however much he insists—correctly, of course—on its symbolic mediation.

### The Ethics and Politics
### of and in Geertz's Work

Starting in the 1970s, questions of power have become central to contemporary scholarship. Geertz seems to have stood apart from that trend. For the most part, as I discuss in my paper, one will not find issues of gender asymmetry, racial discrimination, colonial domination, ethnic violence, and so on in Geertz's work. Going further, Geertz has been accused of maintaining a relatively detached and "disengaged" stance vis-à-vis the problems of power and violence in the contemporary world.[9]

It is certainly the case that Geertz does not put issues of power and domination at the center of his interpretations and that this puts him sometimes startlingly out of phase with work based in feminist, or minority, or postcolonial theory.[10] If one looks back at the fieldnote about Cohen and the sheep that Geertz uses as the basis for his discussion of "thick description," for example, one may feel that it cries out for a more hard-edged interpretation than Geertz gives it.[11] The note describes a series of encounters between a Jewish trader named Cohen, some Berber tribesmen, and a French colonial official. Several people are killed, and in the end Cohen is unjustly jailed by the French, who also confiscate his sheep. Yet Geertz's discussion of the episode is in terms of a "confusion of tongues" and a "clash of cultures" that never significantly engages with the power differentials in play.

Yet to say that Geertz does not engage in nineties-style feminist or Foucauldian or postcolonial analysis (and in all fairness, the discussion of Cohen and the sheep was written at a much more innocent moment of anthropology more generally) is not to say either that he is "disengaged" or that his work does not contain some important implications for the politics of and in anthropology (and beyond). A few words on each point.

Concerning the issue of engagement, first, I think I myself rather casually shared the view, based perhaps on his frequently ironic style of writing, that Geertz's stance toward what he studied was relatively cool and disengaged. I was thus fascinated as the editor of this volume to see paper after paper describing Geertz as a passionate thinker and writer with a range of strong moral and ethical purposes. William Sewell makes the useful distinction between addressing "current social problems" à la Margaret Mead, which Geertz does not do, and addressing "issues of social and moral philosophy," à la Ruth Benedict, which he does do. George Marcus specifically notes the combination of playfulness and deep commitment in Geertz's writing and provides some extraordinary quotes on the wrenching disorientation of personal relationships in fieldwork from Geertz's little-read article "Thinking as a Moral Act."[12]

Renato Rosaldo makes the most extended case for understanding Geertz as a committed moral thinker. Rosaldo accepts Geertz's classic anthropological sense of real difference between cultures (an issue to which I will return) and explores the moral intensity that Geertz brings to articulating the need for, and the importance of anthropology in, the achievement of genuine cross-cultural understanding. Describing Geertz at one point as writing with "concentrated passion," Rosaldo goes on to say that "Geertz renders ethnographically and humanly vivid the force of his ethical vision about mutual engagement accountable to the depth and specific nature of human differences." It will be difficult in light of these discussions to sustain a view of Geertz as intellectually or ethically disengaged.

In addition, I would suggest that although Geertz's work does not address the kinds of issues that for the most part constitute "politics" in the present moment, it nonetheless offers the intellectual grounding for a position of considerable political importance. I refer here to the question of the cultural construction of "agency," of human intentionality and forms of empowerment to act.[13] I take such a notion to be central to any understanding of the dynamics of power, yet there has been in social theory a tendency toward a relatively thin (and often ethnocentric) sense of the cultural and historical specificity of agency in given contexts of "power" and "resistance."[14] What is important in Geertz's work, in turn, is that the makings are there for a culturally and philosophically rich theory of agency. From his insistence that culture must be understood "from the actor's point of view"; to his emphasis on the cultural construction of the needs, desires, and emotions that form the core of personhood in given times and places; to the central role he gives to understanding actors' intentions in the practice of "thick description"—each of these points make Geertz's work particularly productive for theorizing, or simply analytically deploying, "agency" in nonreductive ways.

Some of the possibilities of Geertzian theory for opening up issues of agency may be seen in Natalie Zemon Davis's paper, and in my own. In Davis's paper, we get rich, culturally informed portraits of a seventeenth-century Jewish trader and a rabbi. We see the ways in which they pursue their lives with great consciousness and self-awareness with respect to money, prestige, moral decisions, relationships with relatives and enemies, and the intertwining of all these. Davis argues that these complex ideas cannot be reduced to some simple "ethic" in some simple causal relationship to the emergence of capitalism. Rather, they must be understood as very specific, culturally grounded forms of agency (though Davis doesn't use the term) and intentionality.

My own paper concerns the relationship between Sherpas and international mountaineers on Himalayan climbing expeditions in the context of the ever-present possibility of sudden death on the mountains. The mountaineers control the terms of the expeditions, but the Sherpas mobilize a variety of cultural forms to manipulate the mountaineers and gain some measure of both real and supernatural protection. The analysis is grounded in several Geertzian interpretive strategies adapted for understanding the cultural construction of "agency," which in turn is placed in the service of reaching a more complex understanding of "power" and "resistance."

It may be suggested that the visibility of Geertz's ethical passion and the relevance of his work for a more overtly political agenda are, like his "objectivism" and commitment to some sort of recognizable scientific project, very much matters of figure and ground. In an earlier cultural and political context, the ethical significance of Geertz's (and anthropology's) commitment to cross-cultural understanding and translation was both more visible and more appreciated than it is now, a point to which I will return below.

### The Fate of "Culture"

Clifford Geertz's major contribution to anthropology, and through that to the wider reconfiguration of social theory, was centered on his retheorization of the concept of "culture." This retheorization had two very closely interlocked dimensions—an ontological one (what culture *is*) and an epistemological one (how we can know it). To define culture as a system of meanings embodied in symbols is to say not only that it is, as anthropology had long claimed, a system of world-views, values, and so forth ("meanings"), but also that one gains access to it not through some act of mystical empathy with informants, but through the (recording and) interpretation of the publicly available forms in which it is encoded (the "symbols"). One way to think about the "fate of culture" in the present moment is to consider the possibility that these two dimensions, the ontological and the epistemological, are coming apart.

As Geertz himself has recently noted, the epistemological revolution has been enormously successful: what has been called among other things "the interpretive turn" has "proved a proper revolution: sweeping, durable, turbulent, and consequential."[15] The ontological claims are suffering quite a different fate. As Geertz notes at another point in the same essay, the concept of culture, up to and including his redefinition of it, has come under enormous attack. He is worth quoting at length on this:

Questions rained down, and continue to rain down, on the very idea of a cultural scheme. Questions about the coherence of life-ways, the degree to which they form connected wholes. Questions about their homogeneity, the degree to which everyone in a tribe, a community, or even a family (to say nothing of a nation or a civilization) shares similar beliefs, practices, habits, feelings. Questions about the discreteness, the possibility of specifying where one culture . . . leaves off and the next . . . begins. Questions about continuity and change, objectivity and proof, determinism and relativism, uniqueness and generalization, description and explanation, consensus and conflict, otherness and commensurability—and about the sheer possibility of anyone, insider or outsider, grasping so vast a thing as an entire way of life and finding the words to describe it. Anthropology, or anyway the sort that studies cultures, proceeds amid charges of irrelevance, bias, illusion, and impracticability.[16]

Geertz also goes on to make clear that he stands by that idea of culture:

Everyone, everywhere and at all times, seems to live in a sense-suffused world, to be the product of what the Indonesian scholar Taufik Abdullah has nicely called a history of notion-formation. . . . one can ignore such facts, obscure them, or pronounce them forceless. But they do not thereby go away. Whatever the infirmities of the concept of "culture" ("cultures," "cultural forms" . . .) there is nothing for it but to persist in spite of them.[17]

In the present collection, both Lila Abu-Lughod and George Marcus question and depart significantly from the Geertzian or by now "classic" concept of culture. Both go after the idea of culture as "contained" in a location, and/or attached to a particular group. Marcus, arguing for radically new epistemological bases and practical forms of anthropological fieldwork, criticizes the position held by Geertz and others that "the symbolic and literal domain of fieldwork takes place inside another form of life, entailing crossing a boundary into it, exploring a cultural logic of enclosed difference." Abu-Lughod, discussing her current project on the subject of popular television in Egypt, makes much the same point: "Television is most interesting because of the way it provides material inserted into, interpreted with, and mixing up with local but themselves socially differentiated knowledges, discourses, and meaning systems. Television . . . renders more and more problematic a concept of cultures as localized communities of people suspended in shared webs of meaning."

Several different things are going on in these critiques, and more generally in anthropological self-questioning. Perhaps the most important is precisely the attempt to reconfigure the anthropological project in relation to the study of very complex social formations—nations, transnational networks, discontinuous discourses, global "flows," increasingly hybridized identities, and so forth. How can anthropology hold on to ethnographic work in the deepest sense—long term, intense, linguistically competent, whole-self, participant observation—in a world of these kinds of forms and processes? What kinds of relationship(s) can/may/should obtain between the resolute localness and face-to-faceness of ethnographic work and the vastness, complexity, and especially non- or a-localness of such formations?[18] The suggestion here is that "culture" in the traditional anthropological and upgraded Geertzian sense is simply less and less relevant to the contemporary world.

A different source of skittishness about the idea of "culture" as a deeply sedimented essence attaching to or inhering in particular groups of people emerges from a variety of issues surrounding colonialism and postcolonialism. While, as Abu-Lughod discusses, "the notion of having a culture, or being a culture, has become politically crucial to many communities previously labeled 'cultures' by anthropologists," at the same time many ethnic groups, and many contemporary postcolonial intellectuals, react very strongly against being studied as specimens of cultural difference and otherness. It is in relation to this concern, among others, that both Marcus and Abu-Lughod seek to construct projects in which informants are not understood as representatives of "other cultures" (even when, in some conventional sense, they are), and in which the anthropologist is instead, as Marcus puts it, "complicit" with his or her informants in a variety of ways.

Without denying the profound and far-reaching importance of this critique, I would suggest nonetheless that the issue is not so much one of either banishing the concept of culture, or insisting (even if one agrees with Geertz, as I do, that culture is real and will not go away) on an unreconstructed "classic" ethnographic project. Rather the issue is, once again, one of reconfiguring this enormously productive concept for a changing world, a changing relationship between politics and academic life, and a changing landscape of theoretical possibilities. Specifically, at least the following imperatives for rethinking and reconfiguring "culture" in the contemporary moment are suggested by work inside and outside this volume:

(1) To the move to reduce difference and create complicity, add the move to exoticize and objectify the culture of the ethnographer, placing it in the same analytic frame. An example in this collection would be my own piece, examining the history of encounters in Himalayan mountaineering between Western mountaineers (who appear rather "savage" in this account, insisting, for example, on slaughtering animals for meat on expeditions) and Buddhist Sherpas (not exactly nonviolent themselves, but who have a profound aversion to killing). More generally, and as Renato Rosaldo has argued elsewhere, welcome the ethnographies and histories of "borderlands," of zones of friction (or worse) between "cultures," in which the clash of power and meaning and identities is the stuff of change and transformation.[19] In other words, maintain a strong presumption of cultural difference, but make it do new kinds of work.

(2) Emphasize the issue of meaning-*making* in Geertz (and others), as against the notion of cultural "systems." The question of meaning-making is central to

questions of power and its effects. The idea that symbolic constructions of meaning are actively made by real historical actors was always visible in Geertz's work with respect to issues of political ideology.[20] Abu-Lughod's paper, in which she examines the ways in which Egyptian television programs, made by self-consciously "feminist" urban women, are received and reinterpreted by women in rural village settings, discusses several important complexities in the issue of the relatively self-conscious construction and transformation of meaning.

But there is another side to the question of meaning-making, signaled particularly by Geertz's discussions in "Religion as a Cultural System." There Geertz presents a portrait of human beings as vulnerable creatures who need "meaning," in the sense of order and purpose and reason, in order to survive, that is, in order to grapple with the threat (and sometimes the reality) of chaos and evil. One can push the implications of this point to get beyond the foregrounded discussion of religions as ready-made systems of meaning awaiting interpretation to the more backgrounded point that people are spinning what Geertz called "webs of meaning" all the time, with whatever cultural resources happen to be at hand. Thus, even if culture(s) were never as whole and consistent and static as anthropologists portrayed them in the past, and even if, as many thinkers now claim, there are fewer and fewer in the way of distinct and recognizable "cultures" in the contemporary world (though I am less sure about that), the fundamental assumption that people are always trying to make sense of their lives, always weaving fabrics of meaning, however fragile and fragmentary, still holds. The works of anthropologists who study very poor people or victims of overwhelming violence make it clear that the meaning-making process is of the most profound importance in these circumstances—without it there is rage, dissociation, madness.[21]

(3) As a general rule, situate cultural analysis within and, as it were, beneath larger analyses of social and political events and processes. Cultural analysis can no longer, for the most part, be an end in itself. The production of portraits of other cultures, no matter how well drawn, is in a sense no longer a major option, for the myriad reasons that Geertz summarizes so trenchantly in the passages quoted earlier. The point is not that there is no longer anything we would call "culture" or even "cultures," but that we want cultural interpretation to do different kinds of work. This is where the question of embedding cultural analysis within other kinds of questions and projects comes in.

This embedding is fundamental to a certain kind of cultural history, which William Sewell discusses theoretically, and which Natalie Zemon Davis and Stephen Greenblatt illustrate in practice. It is worth spending a little time on it here, as I take the historians' move(s) with culture to be paradigmatic of a more generalizable enterprise, beyond the fields of history and New Historicist literary criticism. The point is that there is always a story to be told, a story of struggle and change, a story in which actors are differentially situated with respect to power and have differential intentions. "Culture" is the means of understanding the "imaginative worlds" (as Greenblatt calls them) within which these actors operate, the forms of power and agency they are able to construct, the kinds of desires they are able to form, and so forth. The point, as noted earlier in the discussion of agency, is already implicit in Geertz's work, but it becomes explicit in the hands of the historians and New Historicist literary critics like Greenblatt: Culture is not an aesthetic object but the grounds of action and the stakes of action, with real outcomes in the real world and with powerful representations in literature, drama, and art.

The studies of cultural history may be organized in a variety of ways. We may think of them as having, in Sewell's phrase, a "synchronic moment," a space in which the cultural underpinnings of the drama are teased out, before they are put into motion. Yet this need not be the case. A cultural historian's work can be fully synchronic (as Sewell also illustrates), can appear deceptively like a static ethnography of a "culture," yet there is always a difference because historians collectively understand the narrative surrounding the text, the before-and-after that produces and is produced by the lines of force and conceptual structures in the text.

Consider the two examples of this interpretive strategy that appear in this collection. Stephen Greenblatt, first, examines two texts of ghostly apparitions in seventeenth-century England, the first from a deposition to a Yorkshire magistrate by an ordinary man who saw a ghost and fainted, the second from the first act of Shakespeare's *Hamlet*, when the King's ghost appears to Horatio and others on the battlements of Elsinore Castle. Greenblatt's main intention is to illustrate the ways in which the ethnographic-like text and the literary text may be used to illuminate one another, to bring out the shapes of the events within which—given a certain "imaginative universe"—such apparitions tended to appear, the kinds of terror and wonder they produced, the kinds of language in which people talked about them, and so forth. This then is the synchronic moment of the paper. But the cultural analysis is embedded in a larger narrative, which Greenblatt introduces at several points along the way, in this case a narrative of both official state interest in (claims of) ghostly happenings throughout the seventeenth century (which explains why such depositions were being taken down in the first place) and the "continuing, passionate debate . . . about the reality of spectral visitation" that went on in other quarters as well, and that wove in and out of larger political events. The analysis thus moves beyond its immediate contexts to open up the cultural underpinnings of intense and violent social and political conflict in that era.

Natalie Zemon Davis, similarly, addresses several seventeenth century texts: the autobiography of a Jewish woman trader and the biography of a rabbi. She too seeks to illuminate the conceptual and affective underpinnings of a particular local world, in the manner of a classic cultural interpretation. But once again the move has different effects because it is embedded within a narrative (in fact several) of power, difference, and change. Like Greenblatt, Davis appreciates the insight gained through Geertzian interpretation, the ways in which (for example) his discussion of the Moroccan *suq* (market) takes one into the richness and specificity of economic behavior in some real place and time. Like Greenblatt, too, Davis does not spell out all the narratives within which her characters and their thinking are embedded, narratives that give the cultural interpretation a larger political and historical import. Yet various parts of her discussion point precisely toward those larger narratives: the early emergence of capitalism (to be understood in a more complex—"ethnographic and comparative"—way than in the theories of Werner Sombart and Max Weber); and the precarious situation of even wealthy and successful Jews in the seventeenth century and beyond.

"The historic turn" need not, of course, be set in the past.[22] My point here is that the historians' move of embedding cultural interpretation within larger (represented or implied) narratives of social and political existence—of people both gripped by circumstances and transforming them—is another way of making culture do the kinds of work it does best: illuminating the complex motives and complex debates that are the stuff of real lives and struggles. We can see the same moves in various recent works in anthropology and other social sciences, some of which are set in the past, but others of which simply narrativize the present through a frame of struggle and conflict with outcomes that matter.[23]

What I am trying to say is that the fate of "culture" will depend on its uses. The classic ethnography (which Geertz did, along with theory, so brilliantly) no longer carries the kind of epistemological/ethical import—the opening of difference to sympathetic cross-cultural understanding—it once did. "Culture," if it is to continue to be understood as a vital part of the social process, must be located and examined in very different ways: as the clash of meanings in borderlands; as public culture that has its own textual coherence but is always locally interpreted; as fragile webs of story and meaning woven by vulnerable actors in nightmarish situations; as the grounds of agency and intentionality in ongoing social practice. All of these issues continue to assume, however, a fundamentally Geertzian view of human social life: meaning-laden, meaning-making, intense, and real.

## Notes

Deepest thanks to Tim Taylor and Bill Sewell for speedy and thoughtful readings of this introduction, including both valuable editorial comments and general positive support.

1. As Clifford Geertz explains in *After the Fact: Two Countries, Four Decades, One Anthropologist* (Cambridge, Mass., 1995), chap. 5, he spent relatively little of his career in graduate departments of anthropology. He thus did not produce a large number of students, though most of the students he did train have gone on to distinguished careers: Karen Blu, James Boon, Dale Eickelman, Paul Rabinow, Lawrence Rosen, James Siegel. There are no doubt others as well; sincere apologies to anyone inadvertently omitted.
   Sincere apologies also to Robert Darnton. Darnton should certainly be repre-

sented in this collection but, due to various compounding errors on my part, intersecting with his own impossible schedule, this turned out to be impossible. Darnton's is among the very important works in historical studies that have been influenced by Geertz and that was instrumental in launching a new genre of cultural history in the seventies and eighties; see, for example, his prizewinning *The Great Cat Massacre and Other Episodes in French Cultural History* (New York, 1984).

2. I have since moved to Columbia University and am no longer on the Board.

3. Of the group, only I was Geertz's student in a formal sense. A few personal notes may be in order here. Geertz was already legendary by the time I came to the University of Chicago Department of Anthropology in the early sixties. The dittoed manuscript version of what became one of the founding essays of Geertzian anthropology, "Religion as a Cultural System," was circulating hotly among the graduate students during my first year. Yet Geertz did not actually become my advisor until my third year at Chicago, when he agreed by mail from Morocco to take me on. We had very little face-to-face contact as advisor/advisee; he was in Morocco when I was finishing course work, then I was in the field in Nepal, then he was in Princeton deciding whether to take the offer at the Institute for Advanced Study when I came back from the field. It took me a while to realize just how deeply imprinted I was with his perspective(s), in part through his own direct influence, but even more through the impact his thinking had had on the graduate program at Chicago, and how heavily the Chicago graduate program in turn imposed itself (and still does, I think, though of course with other influences) on its students.

   He was an ideal advisor, certainly for me. He was generous (in the double sense of kind and copious) with his comments on my dissertation but never—as far as I can recall—insisted on any particular changes. He has maintained this combination, throughout my career, of being fundamentally supportive without demanding great shows of intellectual loyalty, for which I am deeply appreciative.

4. See E. P. Thompson, *The Making of the English Working Class* (London, 1963); Raymond Williams, *Marxism and Literature* (Oxford, 1977); Paul Willis, *Learning to Labor: How Working Class Kids Get Working Class Jobs* (New York, 1981); and Stuart Hall, "Cultural Studies: Two Paradigms," in Nicholas B. Dirks, Geoff Eley, and Sherry B. Ortner, eds., *Culture/Power/History: A Reader in Contemporary Social Theory* (Princeton, 1995).

5. One further absence. One of the UC Press readers noted that there is very little discussion of Geertz as an ethnographer, both in the essays and (therefore) in this introduction. This is true, and raises many interesting questions, but these must be saved for some other occasion.

6. See Sherry B. Ortner, "Theory in Anthropology Since the Sixties," *Comparative Studies in Society and History* 26, no. 1 (1984): 126–66, for an overview of anthropological theory that begins with the Geertzian revolution in the sixties.

7. His position is first laid out in various essays that began coming out in the sixties, later collected in Clifford Geertz, *The Interpretation of Cultures* (New York, 1973).

8. Clifford Geertz, "The Growth of Culture and the Evolution of Mind," in ibid.

9. Nancy Scheper-Hughes, review of *After the Fact*, by Clifford Geertz, *New York Times Book Review*, 7 May 1995.

10. It is worth noting, however, that Geertz has always seemed to me astonishingly nonsexist as a teacher and adviser. On this matter he reverses the more usual relationship between the talk and the walk.

11. Clifford Geertz, "Thick Description: Toward an Interpretive Theory of Culture," in *Interpretation of Cultures*.
12. Clifford Geertz, "Thinking as a Moral Act," *Antioch Review* 28, no. 2 (1968):139–58.
13. See Sherry B. Ortner, "Making Gender: Toward a Feminist, Minority, Postcolonial, Subaltern, etc., Theory of Practice," in *Making Gender: The Politics and Erotics of Culture* (Boston, 1996).
14. Sherry B. Ortner, "Resistance and the Problem of Ethnographic Refusal," *Comparative Studies in Society and History* 37, no. 1 (1995):173–93.
15. Geertz, *After the Fact*, 115.
16. Ibid., 43.     17. Ibid.; ellipses in original.
18. See especially George E. Marcus, "Ethnography in/of the World System: The Emergence of Multi-Sited Ethnography," *Annual Review of Anthropology* 24 (1995):95–117; Arjun Appadurai, "Global Ethnoscapes: Notes and Queries for a Transnational Anthropology," in *Recapturing Anthropology: Working in the Present*, ed. Richard G. Fox (Santa Fe, N. Mex., 1991).
19. See, e.g., Renato I. Rosaldo Jr., "Border Crossings," in his *Culture and Truth: The Remaking of Social Analysis* (Boston, 1989).
20. Clifford Geertz, "Ideology as a Cultural System," in *The Interpretation of Cultures*.
21. E.g., José Limón, *Dancing with the Devil: Society and Cultural Poetics in Mexican-American South Texas* (Madison, Wis., 1994); and E. Valentine Daniel, *Charred Lullabies: Chapters in an Anthropography of Violence* (Princeton, 1996).
22. Terrence McDonald, *The Historic Turn in the Human Sciences* (Ann Arbor, Mich., 1996); see also Dirks, Eley, and Ortner, *Culture/Power/History*.
23. Examples of such work set in the past include Marshall Sahlins, *Islands of History* (Chicago, 1985); Jean Comaroff and John Comaroff, *Ethnography and the Historical Imagination* (Boulder, Colo., 1992); Sherry B. Ortner, *High Religion: A Cultural and Political History of Sherpa Buddhism* (Princeton, 1989). Examples of works that narrativize the present include, e.g., Faye D. Ginsburg, *Contested Lives: The Abortion Debate in an American Community* (Berkeley, 1989); Jonathan Rieder, *Carnarsie: The Jews and Italians of Brooklyn Against Liberalism* (Cambridge, Mass., 1985); Stephen Gregory, *Black Corona: Race, Class, and the Politics of Place* (Princeton, 1998).

# STEPHEN GREENBLATT

## The Touch of the Real

"ANALYSIS," WRITES CLIFFORD GEERTZ in the essay "Thick Description" that opens his celebrated book, *The Interpretation of Cultures* (1973), "is sorting out the structures of signification—what Ryle called established codes, a somewhat misleading expression, for it makes the enterprise sound too much like that of the cipher clerk when it is much more like that of the literary critic—and determining their social ground and import."[1] Small wonder then that Geertz's account of the project of social science rebounded with force upon literary critics like me in the mid-1970s: it made sense of something I was already doing, returning my own professional skills to me as more important, more vital and illuminating, than I had myself grasped. I perhaps did not wholly appreciate the scientific ambition lurking in the word "determining," but I was excited to find a sophisticated, intellectually powerful, and wonderfully eloquent anthropologist who could make use of the tools in my disciplinary kit and in so doing renew in me a sense of their value.

Within the contentious discipline of anthropology, Geertz has by now been so routinely accused of one or another form of wickedness—such is the cost of academic success—that it is easy to overlook the liberating effect he had on those who came to him, as I did, from the outside and particularly from literary criticism. He did not attempt, of course, to justify the academic analysis of literature, let alone to find in it the radical politics for which I was longing, but he did something that seemed still more important. He argued that our interpretive strategies provided key means for understanding the complex symbolic systems and life patterns that anthropologists studied. The effect was like touching one wire to another: literary criticism made contact with reality. Or rather, as Geertz quickly observed, it made contact, as always, with pieces of writing. But this was writing with a difference: not poetry or fiction but verbal traces less self-consciously detached from the lives real men and women actually live.

The crucial, self-defining move in Geertz's essay on thick description comes when the anthropologist pulls away from Gilbert Ryle's distinction between a twitch and a wink (and between both of these and a parody of a wink or even the rehearsal of this parodic wink). "Like so many of the little stories Oxford philosophers like to make up for themselves," Geertz remarks, "all this winking, fake-winking, burlesque-fake-winking, rehearsed-burlesque-fake-winking, may seem a bit artificial" ("Thick Description," 7). What would be the alternative to such artificiality? How could the distinction between "thin description" and "thick description" (the one merely describing the mute act, the other giving the act its place in a network of framing intentions and cultural meanings) be linked, as Geertz puts it, to something "more empirical"? The answer is still, it turns out, a little story—that is, an anecdote—but now it is not one of the little stories Oxford philosophers make up for themselves but rather one of the little stories anthropologists record, or are supposed to record, in their notebooks during the great disciplinary rite of passage known as fieldwork. "Let me give," Geertz writes, "deliberately unpreceded by any prior explanatory comment at all, a not untypical excerpt from my own field journal" ("Thick Description," 7). There follows, set off in a different typeface, a wonderful short account of an episode of sheep-stealing, murder, and justice, a series of events that occurred in central Morocco in 1912 and were related to Geertz by one of the participants, an old man named Cohen, in 1968.

"A not untypical excerpt": Are such recorded stories typical or not of the contents of the anthropologist's field journal? Geertz's delicate double negative enables the text he quotes to have some representative force without being absorbed into a larger whole. If you understand what it means to interpret this excerpt, you will have some idea of what it means to interpret many roughly comparable excerpts, but you will not thereby possess the entire system. That is, you will not be freed of the obligation to ponder each excerpt individually and (as far as possible) on its own terms, nor will you have comprehended anything like the full range of the materials to be pondered. "Deliberately unpreceded by any prior explanatory comment at all": the excerpt is meant to surprise and to baffle, not to assume a comfortable place in a preexisting analysis of Moroccan culture. It functions then to subvert a programmatic analytical response, a fully systematized methodology, and it helps Geertz call into question, in the midst of his residual allegiance to structuralism, whether either a culture or a method could ever be rendered satisfyingly systematic. The anecdote is, as Geertz puts it, "quoted raw, a note in a bottle" ("Thick Description," 9). As such, it is meant not only to convey the idea of the "empirical" (as distinct from the philosopher's "artificial" stories) but also to arouse the bafflement, the intense curiosity and interest, that necessitates the interpretation of cultures.

Geertz repeats the image of the note in the bottle twice in the essay on thick description. The image nicely serves to emphasize something at once specific to his sheep-stealing anecdote, since it has bobbed up from 1912 and thus from a Morocco that has by now long vanished over the horizon, and more general, since all cultures that are not one's own are always located beyond one's familiar horizon. It thus underscores the promise, implicit in most ethnographic texts and explicit here, that the excerpt has not been invented by the anthropologist, that it comes from "somewhere else."[2] Moreover, the anecdote has not been carefully cooked up, like Ryle's story of winks and twitches, to exemplify an abstract point; it is not only something found, like a note in a bottle, but also, as Geertz puts it, "raw."

Yet Geertz's link to literary criticism depends upon his immediately qualifying, indeed abandoning, this notion of the "raw." For if it is important for the reader to accept Geertz's claim that he is not making up an exemplary tale but rather quoting something told him by one of his "informants," it is at least as important for the reader to grasp that the quotation is itself a story, a story that has been written down in the anthropologist's field journal. This insistence on narrative and on textuality helps to justify the appeal to techniques of literary analysis, but it is not quite the same as an insistence that "there is nothing outside the text." Or rather as soon as you collapse everything into something called textuality, you discover that it makes all the difference what kind of text you are talking about. The collapse licenses a certain kind of attention and invites the questions that literary critics characteristically ask, but at the same time it calls for a sharp attention to genre and rhetorical mode, to the text's implicit or explicit reality claims, to the implied link (or distance) between the word and whatever it is—the real, the material, the realm of practice, pain, bodily pleasure, silence, or death—to which the text gestures as that which lies beyond the written word, outside its textual mode of being.

The "raw" excerpt from the fieldnotes makes a stronger claim to reference— it points more directly to a world that has some solidity and resistance—than Ryle's invented example, but the former is no less a textual construction than the latter. The sheep-stealing anecdote has a quality of strangeness or opacity, but not because it is something mute and shapeless, dug up like a potato from an alien soil. What "we" anthropologists call "our data," Geertz writes, "are really our own constructions of other people's constructions of what they and their compatriots are up to." "This little drama" ("Thick Description," 9), as he calls the passage he quotes from his fieldnotes, is meant to show that there is rather less observation and considerably more explication—*explication de texte*—than anthropologists generally admit to.

Thick description, as Ryle uses the term in his essays on thinking, entails an account of the intentions, expectations, circumstances, settings, and purposes that give actions their meanings.[3] The distinction between a twitch and a wink is secured by the element of volition that is not itself visibly manifest in the contraction of the eyelid; a thin description would miss it altogether. So too with the other layers of framing intentions that Ryle piles on: fake twitches, rehearsals of fake twitches, and so forth. Many of these framing intentions seem to introduce an explicitly aesthetic or representational quality, but such a quality is not essential to the notion of thick description. A thin description of what you are doing when you are pumping up bicycle tires, to cite another of Ryle's examples, would be an account of a series of repetitive physical motions that produce a certain effect. A thick description of those same motions would involve a fuller sense of the significance of what you are doing. If you are pumping up your bicycle tires because you are preparing to go for a bike ride, a thick description of your pumping requires a reference to your intended ride, whether that ride actually occurs or not; if, on the other hand, you are pumping up your bicycle tires because you want to strengthen the muscles of your arms so that bullies will no longer kick sand at you at the beach, the thick description of your pumping would differ accordingly.

Ryle is fascinated by receding planes, a fascination that repeatedly draws him to the game of inventing chains of further complications around what initially seems a simple action: winking (or twitching), clearing your throat, hitting golf balls, playing tennis, cooking, jumping over flower beds. The mental game is not difficult to play: you are not actually intending to go on a bike ride (to continue in Ryle's vein) but only pretending that you are, in order to deceive an observer; or you are rehearsing for a drama in which you will play the part of someone who deceives an observer by pumping up bicycle tires as if in anticipation of a bike ride that your character never really intends to take. And so on. The difficulty lies in accounting persuasively for the relation between these surrounding circumstances and the action as thinly described. Thick description, in Ryle's account, involves two major features: *intention-parasitism* (the intention with which a person undertakes to pump up bicycle tires is ancillary to and hence parasitical upon the person's intention to take a bike ride) and *circumstance-detachment* (the actor rehearsing the part of the tire-pumper need not actually have a pump or a bike on hand—a stick and a table will do just fine for the purpose of rehearsal—but the act of rehearsing only makes sense in reference to the intended performance).

For Ryle, thick description is manifestly a quality of the explication rather than of the action or text that is explicated: it is not the object that is thick or thin, but only the description of it. A thick description thus could be exceedingly straightforward or, alternatively, exceedingly complex, depending on the length of the chain of parasitical intentions and circumstantial detachments. A thin description need not be brief or schematic; it could be quite lengthy and complicated—an adequate account of the physiology and pneumatics involved in pumping tires would take many pages—but it would not concern itself with the agent's framing intentions or the culture within which those intentions acquire their significance. Thickness is not in the object; it is in the narrative surroundings, the add-ons, the nested frames.

As Geertz's famous essay deploys the term, however, thickness begins to slide almost imperceptibly from the description to the thing described. For, though Geertz may wish to imply that his excerpt was chosen virtually at random and that one fragment would have been as good as another, some texts seem far more amenable to thick description than others, and consequently some texts seem "thicker" than others. Thickness no longer seems extrinsic to the object, a function solely of the way it is framed. The sheep-stealing narrative is supposed to be nothing more than the ethnographic equivalent of Ryle's winks and twitches, but in fact they seem profoundly different: Ryle's is a purpose-built illustration of a carefully delimited philosophical point; Geertz's supposedly "raw" excerpt from his field-notes is a complex narrative in which the motivating intentions seem intrinsic. That is, neither of Ryle's key terms, *intention-parasitism* and *circumstance-detachment*, is remotely relevant to Geertz's anecdote, precisely because the intentions and circumstances are not securely situated on the outside of the actions reported.

This slide is not a theoretical proposition, nor is it, in its divergence from Ryle, a mistake; rather, it is part of the disciplinary interest of anthropology. The shift from the philosopher's tale to the "native informant's" tale is for Geertz a shift from the "artificial" toward the "empirical," that is, toward textual constructions, presented as "raw" data or "evidence," that seem less purpose-built, more resistant to simple appropriation and hence more nearly autonomous. As the anthropologist interprets his exemplary texts, these texts seem to be increasingly embedded in the cultures from which they come and to possess within themselves more and more of the culture's linked intentions. In practice (that is, in Geertz's interpretive practice), certain constructions of cultural reality appear *compressed* and hence *expandable*: "From this simple incident," Geertz remarks about the sheep-stealing anecdote, "one can widen out into enormous complexities of social experience" ("Thick Description," 19).

Are these complexities actually inscribed in the textual fragments, or are they brought to bear upon them from the outside in the course of interpretation? Part of Geertz's power was his ability to suggest that the multilayered cultural meanings by which he was fascinated were present in the fragments themselves, just as the literary criticism of William Empson or Kenneth Burke managed to suggest that the dense ambiguities and ironies were present in the literary texts themselves and not only in the acts of interpretation.[4] Those acts of interpretation were not completely supplementary—they helped to create as well as to disclose the effect of compression—but the dense networks of meaning charted in an effective thick description had to be traceable back to the anecdote initially held up for scrutiny.

What I am calling the effect of compression enabled a literary historian like Erich Auerbach to move convincingly from a tiny passage to a sprawling, complex text (and, finally, to "Western literature"). Drawing on literary criticism—Auerbach is cited, along with Samuel Taylor Coleridge, T. S. Eliot, Burke, Empson, R. P. Blackmur and Cleanth Brooks—Geertz did something similar with cultural fragments, small bits of symbolic behavior from which he could "widen out" into larger social worlds.[5] The techniques of literary analysis thus helped to make possible for Geertzian anthropology something akin to what in optics is called "foveation," the ability to keep an object (here a tiny, textualized piece of social behavior) within the high-resolution area of perception. Foveation in cultural interpretation is rather difficult because of problems of both scale and focus. The interpreter must be able to select or to fashion, out of the confused continuum of social existence, units of social action small enough to hold within the fairly narrow boundaries of full analytical attention, and this attention must be unusually intense, nuanced, and sustained.

Geertz grasped that, along with analytic philosophy, literary criticism had for years been honing useful foveation skills. Hence the terms that he uses to describe his piece of thick description not only emphasize its own textuality (in keeping with his insistence that ethnographers are writers) but also repeatedly extend that textuality to the object described: "our sheep story—an assortment of remarks and anecdotes," "a not untypical excerpt from my own field journal," "a note in a bottle," a "passage," "this little drama," "our text," a "social farce," "our pastoral drama," "the rigmarole," a "social discourse," and—moving away from the excerpt and toward what the excerpt is meant to exemplify—"a manuscript—foreign, faded, full of ellipses, incoherencies, suspicious emendations, and tendentious commentaries, but written not in conventionalized graphs of sound but in transient examples of shaped behavior" ("Thick Description," 10). That is, culture is itself an "acted document," whether it takes the form of "a burlesqued wink or a mock sheep raid" (10). The point is that to understand what people are up to in any culture—and, "leaving our winks and sheep behind for the moment," Geertz takes a Beethoven quartet as his example—you need to be acquainted "with the imaginative universe within which their acts are signs" (11).

For the purposes of literary criticism, *imaginative, drama, manuscript,* and *signs* were reassuringly familiar terms, as was the whole emphasis on symbolic behavior, but the specific force of Geertz's work for New Historicism resided in the expansion of these terms to a much broader and less familiar range of texts than literary critics had permitted themselves to analyze. For Geertz this expansion reflected an empowering appropriation of analytical tools, an appropriation that conferred the prestige accorded to the supreme achievements of Western high culture, such as Beethoven quartets, on the flotsam and jetsam in an anthropologist's fieldnotes. At issue was not only prestige—what Pierre Bourdieu famously analyzed as cultural capital—but a transference of the kind of attention paid to canonical works of art to the ordinary and extraordinary behavior of the subjects of anthropology. To construct descriptions, Geertz notes, "of the involvements of a Berber chieftain, a Jewish merchant, and a French soldier with one another in 1912 Morocco is clearly an imaginative act, not all that different from constructing similar descriptions of, say, the involvements with one another of a provincial French doctor, his silly, adulterous wife, and her feckless lover in nineteenth century France" (15–16). If it is not altogether clear at this moment in Geertz's essay whether it is the anthropologist himself or the anthropologist's informant Cohen who is being likened to Gustave Flaubert, this is because both the informant's discourse and the anthropologist's discourse about that discourse (and, for that matter, the series of actions from 1912) are alike fictions, in the root sense of things *made, composed, fashioned.*

My goal in response to Geertz was not exactly to reverse the disciplinary appropriation, that is, to apply to literary analysis the terms and concepts developed by anthropologists. (Such an application, of course, was in fact occurring, especially in literary structuralism's use of Claude Lévi-Strauss.) What I wanted was not social science but ethnographic realism, and I wanted it principally for literary purposes. That is, I had no interest in decisively leaving works of literature behind and turning my attention elsewhere; instead, I sought to put literature and literary criticism in touch with that elsewhere. It is a tribute to Geertz that it was not his method that seemed powerful to me (after all, that method was in part borrowed from literary criticism) but rather the lived life that he managed so well to narrate, describe, and clarify. That lived life, at once raw and subtle, coarse and complex, was the thing that had been progressively refined out of the most sophisticated literary studies, or so it seemed to me at the time. By embracing and displacing literary studies, *The Interpretation of Cultures* provided an impetus for recovering what had been lost. Literary criticism could venture out to unfamiliar cultural texts, and these texts—often marginal, odd, fragmentary, unexpected, and crude—in turn could begin to interact in interesting ways with the intimately familiar works of the literary canon.

To Auerbach's powerful ability to conjure up complex lifeworlds from tiny fragments, Geertz added the anthropologist's strong claim to a hold on the world. That is, it was crucial, as part of the pleasure and interest of reading Geertz, to believe that he had not made up his Mr. Cohen and that Cohen too had not simply made up his story. To be sure, Geertz encourages the reader to grasp that his informant's version of the story is not identical to one that would have been produced by any of the other principals in it and that he may have considerably enhanced the story for rhetorical effect, but Cohen was a real person recounting actual experiences, and his story was *his* story and not the ethnographer's.

"I can call spirits from the vasty deep," claims Owain Glyndŵr, the strange Welsh magus in Shakespeare's *1 Henry IV.* "Why, so can I, or so can any man," is Hotspur's sardonic reply, "But will they come when you do call for them?"[6] So too an anecdote may conjure up reality, but will reality come when it is called? If it is only a matter of rhetoric—the effect of what the ancient rhetoricians called *enargeia*, or vividness—then only a reality-effect is conjured and nothing more. But something more is at stake. Geertz gestures toward that something when he acknowledges that there are important problems of verification or, as he prefers to term it, appraisal. This process of appraisal is largely internal to a particular discipline—I obviously had no way of testing Geertz's interpretation of Moroccan culture nor could I confirm the authenticity of his fieldnotes—but it is in principle significant for the value anthropology could have for literary studies. For the interest was never to collapse anthropology and literary criticism into each other but to draw upon their particular strengths, strengths that depended at least as much upon the differences between their characteristic texts as upon their surprising similarities. Indeed it is an awareness of how those differences are constituted and what they mean—an understanding of the emergence of the literary and the imaginative force of the nonliterary—that has virtually obsessed not only my own work but that of New Historicism in general.

What then should we make of Geertz's claim that an anecdote from the field journal is "not all that different," as an imaginative construction, from *Madame*

*Bovary*? Very little beyond the critical incentive, or rather the imperative, to interpret. To be sure, if it turned out that Geertz's Cohen had taken it upon himself to be the Flaubert of the Maghreb and had made up his entire story, we might still have concluded that we possessed something of ethnographic value: a glimpse of the fantasies of an old man who had been steeped in the symbolic systems of colonial Morocco.[7] If, however, it turned out that Geertz had made up Cohen, I at least would have concluded that as an ethnographer Geertz was not to be trusted, and his work would have immediately lost much of its value. For it is precisely not as a fiction or as a little philosopher's tale that Geertz invites us to read his anecdote; it is as a "raw" sample of his fieldnotes. The frame is really crucial, since in this case it helps us to conjure up a "real" as opposed to "imaginary" world.

Geertz's conjuring of the real seemed to me useful for literary studies not because it insisted upon the primacy of interpretation—that was already the norm in literary criticism—but because it helped to widen the range of imaginative constructions to be interpreted. His thick descriptions of cultural texts strengthened the insistence that the things that draw us to literature are often found in the nonliterary, that the concept of literariness is deeply unstable, that the boundaries between different types of narratives are subject to interrogation and revision. I wanted to argue that human creativity, including narrative and linguistic creativity, only makes sense in the long run because it is a widespread, indeed democratic possession, a possession that is almost impossible to contain within a small elite or sequester from the sweet, familiar light of the everyday. I wanted too to use the anecdote to show in compressed form the ways in which elements of lived experience enter into literature, the ways in which everyday institutions and bodies get recorded. And I wanted, conversely, to show in compressed form the ways in which poetry, drama, and prose fiction play themselves out in the everyday world, since men and women repeatedly find themselves in effect speaking the language of the literary not only in their public performances but also in their most intimate or passionate moments.

I sought something beyond this: I wanted to find in the past real bodies and living voices, and if I knew that I could not find these—the bodies having long moldered away and the voices fallen silent—I could at least seize upon those traces that seemed to be close to actual experience. Literature seemed to me, as to many others, almost infinitely precious because its creators had invented techniques for representing this experience with uncanny vividness, but there were other techniques and other texts, outside the conventional boundaries of the literary, that possessed a nearly comparable power. The greatest challenge lay not simply in exploring these other texts—an agreeably imperial expansion of literary criticism beyond its borders—but in making the literary and the nonliterary seem to be each other's thick description. That both the literary work and the anthropological (or historical) anecdote are texts, that both are fictions in the sense of things made, that both are shaped by the imagination and by the available resources of narration and description helped make it possible to conjoin them, but their ineradicable differences—the fact that neither is purpose-built for the other, that they make sharply different claims upon the actual, that they are incommensurable and virtually impossible to foveate simultaneously—made the conjunction powerful and compelling.

I wanted to recover in my literary criticism a confident conviction of reality, without giving up the power of literature to sidestep or evade the quotidian and without giving up a minimally sophisticated understanding that any text depends upon the absence of the bodies and voices that it represents. I wanted the touch of the real in the way that in an earlier period people wanted the touch of the transcendent.

Let me give a tiny example, my equivalent of the note in the bottle. It comes from a collection of depositions from the Castle of York and is dated 26 June 1668:

John Bowman, of Greenhill, co. Darby, taylor, saith, that upon the Tuesday before Assention Day last, hee was comeing home from Sheffield market on the footway towards Highley; and about the mid-way there was one John Brumhead overtooke him, and they past along until they came against the cutlers bridge. And when they came at the said bridge they had some discourse concerneing an apparition that had beene seene theere, as it was reported, in the shape and corporall forme of a man that they called Earle George. And as they were speakeinge of itt, of a sudden there visibly appeared unto them a man lyke unto a prince with a greene doublet and ruff, and holdinge a brachete in his hande. Whereupon this examinate was sorelye affrighted and fell into a swound or trannce, and contynued in the same, as hee conceiveth, for the space of aboue halfe an houre. And when he awakend he saw a man passinge with two loadend horses, and he went with him towardes Highley.[8]

The interest of this tiny fragment lies in part in the brief but agreeably circumstantial glimpse of the utterly obscure tailor whose ordinary course of life is so violently disrupted by an uncanny visitation. A walk home on a familiar footpath, a conversation with an acquaintance, the arrival at Cutler's Bridge—a whole fabric of the everyday—is suddenly torn apart by the apparition, an apparition that fills poor John Bowman with an anxiety so intense that he loses consciousness. Evidently, the specter did not appear to him alone—he believes, in any case, that John Brumhead witnessed it as well, since the report states that it "visibly appeared unto *them*"— but his companion, who was not deposed by the court, seems not to have waited around during the half-hour that Bowman was unconscious. For the shattered tailor, the human makes its reflux upon the fiendish, to use Thomas De Quincey's phrase, in the form of the "man passing with two loadend horses," in whose company Bowman continues (now presumably on the main road rather than the footpath) toward Highley.

To provide a satisfyingly thick description of this anecdote, of course, we would have to know something more about Bowman and Brumhead, not to mention "Earl George," dressed in his green doublet and ruff and holding a "brachete"—

a hound, presumably for the hunt—in his hand.[9] But even without such knowledge, we could readily extend our understanding beyond an appreciation of simple circumstantiality by reflecting on the power of suggestion to which the narrative inadvertently bears witness. Losing consciousness in terror is an extreme experience of radical isolation, but the ghost's actual appearance occurs, in effect, in a social space, and it materializes, if that is the right word, out of a particular kind of social experience. Two men, heading in the same direction, have encountered each other on a path and entered into conversation. In the course of the conversation, they reach an identifiable and named place where they begin to speak of the specter, and, behold, the specter suddenly appears, at once interrupting and continuing their conversation. That conversation in turn is folded into an official narrative, the record of a public inquiry in which time and place and the identity of the speaker are all duly noted.

The interpretive question, for us as for the Yorkshire magistrate, is how much pressure to apply to any of the details. Does it matter that the specter appears at a bridge? Is there any significance to the proximity of this appearance to Ascension Day, that is, the day on which, forty days after the Resurrection, Jesus, in "the shape and corporall forme of a man" (to borrow the deposition's phrase), was said to have ascended to heaven? What kind of uneasiness, what official or unofficial reservation is being registered in the cautious words used to identify the ghost—"that they called Earle George"—or in the phrase "the shape and corporall forme of a man"? What was the Yorkshire Assize looking for or worried about that they bothered to take some half-crazed tailor's deposition?

It may be that by searching the Yorkshire records we could find at least a few answers to these questions and thereby thicken the description, as we could further do by looking carefully at a series of other textual traces of ghostly apparitions from approximately the same period: *Horrid and Strange News from Ireland* (1643), *News from Puddle-Dock* (1674), *The Rest-less Ghost* (1675), *The Deemon of Marleborough* (1675), *Strange and Wonderful News from Lincolnshire* (1679), *A Strange and Wonderfull Discovery of a Horrid and Cruell Murther* (1662), *A Narrative of the Demon of Spraiton* (1683), and so forth.[10] One line of inquiry would lead us to the politics of haunting, and in particular to the ways in which ghosts can appear to disclose or protest against crimes committed by those in high places. Hence, for example, in the immediate wake of the restoration of the monarchy, a pamphlet appeared giving an account of a poltergeist that haunted the Parliamentary commissioners who had come in 1649 to compile an inventory of the king's possessions in his manor house at Woodstock. If anyone should ask, the anonymous author writes, why the account was not printed closer to the time of the alleged events, the answer lies in the pressures of "the tyrannical times of that detestable usurper Oliver Cromwel . . . who had raked up such Judges, as would wrest the most innocent language into high Treason."[11] Another line of inquiry would lead to the continuing, passionate debate in the seventeenth century about the reality of spectral visitation, a debate that reached something of a climax in Joseph Glanvill's *Saducismus Triumphatus* (1681). But for my purposes, the crucial text to be invoked, both to intensify the impact of Bowman's deposition and reciprocally to be intensified by it, comes from an earlier time, more precisely from 1600 to 1601.

"What, has this thing appeared again tonight?" (*Hamlet*, 1.1.19), asks Marcellus on the battlements of Elsinore. Horatio, accompanying the watch, has scoffed at the reports and has attributed the sightings to mere fantasy. In response, the soldiers declare that they will reiterate their account: "Sit down a while," says Barnardo,

> And let us once again assail your ears,
> That are fortified against our story,
> What we two nights have seen. (1.1.28–31)

The narrative begins with the flourish of circumstantiality that we saw in the Yorkshire document:

> Last night of all,
> When yon same star that's westward from the pole
> Had made his course t'illume that part of heaven
> Where now it burns, Marcellus and myself,
> The bell then beating one—(1.1.33–37)

only to break off with the sudden appearance of the Ghost "in the same figure like the King that's dead" (1.1.39). No one faints at this apparition, as the unfortunate tailor did under comparable circumstances, though we are told that the soldiers had been "distilled / Almost to jelly with the act of fear" (1.2.204–5) by an earlier haunting, and Horatio evidently comes close to losing consciousness: "How now, Horatio?" asks the vindicated Barnardo, "You tremble and look pale" (1.1.51). There follows an anxious inventory of the Ghost's dress and a still more anxious series of speculations as to "some strange eruption to our state" (1.1.69) that the spectral visitation may portend.

Bowman's deposition alerts us to the odd blend of anticipation and astonishment that marks the Ghost's appearance in *Hamlet*, the way in which the specter at once fulfills and radically disrupts the conversation. It alerts us to the charged nature of certain places (the bridge, the battlements), to the intense attention paid by the witnesses to the Ghost's costume (the green doublet and ruff, the armor "cap-à-pie"), and to the peculiar way in which terror is oddly conjoined to repetition, that is, to the uncanny predictability and reiterability of the visitation. And it alerts us too to the element of testifying, the quasi-legal tone, of the exchanges between Horatio and the soldiers in the wake of the apparition. Asked upon the Ghost's departure to account for the intensive arms manufacturing in Denmark, Horatio explains that old Fortinbras of Norway

> by a sealed compact
> Well ratified by law and heraldry
> Did forfeit, with his life all those his lands
> Which he stood seized on to the conqueror;
> Against the which a moiety competent
> Was gagèd by our King, which had returned
> To the inheritance of Fortinbras,
> Had he been vanquisher, as by the same cov'nant
> And carriage of the article designed
> His fell to Hamlet. (1.1.85–95)

Shaken by the eruption of the inexplicable, the small community constituted by the group on the battlements attempt to stabilize themselves by means of a long historical and legal discourse (some forty lines in the folio text and longer still in the second quarto), only to have that discourse itself interrupted by the Ghost's second appearance. At this point, Horatio, directly questioning the Ghost, advances a series of possible reasons that may have caused it to return to earth, but this attempted interrogation is met only with silence.

Bowman's deposition is hardly the key to unlock *Hamlet*'s mysteries. Indeed its invocation here comes perilously close to confirming the charge of "arbitrary connectedness"—in effect, an irresponsible hermeneutical surrealism—sometimes leveled at New Historicism. Recorded in a different city almost seventy years after Shakespeare's tragedy and concerning people unlikely to have had any encounter with the professional theater or knowledge of Shakespeare's existence, it is an utterly marginal document, too fragmentary and odd to be adduced as a piece of solid evidence for anything. The most gossamer touch of the real, its only virtue in the present context is its very marginality, its stretching to the limit the possibility of a meaningful link, its distance from the kind of historical document more conventionally adduced to illuminate a work of art. Such a document usually precedes the work in question or is closely contemporary with it; it often comes from the same geographical and social setting; and, most satisfying of all, it may offer a direct philological link. Thus the relationship between Samuel Harsnett's *Declaration of Egregious Popish Impostures* (1603) and *King Lear* (1605) is attested to in a mass of *Lear*'s verbal borrowings and echoes ("Modu," "Mabu," "Flibbertigibbet," and so forth); the link between Reginald Scot's *Discovery of Witchcraft* (1584) and *Macbeth* (1606) is established, among other means, by Shakespeare's appropriation of the strange phrase "auger hole"; the connection between William Strachey's privately circulated report on the "Wrack and Redemption of Sir Thomas Gates" (1610) and *The Tempest* (1611) is secured by the precise depiction of the tremendous sea storm, by Ariel's reference to "the still-vexed Bermudas," and by many other details. The interpretive tact here involves deciding how far the relationship extends beyond tiny formal features and allowing the contextual documents to have their own imaginative life and argumentative power. Far from constituting a defect, the secure conventionality of such conjunctions is part of their extraordinary appeal: the three instances I have just cited have served, as it happens, as the objects of my most sustained and passionate attention.

But traditional source texts are not the only documents for the literary historian's attention. Geertz's work in the 1970s began to open up ways in which it would be possible to pay attention to odd fragments such as Bowman's, to understand them as symbolic actions and to consider what light they might cast upon the imaginative universe in which they were recorded. The tailor's walk home from the market, the conversation at the bridge, the apparition of Earl George, the fainting fit, and the subsequent legal interrogation that left its tiny textual trace in the records kept in Yorkshire Castle are cultural signs that can, Geertz urges us, be interpreted with some of the same tact and skills with which one would interpret a literary text. I have quoted the trace "raw, a note in a bottle" because that is how I encountered it, but also because it serves to convey the crude shock of the real and at the same time to insist that what seems raw is in fact a narrative, a narrative in all probability crafted collaboratively by Bowman and the officials to whom he gave his testimony.

As I have already sketched, there are several reasons why even so minor a narrative as Bowman's might serve to alert us to important features of so major a text as *Hamlet*, but I cannot pretend that those features could only be made visible by a ramble through the Yorkshire archives. So why bother at all? In part the answer lies in Geertz's observation that the "famous anthropological absorption in the (to us) exotic" is "essentially a device for displacing the dulling sense of familiarity with which the mysteriousness of our own ability to relate perceptively to one another is concealed from us" ("Thick Description," 14). Anthropology is, in this account, a sustained practice of "estrangement," as literature itself was said to be by the Russian formalists. The twist is that celebrated works of literature— and *Hamlet* is probably the supreme example—by virtue of their fame run the risk of losing their ability at once to seem strange and to estrange. A tiny anecdote such as Bowman's deposition can, to use Geertz's cautious phrase, displace the familiarity of the canon and thus return to art one of its principal powers.

Moreover, it is striking that several generations and a political revolution after *Hamlet* was first performed, we find in the actual life-experience of Bowman and a number of other seventeenth-century men and women weird encounters oddly similar to those staged. Does it make a difference that in *Hamlet* we are not dealing only with a literary convention, something received from Seneca or from Thomas Kyd? Yes, to me it makes a huge difference. The difference in this case obviously has nothing to do with the positing of an extra-literary "source" for the theatrical text, the attempt to ground a literary fantasy in a preexisting reality. I have deliberately chosen a document from a period later than *Hamlet* to emphasize the fact that the real, as we perceive and respond to it, is not securely prior to language, nor is it the stable, prosaic, solid foundation upon which the imagination builds its airy castles. Bowman's encounter with the ghost of Earl George is one sign among many of the imaginative universe that enabled Shakespeare's play to be conceived, written, and performed successfully, one index of the purchase that the drama could claim upon human experience, one piece of an embodied reality that at once pressed in upon and was shaped by staged performance.

The point is not that Bowman's ghost is the "thing itself" as opposed to *Hamlet*'s merely represented ghost. Shakespeare's tragedy powerfully calls into question the whole distinction between representation and reality: Hamlet struggles to verify the authenticity of the Ghost, which has appeared in the form or semblance of his father, by staging a play and then carefully observing the play's physiological effects upon the royal spectator. Moreover, for centuries now, *Hamlet* has had an unprecedented, unrivaled cultural impact, so that it has itself been able to lay claim to reality and to shape the perception of the world that lies about it. Hence, after all, my own interest in Bowman's deposition is thoroughly conditioned by Shakespeare's play, as is the very desire for the "real" that drove me outside the boundaries of the play. And, of course, what I find outside those boundaries are more narratives, other texts. For Geertz's work would remind us, if we needed a reminder, that the Yorkshire deposition is a representation, a reconstruction of a terrifying experience, and, as we have earlier observed, this terrifying experience was already caught up in discursive representation. It is no accident that the Ghost made his appearance precisely at the moment that the two men were talking over the story of his appearance. For though the appearance of a ghost may be as sudden and involuntary as a twitch, we are never in fact very far from winks, fake winks, burlesque-fake-winks, and so forth. The state was interested in ghost stories— interested enough to take down depositions throughout the seventeenth century and into the eighteenth—not only credulously but also skeptically: ghostly apparitions, like other forms of spirit-possession and bewitchment, were fertile grounds for imposture, chicanery, and fraudulent performance, possibly with heretical or seditious intent.

Throughout the sixteenth and seventeenth centuries, there were repeated debates about the reality of ghosts, debates that we of course know principally from printed sources but that must have occurred all the time in casual conversation.[12] "Upon a relation of Dr. Lambes execution," Thomas Crosfield noted in his diary on 17 December 1627, "the question disputed whether spirits really and substantially appeare, i.e. the ghosts of the deceased."[13] The debate centered sharply on the doctrinal differences between Catholics, for whom souls in Purgatory could take on human shape and return to the earth, and Protestants, for whom in principle at least there could be only demons masquerading as ghosts. Hence, for example, in the late 1570s, the vicar of Lostwithiel in Cornwall was suspected of being a Catholic because at dinner he had "maintained the apparition of souls after their departure out of this life, and for proof affirmed that Sir Walter Mildmay was desirous to see Cardinal Pole after his death, and one by conjuration caused the said Cardinal to appear unto Sir Walter. Then the conjurer asked of Sir Walter Mildmay what he did see, and Sir Walter answered him 'a man much like the cardinal.' "[14] But skepticism, an awareness of theatrical imposture, a sense of the manipulation of appearances were by no means exclusively Protestant.

Here once again Geertz's essay on thick description can be of use, for the thickness in his sheep-stealing anecdote seems to depend upon a high degree of social conflict, and social conflict, he writes, "is not something that happens when, out of weakness, indefiniteness, obsolescence, or neglect, cultural forms cease to operate, but rather something which happens when, like burlesqued winks, such forms are pressed by unusual situations or unusual intentions to operate in unusual ways" ("Thick Description," 28). Bowman's deposition and the many anecdotes like it are reminders that ghostly apparitions were not obsolescent or merely "literary" in Shakespeare's time and in the generations that followed; they were mercifully rare experiences, but they continued to occur in the real lives of men and women and to arouse the interest of the state and the church. That interest was in part at least the consequence of a prolonged and often murderous conflict about the nature of spiritual experience, a conflict that in turn pressed certain cultural forms, such as ghosts, to operate in highly unusual ways. And from here we can return, with a heightened sense both of the real and of the imaginary, to *Hamlet*.

# Notes

1. Clifford Geertz, "Thick Description: Toward an Interpretive Theory of Culture," in *The Interpretation of Cultures* (New York, 1973), 9.
2. The promise is conveyed, among other means, by such features as the changed typeface (used, in the case of such a long excerpt, instead of quotation marks) and the brackets that denote the writer's scrupulousness in signaling any additions or alterations to what he had originally written in his journal: "The French [the informant said] had only just arrived." Such printing conventions do a considerable amount of work in establishing the particular nature of the piece of writing.
3. Gilbert Ryle, "Thinking and Reflecting" and "The Thinking of Thoughts: What is 'Le Penseur' Doing?" in *Collected Papers*, vol. 2, *Collected Essays, 1929–1968* (London, 1971), 465–96.
4. For a critique, from the standpoint of social science, of Geertz's way of suggesting the vital presence in the cultural texts themselves of their range of meanings, see Mark A. Schneider, *Culture and Enchantment* (Chicago, 1993), 55–82.
5. Clifford Geertz, "Ideology as a Cultural System," in *Interpretation of Cultures*, 208.
6. *1 Henry IV*, 3.1.51–53. All citations to Shakespeare are from *The Norton Shakespeare*, ed. Stephen Greenblatt et al. (New York, 1997).
7. It is not the case that Gustave Flaubert's novel lacks ethnographic interest, but the level of self-conscious mediation is completely different from what we hope to find in a native informant's narrative.

8. *Depositions from the Castle of York*, Surtees Society, vol. 40 (Durham, Eng., 1861), 161–62.

9. The editor of the Yorkshire assize papers notes that the ghost must be Earl George of Shrewsbury who died in 1590: "He was a distinguished and prudent statesman and a person of the highest rank and consequence" (161). But why his consequence should extend to spectral visitations, almost eighty years later, is not clear.

10. We could also look at a much longer history of apparitions in Yorkshire, which appears to have been particularly haunted by ghosts throughout the Middle Ages. See the numerous sightings discussed in Jean-Claude Schmitt, *Les revenants. Les vivants et les morts dans la société médiévale* (Paris, 1994).

11. *The Just Devil of Woodstock. Or, A True Narrative of the Several Apparitions, the Frights and Punishments, inflicted upon the Rumpish Commissioners* (London, dated 1649 but published in 1660), A2r.

12. We can establish convenient (and more or less arbitrary) starting and ending points. At one end, we can cite Erasmus's *Colloquy* called "Exorcism, or The Specter" (1524), in which a superstitious parish priest is made the object of a sly theatrical imposture. At the other end, we can take the 19 May 1694 diary entry of the Yorkshire antiquary Abraham de la Pryme, in which he relates the story of a ghost that supposedly haunted a house in Cambridge and frightened hundreds of people, including one of the local ministers, who gathered around the house and crowded in at the door. The diarist provides a fascinating glimpse of Isaac Newton: "On Monday night likewise there being a great number of people at the door, there chanced to come by Mr. Newton, fellow of Trinity College: a very learned man, and perceiving our fellows to have gone in, and seeing several scholars about the door, 'Oh! yee fools,' says he, 'will you never have any witt, know yee not that all such things are meer cheats and impostures? Fy, fy! go home, for shame,' and so he left them, scorning to go in"; *The Diary of Abraham de la Pryme* (London, 1870), 42.

13. *The Diary of Thomas Crosfield* (1602–63), ed. Frederick S. Boas (London, 1935), 17. The slightly odd locution "visibly appeared" in the Bowman deposition is a variation, it seems, on this question of whether spirits are "really and substantially" present.

14. Quoted in A. L. Rowse, *Tudor Cornwall: Portrait of a Society* (London, 1943), 335.

# RENATO I. ROSALDO JR.

# A Note on Geertz
# as a Cultural Essayist

Rᴇᴀᴅᴇʀs ᴏғ ᴄʟɪғғᴏʀᴅ ɢᴇᴇʀᴛᴢ's ᴇssᴀʏs fall roughly into two camps, those who find them lucid and those who find them opaque. Because his essays repay a close reading, I often peruse them slowly and attentively. They make such good sense to me that I find myself puzzled that anyone should puzzle over them. No doubt this is a case of overlapping versus disjunctive disciplinary frameworks where, on the model of different cultures, one could argue that what appears to be a matter of one world's lucid common sense becomes the opaque exotic Other from the perspective of another discipline. What follows is an attempt to reduce the puzzlement for readers of good faith who have grappled with Geertz's essays (intolerant positivist polemicists are another matter for another occasion).

For Clifford Geertz, the essay has been the vehicle of choice for conveying his sense of method and craft in ethnographic understanding. "For making detours and side roads," as he put it, "nothing is more convenient than the essay form."[1] My brief sketch explores three characteristics of Geertz's essays as a means of elucidating what they are most centrally about. The characteristics of the essays (let us call them telling "detours and side roads") I should like to consider are the local (or "native") points of view, the uses of context in elucidating local knowledge, and the purposes of comparison.

## The Local Point of View

For Geertz, the study of culture begins with the understanding of how people understand themselves. If ethnographers study the stories people tell themselves about themselves, their job is to look over people's shoulders as they tell these stories and record them accurately. The idea is to get it right and not to misquote and, beyond that, to aspire to get to the heart of the matter, to distinguish the important from the trivial issues. The task of cultural understanding, as Geertz often insists, involves observing what occurs between people in the intersubjective realm. These exchanges take place in the clear light of public interactions; they do not entail the mysteries of empathy or require extraordinary capacities for going inside people's heads or, worse, their souls.

Collectively formed self-understandings articulated in local vernacular terms (what Geertz, borrowing from Heinz Kohut, calls "experience-near") cannot be left out of an ethnography, but they must be supplemented by, among other things, analogies ("experience-distant") introduced by the ethnographer.[2] One thinks, as Geertz says, of falling in love as experience-near and object cathexis as experience-distant. In "Blurred Genres: The Refiguration of Social Thought," Geertz explores the analytical analogies of gaming, staging, and reading.[3] In relation to gaming, he discusses Erving Goffman; to theater, a synthesis of Victor Turner and Kenneth Burke; to reading, Paul Ricoeur, Alton Becker, and himself. Such analogies can prove useful as vehicles for describing social worlds or as accounts of one's mode of social analysis or both together. In a manner surprising for a writer of such wit and crafted poetic diction, Geertz is too often read flatly and literally. As with any analogy, he does not imagine the world literally to be a text; this is not a question of realism or how the world, in essence, really is. The questions instead are: What does the textual analogy bring into view that other analogies do not? What other questions does it lead to (as another idiom has it, a productive hypothesis is one that generates further productive hypotheses)? What topics does it bring into focus that otherwise would remain blurred?

The notion of self-understanding as an ethical project calls for the universal human perception that each person or group is an other among others. That is, nobody has a monopoly on truth. All knowledge is local, no matter what its pretensions. *Esprit humaine* thus becomes a local product that requires ethnographic explication in its Parisian contexts, rather than an accurate portrayal of the universal human spirit. In this sense we are all condemned to parochialism, ethnocentrism, and presentism unless we find a means to broaden our visions by learning about other local knowledges. Geertz puts the matter vividly:

To see ourselves as others see us can be eye-opening. To see others as sharing a nature with ourselves is the merest decency. But it is from the far more difficult achievement of seeing ourselves amongst others, as a local example of the forms human life has locally taken, a case among cases, a world among worlds, that the largeness of mind, without which objectivity is self-congratulation and tolerance a sham, comes.[4]

Only the cultural polyglot who studiously apprehends other local knowledges in the mutual give-and-take of engaged conversation can hope to inhabit a world broader than her or his parish of birth.

### Contexts

To provide a "telling" interpretation the ethnographer must find appropriate contexts for elucidating the phenomenon under study. The idea is that in their local contexts matters can be made intelligible, even when they at first glance appear outlandish, exotic, or simply opaque to people encountering them in other times and places. In "Art as a Cultural System," for example, Geertz invokes Michael Baxandall's studies of quattrocento Italian art, where the relevant contexts for interpretation, drawn from the fifteenth-century form of life, include relations between pictorial images and religious ideas, social dancing, and gauging (the practical commercial skill of accurately estimating amounts and volumes when containers and measuring devices are idiosyncratic and wildly various).[5] The appropriate interpretive contexts are not universal for all times and places; they are not limited to an autonomous sphere, say, that of the aesthetic; rather, they permeate the general experience of life in such a way as to make it seem as natural to quattrocento painters and their viewers as they seem startling to late-twentieth-century readers of Baxandall. Who would have thought this disparity posssible? Yet Geertz shows that situating unfamiliar ways of doing things in appropriate contexts can render them intelligible.

Geertz's most recent book, *After the Fact*, studies two towns, one in Morocco and the other in Java, at opposite ends of the Moslem world.[6] He explores the towns, among other ways, within the context of their respective countries and within the international system of inequalities among nations. Throughout, he tacks between general concerns, such as nationalisms and hegemonies, and the most local and micro situations within which they can be elucidated. He attempts to ground larger concerns in local settings and to elucidate the most particular of particular cases through their often surprising playing out of larger concerns. The local rarely is as the metropolis imagines it to be, but it is not devoid of such broad human matters as ethics and aesthetics, contrary to what the civilized-me/brute-savage-Other school of thought might suppose.

### Comparisons

Geertz proclaims himself to be a cases-and-interpretations type of anthropologist, one concerned above all with the specifics of local cultures. He uses terms such as *circumstantiality* and *thick description* to characterize his ethnographic goals.[7] Yet virtually all of his essays, in a way that is rarely remarked upon, also rely centrally on comparisons to bring their subject matter into view. His analyses take central concepts in social theory and explore their range of meanings (through ethnographic exemplification and application) in a plurality of human forms of life—as evidenced in the wide variety of subjects the essays engage: art, ritual and social change, religion, ethos and worldview, charisma, ideology, nationalism, primordial sentiment, law, politics, common sense, the moral imagination, social thought. Geertz's method is to enlarge the sense of human possibilities and the conceptual range of central terms simultaneously.

The near paradox, the simultaneous specification/comparison goal of Geertz's essays, has received little notice, especially given the notoriety of his so-called particularism and relativism. Perhaps the reason is that his comparisons are unfamiliar in method and purpose to certain readers who expect Durkheimian studies in concomitant variation (showing, for example, how the rate of suicide varies with religious affiliation or marital status or both together). He resists both descent to the lowest common denominator—a distinctive feature that "art" in all places and in all times has in common—and ascent to an abstract universal definition of art derived from theoretical treatises or universal postulates for the human processes of thought.

Ludwig Wittgenstein's notion of family resemblances informs Geertz's comparisons. Wittgenstein's idea is that two cousins, for example, may resemble each other in their hair, eyes, and ears, and two other cousins may resemble each other in their lips, teeth, and noses. As a total group of cousins, they probably do not have any single feature in common; there is no lowest common denominator that unites all family members. Instead, the strength of their connections resides in the significant, if incomplete, overlap of such features. Rather than confining himself to the vertical dimension, either descending to the lowest common denominator or ascending to abstraction, Geertz moves laterally to expand his readers' sense of human possibilities. Art, for example, is variously embedded in the collective social activities and forms of life that it shapes and by which it is shaped. Geertz intentionally violates notions of high and low art when he compares the cultural productions of quattrocento Italy, the Yoruba people, and the Abelam of Papua New Guinea with, say, Moroccan popular verse. His idea is to show that the similarities and differences that occur in actual human lifeways range beyond what a person could imagine without studying the human record. The human imagination is as culture-bound as any other cultural artifact.

Geertz takes the barriers erected by cultural difference more seriously than most observers. He sees people—whether they are positivist or interpretive social scientists by profession, or Javanese or Moroccan by nationality—as inhabiting different worlds governed by distinct assumptions, concepts, and sociohistorically constructed forms of life. At the same time he holds out utopian hopes for the possibility of communication between such mutually disjunctive worlds. In speaking of the extraordinary diversity of modern thought, for example, he maintains (the viciousness of academic warfare notwithstanding) that it is possible for "people inhabiting different worlds to have a genuine, and reciprocal, impact upon one another."[8] Ethnography is a tool through which people, as he says, can come to know the depth of differences separating them, grasp the precise nature of these differences, and construct a public vocabulary through which they can seriously talk to one another.

The tensions between the doctrine of cultural uniqueness and his insistence on cross-cultural comparisons constitutes the point of departure for Geertz's ethical vision. This ethic recognizes the deep gaps between distinct forms of life and thus foregrounds the corresponding urgency of working with care and attention (of the kind that, for example, mastering a foreign language requires) in order to engage in mutual comprehension and give-and-take across such gaps. Rejecting the alternative ethic of subordination of the different, Geertz aspires to engage in processes analogous to meaningful egalitarian conversation across cultural boundaries.

Speaking with concentrated passion, Geertz renders ethnographically and humanly vivid the force of his ethical vision of mutual engagement. It is a vision accountable to the depth and specific nature of human differences in a compelling case history, told in the following complex single sentence about a bereaved man's extraordinary (at least to non-Javanese) achievement of literal self-composure:

Only when you have seen, as I have, a young man whose wife—a woman he had in fact raised from childhood and who had been the center of his life—has suddenly and inexplicably died, greeting everyone with a set smile and formal apologies for his wife's absence and trying by mystical techniques, to flatten out, as he himself put it, the hills and valleys of his emotion into an even, level plain ("That is what you have to do," he said to me, "be smooth inside and out") can you come, in the face of our own notions of the intrinsic honesty of deep feeling and the moral importance of personal sincerity, to take the possibility of such a conception of selfhood seriously and appreciate, however inaccessible it is to you, its own sort of force.[9]

## Notes

I am indebted for comments on this paper to Mary Louise Pratt. My piece was written while still in recovery from a stroke I suffered at the end of September 1996. I am delighted that a note honoring Clifford Geertz was the occasion for my return to anthropological writing.

1. Clifford Geertz, *Local Knowledge: Further Essays in Interpretive Anthropology* (New York, 1983), 6.
2. Ibid., 57.   3. Ibid., 19–35.   4. Ibid., 16.   5. Ibid., 94–120.
6. Clifford Geertz, *After the Fact: Two Countries, Four Decades, One Anthropologist* (Cambridge, Mass., 1995).
7. Clifford Geertz, *The Interpretation of Cultures* (New York, 1973), 3–30.
8. Geertz, *Local Knowledge*, 161.
9. Ibid., 61.

WILLIAM H. SEWELL JR.

# Geertz, Cultural Systems, and History: From Synchrony to Transformation

CLIFFORD GEERTZ IS SURELY THE MOST INFLUENTIAL American anthropologist of his generation. Although others—for example, Marshall Sahlins or Victor Turner—may rival his standing within anthropology, none approaches his influence on readers outside his home discipline.[1] As Renato Rosaldo once remarked, Geertz has become the "ambassador from anthropology."

The ambassador's slot was already in existence when Geertz emerged as an anthropological superstar in the early 1970s. It had previously been occupied by Ruth Benedict and Margaret Mead. Mead, whose ambassadorial service overlapped Geertz's, had gained a huge popular following, writing a regular column in *Redbook* and dispensing advice in various media on topics as wide-ranging as the nuclear arms race, juvenile delinquency, world hunger, and sex education. Geertz's ambassadorial role has been much closer to that of Ruth Benedict, who, like Geertz, was more interested in the bearing of anthropology on issues of social and moral philosophy than on current social problems. Like Geertz, Benedict was a gifted literary stylist with a penchant for ethnographic *contes philosophiques*—her superb essays on the Zuni, Dobu, and Kwakiutl in *Patterns of Culture* are surely among the classics of a genre that Geertz has subsequently made his own. But Geertz and Benedict have been ambassadors to somewhat different publics. *Patterns of Culture*, in particular, was intended for and read by the educated public at large.[2] Geertz may well have been aiming for such a public, but his major impact has actually been on practitioners and students of other academic disciplines—the social sciences, literary studies, philosophy, and beyond.[3]

Geertz's rise to ambassadorial dignity has given him an iconic status in the American academy. This has also made him vulnerable to iconoclasm, particularly in his home discipline of anthropology, where he is a favorite target of critique among anthropologists of the most varied intellectual provenances—he has been attacked by positivists, postmodernists, and materialists alike.[4] The positivists criticize Geertz for abandoning the scientific values of "predictability, replicability, verifiability, and law-generating capacity" in favor of the more "glamorous" or "alluring" qualities of interpretive method.[5] The postmodernists, by contrast, reproach him for not pushing his interpretive method far enough—in particular, for failing to subject his own interpretive ethnographic practice to critical interpretation.[6] The materialists, finally, criticize him for his neglect of history, power, and social conflict.[7]

This rather edgy relationship between Geertz and his anthropological colleagues is in sharp contrast to his relationship with historians, who embraced his ambassadorial efforts early and warmly. Historians have generally simply quoted him favorably and then gone about applying his methods or ideas in their own work.[8] Of course, historians are generally far less prone than anthropologists to engage in theoretical disputes, and it is also true that Geertz does not serve as a marker in generational struggles among historians. Moreover, the history profession has never had many convinced positivists nor, at least until very recently, many convinced postmodernists. Nevertheless, it seems odd, on reflection, that some version of the materialist critique of Geertz has not been embraced by more historians.

The materialist critique—as elaborated, for example, by William Roseberry in "Balinese Cockfights and the Seduction of Anthropology"—should be quite compatible with the theoretical and methodological commitments of most social and cultural historians. Roseberry argues that Geertz, by conceptualizing culture as a text, adopts an effectively idealist position, separating cultural products from their historical production and from the relations of power and domination in which they are necessarily enmeshed. He points out that Geertz fails to indicate how the contemporary Balinese cockfight has been shaped by gender relations, by the legal regulations of the Dutch colonial and Indonesian states, or by the changing politics of Balinese status formation—all of which are referred to, but never really taken up, in Geertz's text.[9] The cockfight, Roseberry asserts, "has gone through a process of creation that cannot be separated from Balinese history," but in Geertz's account it is in fact separated from that history by being treated as a text.[10] Rather than conceptualizing culture as a text, Roseberry suggests, we should think of it as a "material social process," as "production" rather than as a "product," constantly asking how, by whom, and for what ends it is being produced.[11] This, Roseberry asserts, would "move cultural analysis to a new level" and would render "the old antinomies of materialism and idealism irrelevant."[12]

Most of Roseberry's specific criticisms of Geertz's cockfight essay are bound to resonate with historians' predilections. However, his proposal that we overcome the "antinomy between the material and the ideal" by adopting a "materialist" concept of culture hardly seems promising: one doesn't normally overcome an antinomy by simply embracing one of the antinomic poles.[13] But on closer inspection the issue of materialism versus idealism is quite beside Roseberry's real point, which has more to do with diachrony versus synchrony. The problem is not a matter of Geertz's metaphysical commitments—indeed, I shall later argue that his materialist metaphysical credentials are impeccable—but of his methodological practices. By treating a cultural performance as a text, Roseberry points out, one fixes it and subjects it to a synchronic gaze, bracketing the question of the processes that produced it in order to work out its internal logic.

I would argue that every cultural analysis *necessarily* entails a synchronic moment of this sort, but I would also argue that the synchronic moment should be dialectically related to an equally necessary diachronic moment.[14] And I agree with Roseberry that Geertz's practice of cultural interpretation too often slights the diachronic—that, as I would put it, in Geertz's work the necessary dialectic between synchronic and diachronic tends to be seriously truncated. A number of Geertz's essays, including the cockfight article, feature an event in real historical time, in which particular individuals in specific social and political relations engage in interested social action—in this case, a police raid that scatters observers of a village cockfight. But introduction of such temporal and social particulars serves Geertz as a literary device to move the essay to the real goal: specifying the synchronic and aesthetically satisfying coherence that underlies the cultural practice in question. Geertz does not usually circle back from the synchronic analysis to enrich our understanding of the contingent historical circumstances or structured social tensions that produced the cultural performance in the first place.[15] Thus, although I believe that Roseberry's invocation of the problem of materialism and idealism is confused, I find his critique of Geertz considerably more troubling than those of the positivists or the postmodernists. It gets at precisely the kinds of weaknesses that are bound to seem serious to a social historian.

### Geertz and Historians

Yet social historians, myself included, have been enormously responsive to Geertz's work. Roseberry's critique therefore poses a paradox: why should so many historians, who are professionally concerned with questions of change over time, be so strongly influenced by an anthropologist whose work is insistently synchronic?

In her pathbreaking article "The Traffic in Women," Gayle Rubin thanks her undergraduate teacher Marshall Sahlins for what she calls "the revelation of anthropology."[16] The phrase is apt. The revelation, I take it, is that our world is contingent rather than necessary; that there exist forms of life radically different from ours that are nonetheless fully human, and that, consequently, our own future is potentially more open than we usually imagine. This is the perennial message of anthropology to the world, and its delivery is the core duty of its long-standing ambassadorial function, certainly as carried out by Benedict, Mead, and Geertz. Indeed, I suspect that virtually all anthropologists were initially "allured" or "seduced" into their field by the exhilaration of discovering simultaneously the radical otherness and human comprehensibility of exotic cultures. Most have learned in the course of their professional training to suppress this initial thrill of recognition-in-difference, to replace it with an effort to encompass exotic facts in supposedly universal but actually very Western scholarly codes. Geertz, like Benedict before him, has striven to keep alive and to communicate to his readers the revelation of anthropology. It is precisely this quality that has made him so effective as an ambassador.

If historians have been particularly susceptible to Geertz's charms, it is partly because history is built on an analogous seduction. In the pasts they study, historians find worlds structured differently from ours, worlds where people's motives, senses of honor, daily tasks, and political calculations are based on unfamiliar assumptions about human society and the cosmic order. Many of the greatest works of history—Jacob Burckhardt's *The Civilization of the Renaissance in Italy,* Johan Huizinga's *The Waning of the Middle Ages,* Marc Bloch's *Feudal Society,* E. P. Thompson's *The Making of the English Working Class,* Emmanuel Le Roy Ladurie's *Montaillou*—reveal to us worlds hardly less strange than Bali, Zuni, or the Trobriands.[17] History, like anthropology, specializes in the discovery and display of human variety, but in time rather than space. It reveals that even our own ancestors lived lives stunningly different from ours. Geertz's brand of anthropology, which attempts to plumb the cultural logic of exotic societies, was thus prealigned with an important form of historical sensibility.

Anthropology had an additional claim on history as it was being practiced in the early 1970s, when Geertz published *The Interpretation of Cultures.* Geertz's emergence as an academic superstar took place at a time when social history was approaching dominance in the history profession. The rise of social history introduced fundamental changes to the field, representing a shift from the study of high politics and the actions of political and cultural elites to the study of social structures and the actions of ordinary people. In the United States, the first wave of social history was marked above all by the borrowing of theories and methods (particularly quantitative methods) from sociology, but by the early seventies a second generation of American social historians, myself among them, were beginning to feel that purely quantitative approaches could never grasp adequately the textures and meanings of ordinary people's lives.[18] Anthropology, as practiced by Geertz, seemed to offer a means of reaching deeper. Like social history, it was focused not on the practices of political leaders and intellectuals but on those of ordinary people. And it revealed—in their rituals, social conventions, and language—lives rich with complex symbolism and overflowing with meaning.

But anthropologists had a huge advantage over historians when it came to studying the kinds of people whose thoughts and deeds are seldom recorded in writing. They could live with them, learn their languages, engage them in conversation, observe their rituals, and participate in their daily routines. Historians working on peasants, workers, slaves, women, or colonized peoples were limited to what was written down and saved in archives or libraries—often not in such people's own words but in those of their "betters" or governors. But here Geertz's particular theory of culture gave historians reason for hope—and for emulation. Geertz continually stressed that meaning was not locked away in actors' heads but was embodied in publicly available symbols. He insisted that the symbol systems that make up a culture "are as public as marriage and as observable as agriculture."[19] Good ethnographic fieldworkers, Geertz told us, do not achieve some miracle of empathy with the people whose lives they briefly and incompletely share; they acquire no "preternatural capacity to think, feel, and perceive like a native."[20] The ethnographer does not "perceive what his informants perceive. What he perceives, and that uncertainly enough, is what they perceive 'with'—or 'by means of' or 'through.'" He or she does this "by searching out and analyzing the symbolic forms—words, images, institutions, behaviors—in terms of which, in each place, people actually represented themselves to themselves and to one another."[21]

It should be apparent that such a conceptualization of the study of culture is epistemologically empowering to social historians. It is obvious that those of us who study the dead cannot hope to share their experiences directly, as a naive ethnographer might imagine she or he directly shares the experiences of her or his "natives." But some of the symbolic forms through which the dead experienced their world are available to us in surviving documents—often piecemeal and secondhand, to be sure, but by no means beyond recovery. Geertz's particular conceptualization of culture as made up of publicly available systems of symbols provided an important epistemological guarantee to social historians. It powerfully authorized the use of anthropological methods in studies of past societies.


## The Uses of Synchrony

The vein of anthropological revelation opened up to historians by Geertz's methods was essentially synchronic in character. What Geertz analyzes most brilliantly, or describes most thickly, are what he frequently called "cultural systems."[22] To portray an ensemble of symbols and the practices in which they are employed as a cultural system is to trace how these symbols and practices mutually sustain each other as an integrated whole. For instance, the cultural system of a religion is composed of two complementary symbolic orders—an ethos (a people's "moral and aesthetic style and mood") and a worldview ("their picture of the way things in sheer actuality are")—that mutually imply one another.[23] Thus, for Navahos, "an ethic prizing calm deliberateness, untiring persistence, and dignified caution complements an image of nature as tremendously powerful, mechanically regular, and highly dangerous." And for Hindus, "a transcendental moral determinism in which one's social and spiritual status in a future incarnation is an automatic outcome of the nature of one's action in the present, is completed by a ritualistic duty-ethic bound to caste."[24] Religions, in short, seek to harmonize a people's conceptions of the real with their conceptions of the appropriate way to live. It is this mutual reinforcement that gives religions their systemic character.

But such systems of mutual implication are by no means limited to the sphere of religion. Geertz argues in "Person, Time, and Conduct in Bali" that Balinese naming practices fit tightly with Balinese modes of calendrical reckoning and that both reinforce a particular mode of conduct; the three symbolic domains "are hooked together by a definable logic."[25] Again and again, whether the subject is religions, conceptions of persons, hermaphroditism, aesthetic practices, cockfights, ideologies, state funerals, or royal progresses, Geertz's version of cultural analysis constantly returns to the trope of culture as interlaced and mutually sustaining systems of meaning.

Analyzing culture in this way is a synchronic intellectual operation. Although a synchronic description or analysis is often glossed as a "snapshot" that "freezes" time or as a "slice" of time, this is not quite right. Such a description is, rather, one in which time is *suspended* or *abolished* analytically so that things that actually occur in the flow of time are treated as part of a uniform moment or epoch in which they simply coexist. Just as "synoptic" means that all views are present in a single glance (as in one of those medieval paintings in which the far-flung scenes of a saint's life and martyrdom are depicted in a single continuous landscape), so "synchronic" means that different times are present in a continuous moment. To put it otherwise, in synchronic description acts of cultural signification, rather than being treated as a temporal sequence of statement and counterstatement or as linked by causal chains of antecedent and consequence, are seen as components of a mutually defined and mutually sustaining universe of (at least momentarily, until the analytic spell breaks) unchanging meaning.

Such a procedure of suspending time would appear on the surface to be unhistorical, but this is not necessarily the case. The term "historical" actually has two quite distinct meanings in contemporary speech. On the one hand, it has the obvious adjectival meaning derived from its root "history"—that is, it designates happenings that take place over time, as in "historical sequence," "historical continuity," or "historical narrative." But historical also implies "in the past," standing at a distance from the contemporary world—as in "historical novel," "historical costume," or "historical significance." I would argue that this is actually the primary meaning of the term in both everyday and academic language, since it is only when connected to nouns that themselves imply temporal flow, like "sequence," "continuity," or "narrative," that "historical" implies the continuous passage of time. Consequently, when we admonish someone to "think historically," we give an ambiguous message. We might mean "recognize more consciously and explicitly the 'pastness' of the past you are thinking about." Or we might mean "place the happening you are thinking about in a temporal sequence of transformations." Or we might mean both.

These two meanings of "historical" and "history"—what we might call "history as temporal context" and "history as transformation"—are the synchronic and diachronic faces of history. History as temporal context is historical in the sense that it is placed in some past era, but it is concerned not with the process of change during that time but with the distinct character and atmosphere of what we might call a *block* of time. Indeed, we convince our readers—and ourselves— that we have truly understood the pastness of that time by showing how a wide range of different beliefs, practices, judgments, and forms of action were linked by some common but now foreign logic.

Both history as transformation and history as temporal context are recognized in the practice and training of professional historians. We would regard as incompetent any historian not capable of arguing in both modes. But as in ordinary language, it is actually the synchronic mode that is privileged in historical judgments, not the diachronic. A historical work that makes no effort (or only the most passing effort) to explicate or explain a historical transformation but portrays effectively the context of some past lifeworld can be hailed as a masterpiece. Think of Louis Namier's *The Structure of Politics at the Accession of George III*, Emmanuel Le Roy Ladurie's *Le carnaval de Romans*, the already mentioned works by Huizinga and Burckhardt, or Robert Darnton's essay on the "Great Cat Massacre" (a work that was strongly influenced by Geertz).[26] By contrast, a history that recounted a series of changes over time but failed to indicate the distance of the lifeworld being described from the present would be dismissed out of hand as "anachronistic"— the historian's equivalent of the anthropologist's "ethnocentric" and perhaps the most damning term in the historian's lexicon of judgment.

It is significant that *anachronism*, which means "in the wrong time," is an indispensable term in the historian's vocabulary and has unambiguously negative connotations, whereas *achronism*, a perfectly good word that means "without time," has no negative connotations—indeed, is not a part of the historian's critical vocabulary at all. Here, as any good Geertzian would expect, the language used by historians tells us something about the shape and meaning of their lifeworld.[27] It tells us, perhaps surprisingly, that adequately realized synchrony is more important to good historical analysis than adequately realized diachrony. In the eyes of professionals, it is more important for a historian to know how to suspend time than to know how to recount its passage. Geertz's synchronic methods, therefore, may be just what historians need.

But even if historians' language indicates that they value synchronic adequacy over diachronic adequacy, most also care about history as transformation. Here Geertz is of little direct assistance, but indirectly his synchronic methods remain extremely valuable.[28] I would argue that the study of history as transformation has typically been haunted by an *excess* of diachrony. It was not without reason that insurgent social historians, whether the American "new social historians" or the French historians of the *Annales* school, consistently defined themselves against "narrative history."[29] And even though it was the social historians (and their successors, the cultural historians) who won these battles, historians' long-standing habit of trying to narrate themselves out of tight conceptual spots has hardly disappeared. If I think of the many history articles I have advised journals not to publish in the course of my long service as a peer reviewer, their most common failing by far was attempting to solve—or to avoid—a conceptual problem by retreating to the obvious archival sources and stringing together a narrative of "what actually happened." My ethnographic research in the daily routines of "historyland," in other words, tells me that leaving the synchronic element out of historical analysis—neglecting to pause long enough to work out the structure of a given historical moment—remains an extremely common failing of historical research and writing.[30]

A proper appreciation of synchrony is the secret ingredient of effective diachronic history. I would argue that no account of a historical transformation can be cogent unless it performs a dialectical oscillation between synchronic and diachronic thinking. We should, in my opinion, pay more literal attention to the word "transform," whose two roots—"trans" and "form"—signal precisely the necessary joining of diachrony and synchrony. Unless we can represent to ourselves and our readers the *form* of life in one historical moment or era, unless we can describe systematically the interlocking meanings and practices that give it a particular character, how are we to explain its transformation—or, for that matter, even to recognize when and how it has been transformed? An account of historical change typically shows how initial changes in some particular sector or sectors of a lifeworld have ramifying effects on others, with the ultimate consequence that the lifeworld as a whole is cast into a different shape. An account of this sort can only be convincing if the pretransformation interrelationships have already been cogently demonstrated: otherwise the claims about ramifying effects of initially local changes will seem insubstantial. No account of change will be judged deep, satisfying, rich, or persuasive unless it is based on a prior analysis of synchronic relations.

In short, the fact that Geertz's work is so resolutely synchronic hardly makes it irrelevant to historians. Indeed, the most signal virtue of his work for historians may be its cultivation of a synchronic sensibility. If the trope of the cultural system, the image of deep play, or the ideal of thick description can enable historians to suspend time more effectively—and consequently to portray past lifeworlds and their transformations with greater clarity, complexity, consistency, or depth—then they have been far from foolish to take seriously even Geertz's most unrelentingly synchronic work.

### Cultural Systems as a Material Fact

Geertz's concept of the cultural system posits a very tight fit between publicly available clusters of symbols and the moods, motivations, affects, and activities that these symbols shape. It is this assumed tightness of fit that makes his theorization of culture problematic for explaining cultural change. Geertz never explicitly raises the question of why cultural systems determine human behavior so closely. But I think the basic assumptions can be found in two essays written in the 1960s: "Religion as a Cultural System" and, especially, "The Growth of Culture and the Evolution of Mind," one of the most brilliant and underappreciated essays in *The Interpretation of Cultures*. In these essays, Geertz argues that cultural patterning must be understood as an analogue of genetic programming.

Although I disagree with Geertz's conclusions about the overwhelmingly determining character of cultural systems, I regard his extended meditation on the relationship of genes and symbols as the necessary starting place for any theory of culture. This meditation, moreover, provides the vindication of Geertz's materialist metaphysical credentials that I promised earlier. It does so by demonstrating that "mind"—seemingly a suspiciously "idealist" concept—has a substantial biological basis in human evolution. I will therefore present Geertz's fundamental theory of the symbolic patterning of behavior in some detail in this section before going on to criticize and modify it in the next.

Systems or complexes of symbols, Geertz writes in "Religion as a Cultural System,"

are extrinsic sources of information. By "extrinsic," I mean only that—unlike genes, for example—they lie outside the boundaries of the individual organism as such in that intersubjective world of common understandings into which all human individuals are born, in which they pursue their separate careers, and which they leave persisting behind them after they die. By "sources of information," I mean only that—like genes—they provide a blueprint or template in terms of which processes external to themselves can be given a definite form. As the order of bases in a strand of DNA forms a coded program, a set of instructions, or a recipe, for the synthesis of the structurally complex proteins which shape organic functioning, so culture patterns provide such programs for the institution of the social and psychological processes which shape public behavior.[31]

This analogy between genes and culture is not a mere metaphor, Geertz claims: it has a basis in the biology of human evolution.

[The] comparison of gene and symbol is more than a strained analogy of the familiar "social heredity" sort. It is actually a substantial relationship, for it is precisely because of the fact that genetically programmed processes are so highly generalized in [humans], as compared with lower animals, that culturally programmed ones are so important; only because human behavior is so loosely determined by intrinsic sources of information that extrinsic sources are so vital.[32]

Human cultures, or systems of symbols, provide a supplementary source of information that is not just a convenience to humans but a physiological necessity of our biological endowment.

As against an earlier view that culture arose in human evolution only after the huge cerebral cortex had developed, Geertz, following the lead of such anthropologists as S. L. Washburn and W. W. Howells, argues persuasively that culture and the human brain must have evolved in tandem. In the Pleistocene period, early hominids began to manufacture and use primitive tools and, relatedly, to engage in symbolic communication. Evolutionary pressures then selected for the kinds of neural structures that made such behavior possible, thereby enabling more sophisticated cultural patterns to develop, which in turn increased the selective pressures favoring cerebral development. Eventually, when the growing forebrain had allowed culture to accumulate to the point that "its importance as an adaptive factor almost wholly dominated its role as a selective one," the organic changes in neural structures effectively ceased. From that time forward, having long since acquired language, religion, moral regulation, and the incest taboo, *Homo sapiens* has remained more or less neurologically constant. It was, in short, the development of culture that called into existence the large forebrain that distinguishes our nervous system from that of the earliest hominids.[33]

Not only did culture and the large forebrain evolve together, but they remain organically linked today. "Man's nervous system does not merely enable him to acquire culture, it positively demands that he do so if it is to function at all."[34] Culture, extrinsic information coded in symbols, is a condition of our viability as a species. This is true because the large and astoundingly complex human brain responds to stimuli not by producing specific behavioral responses but rather with highly general affects.

The lower an animal, the more it tends to respond to a "threatening" stimulus with an intrinsically connected series of performed activities which taken together comprise a comparatively stereotyped . . . "flight" or "fight" response. Man's intrinsic response to such a stimulus tends to consist, however, of a diffuse, variably intense, "fear" or "rage" excitability accompanied by few, if any, automatically preset, well-defined behavioral sequences. Like a frightened animal, a frightened man may run, hide, bluster, dissemble, placate, or, desperate with panic, attack; but in his case the precise patterning of such overt acts is guided predominantly by cultural rather than genetic templates.[35]

The only way for humans to produce specific behavior appropriate to the challenges thrown up by their environment is to use the manifold cultural codes that their peculiar neural structure has made possible. Because humans' genetically programmed responses are so generalized, they need the extrinsic information supplied by culture in order to accomplish the diverse tasks of life—whether those be responding to threats, constructing shelter, reproducing the species, seeking companionship, killing other species for food, or constructing political regulations. Humans proceed, and can *only* proceed, by gathering and manipulating information (including information about how to gather information), which is stored not in the physiological structure of the body but in the intersubjective space of human signifying practice and in the objects—books, maps, clothing, tools, sacred goods, illustrations, the built environment—that give it material form.

Intellectually unviable without culture, humans would be emotionally unviable without it as well. Geertz remarks that "man is the most emotional as well as the most rational animal."[36] He might have added the most emotional *because* the most rational. The emotional diffuseness or uncertainty of the human neural response to stimuli is the flip side of the existence of the complex neural apparatus that makes us capable of reasoning. The response to stimuli *can* be diffuse because our reasoning brain makes possible tremendous and adaptively useful flexibility in how we deal with a problem; it *must* be diffuse if we are to deal with a problem flexibly rather than in a stereotyped fashion. But this makes the human "a peculiarly high-strung animal," subject to all sorts of emotional excitement but lacking built-in patterns to guide responses to that excitement.[37] It is cultural patterns that provide the necessary control of emotionally upsetting stimuli. They give "specific, explicit, determinate form to the general, diffuse, ongoing flow of bodily sensation," thereby "imposing upon the continual shifts in sentience to which we are inherently subject a recognizable, meaningful order, so that we may not only feel but know what we feel and act accordingly."[38]

This provision of specific form for diffuse and unsettling human emotion is, according to Geertz, precisely what religions are about. They provide us with conceptions and practices that enable us to live with the ever-present threat of chaos. In "Religion as a Cultural System," Geertz specifies three sources of such threat: events or problems that seem beyond our powers of explanation, suffering that seems impossible to endure, and ethical paradoxes that seem impossible to resolve. What religious symbolism does is not to deny the existence of the uncanny, of suffering, or of evil, but to provide concepts that make them thinkable (such as divine mystery, imitation of Christ, or original sin) and ritual practices that give them an experiential reality (such as the Eucharist, extreme unction, or penance). Religious doctrine, mirrored and experienced in ritual acts, does not, for example, spare us from suffering: it teaches us "how to suffer, how to make of physical pain, personal loss, worldly defeat, or the helpless contemplation of others' agony something bearable, supportable—something, as we say, sufferable."[39] In short, our neural organization necessitates as well as makes possible the shaping of both our cognitive and emotional lives by systems of symbols.

This account of the evolutionary origins and the biological necessity of human culture is a brilliant piece of materialist argumentation. It transcends the material/ideal dichotomy not by some verbal formula but by a substantial, scientifically based account of the inescapable complementarity of "material" and "ideal" in the human condition. It enables us to recognize the simultaneous rootedness of culture (or "mind") in bodily needs and its irreducibility to bodily needs. It enables us to pursue the autonomous logic of cultural systems without worrying that we are becoming "idealists" and therefore losing touch with the "real" world. If Geertz is right, as I firmly believe he is, semiotic systems are not unworldly or ghostly or imaginary; they are as integral to the life of our species as respiration, digestion, or reproduction. Materialists, this suggests, should stop worrying and love the symbol.

## How Cultural Systems Change

The theory of culture Geertz builds on this impressive ontological foundation provides wonderful tools for analyzing synchronic cultural relations but clumsy tools for explaining cultural change. This means that a historian who wants to take advantage of Geertz's synchronic insights but also wants to investigate cultural transformations must modify Geertz's concepts in practice. This is precisely what historians—or historically inclined anthropologists—ought to expect: after all, virtually none of the social theory we use in our work has been developed to deal with problems of historical change. The overriding problem posed by most social theory has been accounting for social order or structure. This is true, for example, not only of Geertz's work but of nearly all of anthropology before 1980; of the entire Durkheimian tradition; of Claude Lévi-Strauss, Roland Barthes, Michel Foucault, and Pierre Bourdieu; of Talcott Parsons, Robert Merton, and Erving Goffman. And even those theorists who have made the explanation of change a central problematic—principally Karl Marx, Max Weber, and such successors as Louis Althusser, Jürgen Habermas, or Immanuel Wallerstein—have usually employed such teleological notions of temporality that their concepts must be extensively revised to be useful to historians.[40]

What is needed is a theoretical critique that acknowledges and embraces what is most valuable in Geertz—for example, his epistemology of ethnographic research, his powerful sense of synchronic relations, and his ontological founding of the concept of culture in human biology—but that modifies his theories so as to make the possibility of change in cultural systems not an afterthought or an externality but integral to the very notion of culture.[41]

A useful starting point for such a critique is Geertz's famous statement that symbols are both "models of" and "models for" reality. They are "models for" in the sense that they are templates for the production of reality—whether architectural ideals that guide the construction of houses or male- and female-coded forms of public behavior that guide the construction of men and women. But they are at the same time "models of" reality: the architectural principles used to construct houses are also used to make sense of or judge existing buildings, and the difference between men's and women's public behavior is taken as an index of the difference between the sexes. This double quality of symbols, Geertz points out, makes them different from genes, which are only models for, not models of.[42]

This is an exceptionally fruitful observation, but in my opinion Geertz fails to exploit some of its most interesting implications. He concludes that the "model of" and "model for" doubleness of symbols means that they give "objective conceptual form to social and psychological reality both by shaping themselves to it and by shaping it to themselves."[43] He assumes, in other words, that the models *of* the social world will simply reflect back the reality that models *for* the social world have produced—and, correlatively, that models for the social world will simply produce in the world the "realities" that models of the social world describe. He assumes a relationship of mirroring or circularity, of complementarity and mutual tuning.

What Geertz fails to explore is that the doubleness of symbols also raises the possibility of a *disjunction* between their "model of" and "model for" aspects, a disjunction that opens up for actors a space for critical reflection about the world. The disjunction could open up on either of the symbol's two sides. To say that symbols are models *of* reality means that they are the product of humans' attempts to make sense of or represent the world. The "model of" dimension of the symbol implies active human thought or consciousness, the very process of intellection that our large brains and diffuse responses to stimuli render both possible and imperative. This process of representation employs the symbols made available by the culture, of course, but these symbols may be used in a creative or open-ended fashion. One makes sense of and evaluates buildings by using the existing store of architectural principles, but doing so might lead the evaluator to discover, to formally elaborate, and to integrate into architectural theories hitherto unrecognized principles that she discovers in the buildings being evaluated. The result is a change in architectural principles.[44] Because the world is always far more manifold than our representations of it, the representations are always potentially susceptible to change.

There is also a possibility of disjunction on the "model for" side. "Social reality," as Geertz would insist, is produced by shaping human action in the world according to cultural templates. But the world may prove quite recalcitrant to our attempts to shape it. After all, every attempt to apply a template takes place in a situation not quite the same as those in which the template was initially constructed. Hence, even if we assume that people always try to reproduce conscientiously that which they have known, what they actually produce is bound to vary— sometimes significantly—from what is intended. An attempt to produce men and women whose forms of public behavior fit the existing pattern may prove impossible if new forms of employment open up for women—say, in spinning mills—in which existing "feminine" forms of public behavior are no longer adequate. When this happens, a gap opens up that can be closed only by some change in the gender coding of forms of public behavior.[45] Because the world so frequently resists our attempts to shape it, cultural symbols that model the world (in both senses) are, once again, susceptible to change.[46]

What this implies is that we cannot unproblematically assume that the "model of" and "model for" aspects of symbols or symbol systems will automatically mirror each other. That they frequently do so, or even that humans normally attempt to make them do so, may well be true; I am no less inclined than Geertz to believe that people normally attempt to impose coherence on their world. But as the notional examples given above would seem to indicate, this attempt to impose coherence can be a force for *transformation* of cultural systems no less than a force for stability. The double character of symbols, far from constituting a guarantee of stability, guarantees that whatever stability is achieved can only be impermanent.

Geertz's ideas about the relations between culture and human neural structure may also be interpreted as implying a certain potential for instability in cultural systems. They do so because they imply considerable variation among individuals in response to a given problem. Because humans react to environmental stimuli in diffuse or general rather than in specific and biologically programmed fashions, they must search for extrinsic information in order to find solutions to challenges. In some cases, cultural codes are so highly stereotyped that this search for information will be very brief, determinate, and uniform for all persons facing the same stimuli. But this is certainly not always the case. Because initial neural responses are diffuse, because there is often ambiguity about what cultural code might apply, and because there is considerable flexibility about precisely how it might be applied, any stimulus is likely to be met by a range of responses, some of which might be quite innovative. If for some reason an innovative response gains salience—for example, because it is particularly successful in dealing with the problem at hand or because the person who responds innovatively is powerful or influential—the cultural codes might be permanently altered. The kind of reproductive mirroring of cultural pattern and social action that Geertz implicitly assumes as the norm may indeed be the norm. But Geertz's explicit ontological model of human cognitive activity seems to imply that significant departures from reproductive mirroring are bound to occur as well.

A similar point might be made about the emotional implications of Geertz's model of the person. He stresses that humans are peculiarly high-strung, that without the assistance of cultural patterns a human "would be functionally incomplete . . . a kind of formless monster with neither sense of direction nor power of self-control, a chaos of spasmodic impulses and vague emotions."[47] Geertz moves from this insight about the fundamental emotional instability of the human condition to an account of how culture provides the controls that are somatically lacking. He points out—very astutely, in my opinion—that the control does not always or even primarily take the shape of repression, but rather of channeling emotions into knowable forms: the flamboyant courage of the Plains Indian, the Manus' guilt-ridden compunctiousness, or the quietism of the Javanese.

But if the organic human emotional response to the environment is so diffuse and unstable, it hardly seems plausible that even the culturally thick, aesthetically appealing, and affectively powerful patterns of emotional self-expression that Geertz analyzes in so many of his articles could consistently generate patterns of behavior that are genuinely constant over time.[48] Instead, one might expect the fundamentally vagrant quality of human emotion to lead to occasional experimentation with new forms of emotional patterning; to periodic dissatisfaction with existing moral and religious systems; and to spasmodic bouts of intense political, religious, and artistic activity. Here, as Geertz himself so often does, we might turn to the theoretical legacy of Weber, who insisted on the crucial role of charisma in certain cases of profound historical change. The emergence of prophets, heroes, congregations of disciples, or bands of revolutionaries can harness diffuse emotional energies into specific, historically potent social forces.[49] Both the emotional and cognitive dimensions of Geertz's theory of mind imply that cultural systems will not be reproduced automatically. An animal so high-strung and so prodigiously talented as the human is bound to produce significant episodes of cultural transformation.

One reason Geertz's cultural systems appear impervious to change is that few of his works explore differences or variations in the beliefs, values, or idioms embraced by different groups within societies. On this point, the practices of cultural anthropologists have diverged sharply from Geertz's over the past decade and a half: examination of cultural difference has become one of their major preoccupations. Probably the most important source of the interest in difference has been feminist anthropology, which has problematized the apparent unity of cultural systems by demonstrating that cultures look very different from the perspective of women than they do from that of men.[50] But the interest in difference has also been central to "reflexive anthropology," which has advocated the ethnographic representation of multiple voices, and to the anthropology of colonialism, which has focused on the freighted cultural negotiations between European rulers and their colonial subjects.[51] Social historians, of course, have been interested in questions of difference for some time: "history from below," as practiced ever since the 1960s, explicitly endeavors to rescue the voices of the poor and marginalized and to relate their cultural experiences to those of the dominant classes.[52] Indeed, the more recent anthropological practices of multivocality have surely been influenced in part by the example of social history.[53]

As much of this anthropological and historical work demonstrates, cultural change often arises out of conflict, communication, rivalry, or exchange between groups with different cultural patterns and social relations. Group difference implies the possibility of conscious challenges to practices or values that might otherwise be reproduced automatically, and of continual negotiations or struggles about meanings. Moreover, internal social differentiation also makes possible the development in specific social niches of new cultural complexes. It is usually the case that cultural innovations do not take place uniformly over an entire society but are concentrated in or originate from specific social and geographical locations. The possibility of a workers' revolt, which haunted European politics for the better part of the nineteenth and twentieth centuries, initially arose out of a very particular dispute between weavers and silk merchants in Lyon in 1831; the cultural innovations we think of as the Renaissance were remarkably concentrated in the town of Florence; the early-twentieth-century transformation of Sherpa Buddhism was initiated by a handful of wealthy traders and monks.[54]

Geertz certainly does not deny the existence or the significance of internal difference, but he usually brackets such difference in his texts. The difference he emphasizes is that *between* societies or peoples—between "the Plains Indian's bravura, the Hindu's obsessiveness, the Frenchman's rationalism, the Berber's anarchism, the American's optimism."[55] It is remarkable how frequently Geertz makes assertions about "the Balinese," "the Javanese," "the Berbers," "the French," "the Hindus," "the Manus," or "the Zuni" without considering the possibility that there are culturally important differences within these categories—of outlook, belief, and comportment, or of wealth, gender, power, and status.

Yet here again, there are theoretical resources in Geertz's work for conceptualizing cultural difference at the intrasociety as well as intersociety level. For example, Geertz argues that the sort of cultural diversity that makes possible such different lifeworlds as those of the Plains Indians, the Hindus, the Manus, and the French is a consequence of humans' inescapable reliance on extrinsic cultural codes. Although the neural equipment of humankind is everywhere essentially the same, the cultural codes that provide our minds with specific content are fundamentally diverse. "To be human," Geertz states, "is thus not to be Everyman; it is to be a particular kind of man, and of course men differ: 'Other fields,' the Javanese say, 'other grasshoppers.'" According to Geertz, it is the anthropologist's particular calling to study the different modes of being human; it is only by understanding the particulars of these forms of life that "we shall find out what it is, or can be," to be human.[56]

To this I would add three points. First, the cultural production of different forms of life takes place at many levels, not just at the level of the "society" or the "people." Differences between the forms of life of peasants and landlords, workers and students, men and women, priests and nobles, or slaves and masters are as legitimate an object of anthropological scrutiny as those between "societies." Second, examining the relations between such different categories of people—whether of conflict, domination, exchange, emulation, or self-conscious differentiation—is a crucial task for cultural analysis. And third, the value of studying relations between categories of people is as great for what we conventionally label "societies" as for classes, genders, or status groups. "Societies" are themselves interpenetrating and mutually constituting social categories, in this respect analogous to the classes, genders, or status groups that constitute them. And they too are animated by relations of conflict, domination, exchange, emulation, and self-conscious differentiation with one another.

Geertz actually provides a good metaphor for the sort of dynamic, relational, differentiated cultural analysis I am advocating here. In "Thick Description: Toward an Interpretive Theory of Culture," he explicates and draws lessons from the tangled Moroccan story of the Jewish peddler Cohen, a tribe of Berber horsemen, and a French colonial official—a story whose "confusion of tongues" he takes as paradigmatic for the situation facing the ethnographic interpreter.[57] In this instance, the confusion of tongues arises from the encounter of three "peoples" in the traditional anthropological sense: Jews, Berbers, and the French. But the metaphor could easily be extended. Analogous cultural misunderstandings, conflicts, and negotiations occur all the time among people who share language, religion, territory, or a sense of ethnic identity but differ in status, gender, class, age, power, caste, or occupation. And it is precisely in these various episodes of confusion of tongues—where social encounters contest cultural meanings or render them uncertain—that cultural systems are transformed. Once we admit social diversity, we can no longer see cultural systems as always self-reinforcing; instead, they must also be seen as sites of conflict, dialogue, and change.

To make sense of historical transformations, then, we must adopt a different theory of culture than Geertz's. But unlike Roseberry and many other of Geertz's anthropological critics, I think we would be gravely mistaken to respond by rejecting his theory outright. Instead, I think we should *appropriate* his theoretical categories—engaging them, weighing their strengths and weaknesses, reworking them from within, but also supplementing them where necessary with foreign grafts. There is still enough untapped richness, insight, and analytical power in Geertz's work to make it a continuing inspiration for historical analysis.

## Notes

1. For example, a quick check of the *Social Sciences Citation Index, 1995 Annual* (Philadelphia, 1996) indicates that Marshall Sahlins was cited slightly more often than Clifford Geertz in anthropology journals, but that Geertz received more than twice as many citations overall (roughly 350 as opposed to 150), including citations in journals in fields as far-flung as agriculture, nursing, environmental studies, business, social work, information science, gerontology, and public relations.
2. Ruth Benedict, *Patterns of Culture* (New York, 1934), and Ruth Benedict, *The Chrysanthemum and the Sword* (New York, 1946).
3. This difference between Benedict's and Geertz's audiences probably reflects the changing contours of American intellectual life more than it does their own specific proclivities: the community of lay public intellectuals for whom Benedict could write in the 1930s hardly exists in the present—it has increasingly been either snuffed out by the rampant commercialization of the media or engulfed by universities.
4. Again a comparison with Marshall Sahlins is revealing. Sahlins is as frequently cited as Geertz by anthropologists, and his work is highly controversial. See, especially, Gananath Obeyesekere, *The Apotheosis of Captain Cook: European Mythmaking in the Pacific* (Princeton, 1992), and Marshall Sahlins's response, *How "Natives" Think: About Captain Cook, for Example* (Chicago, 1995). Yet the eleven annual volumes of *Anthropological Literature* (Cambridge, Mass., 1984–94) since 1984 list twenty-four critical works on Geertz and only ten on Sahlins.
5. The quotations are from Paul Shankman, whose "The Thick and the Thin: On the Interpretive Theoretical Paradigm of Clifford Geertz," *Current Anthropology* 25, no. 3

(1984): 261–79 (quotes from 264, 270) is the most systematic critique from a positivist perspective. As is the norm in this journal, the article itself is followed by comments from an assortment of scholars and a response by the author. Five of the fifteen published comments—those of Erika Bourguignon, Linda Connor, John R. Cole, A. D. Fisher, and Robin Riddington—indicate that Shankman's positivist distrust of Geertz is far from unique among anthropologists. Shankman's thorough bibliography is a good guide to the critical literature on Geertz as of 1984.

6. See, e.g., Vincent Crapanzano, "Hermes' Dilemma: The Masking of Subversion in Ethnographic Description," in *Writing Culture: The Poetics and Politics of Ethnography*, ed. James Clifford and George E. Marcus (Berkeley, 1986), 68–76; James Clifford, "On Ethnographic Authority," in *The Predicament of Culture: Twentieth-Century Ethnography, Literature, and Art* (Cambridge, Mass., 1988), 40–41; Graham Watson, "Definitive Geertz," *Ethnos* 54, nos. 1 and 2 (1989): 23–30; and Graham Watson, "Rewriting Culture," in *Recapturing Anthropology: Working in the Present*, ed. Richard G. Fox (Santa Fe, 1991), 80–81.

7. Examples are William Roseberry, "Balinese Cockfights and the Seduction of Anthropology," *Social Research* 49, no. 4 (1982): 1013–28, republished in *Anthropologies and Histories: Essays in Culture, History, and Political Economy* (New Brunswick, N.J., 1989), 17–29; and Talal Asad, "Anthropological Conceptions of Religion: Reflections on Geertz," *Man* 18, no. 2 (1982): 237–59. See also Talal Asad, *Genealogies of Religion: Discipline and Reasons of Power in Christianity and Islam* (Baltimore, 1993), esp. chap. 1.

8. Ronald Walters gives an account of Geertz's early reception by historians in "Signs of the Times: Clifford Geertz and the Historians," *Social Research* 47, no. 3 (1980): 537–56.

9. Roseberry, "Balinese Cockfights," 1020–23. Roseberry's critique centers on Clifford Geertz's "Deep Play: Notes on the Balinese Cockfight," in *The Interpretation of Cultures* (New York, 1973), 412–53. This article is the sole or primary example discussed in a number of critical articles devoted to Geertz—including those by Clifford and Crapanzano cited earlier. Although there is far more to Geertz than the cockfight article, there is a certain poetic justice in the way critics have treated as a synecdochic representation of Geertz an article in which he claims that the cockfight synecdochically represents Balinese culture.

10. Roseberry, "Balinese Cockfights," 1022.

11. Ibid., 1023–24.      12. Ibid., 1026–27.

13. Ibid., 1024. For a discussion of Roseberry quite consonant with mine, see Nicholas B. Dirks, "Is Vice Versa? Historical Anthropologies and Anthropological Histories," in *The Historic Turn in the Human Sciences*, ed. Terrence J. McDonald (Ann Arbor, 1996), 17–52.

14. On the necessity of synchronic moments in historical analysis, see William H. Sewell Jr., "How Classes Are Made: Critical Reflections on E. P. Thompson's Theory of Working-Class Formation," in *E. P. Thompson: Critical Perspectives*, ed. Harvey J. Kaye and Keith McClelland (Oxford, 1990), 57–59.

15. The only exception that comes to mind is an article written early in Geertz's career (1959), which treats a politically fraught funeral: "Ritual and Social Change: A Javanese Example," in *Interpretation of Cultures*, 142–69. This article was written before Geertz had freed himself from his Parsonian heritage, at a time when he was preoccupied with the problematic of modernization. Although it is now fashionable to equate modernization theory with an unreflexive teleology, Geertz used it in this article and in a number of his early works to examine the contradictions of a Javanese society that,

in the 1950s, was experiencing the throes of transition from colony to independent state. See, e.g., *Agricultural Involution: The Process of Ecological Change in Indonesia* (Berkeley, 1963), *Peddlers and Princes: Social Change and Modernization in Two Indonesian Towns* (Chicago, 1963), and *The Social History of an Indonesian Town* (Cambridge, Mass., 1965). In an exceptionally subtle critical evaluation of Geertz's work, Diane J. Austin-Broos points out the contrast between Geertz's early work on Java, which was undertaken from a modernization perspective but treated culture as ambiguous and manipulable, and his later work on Bali and Morocco, which is characterized by a "new stillness" that results from "the rendering of life as aesthetic." "Clifford Geertz: Culture, Sociology, and Historicism"; in *Creating Culture: Profiles in the Study of Culture*, ed. Diane J. Austin-Broos (Sydney, 1987), 156.

16. Gayle Rubin, "The Traffic in Women: Notes on the 'Political Economy' of Sex," in *Toward an Anthropology of Women*, ed. Rayna R. Reiter (New York, 1975), 157.

17. Jacob Burckhardt, *The Civilization of the Renaissance in Italy* (New York, 1958); Johan Huizinga, *The Waning of the Middle Ages: A Study of the Forms of Life, Thought, and Art in France and the Netherlands in the Fourteenth and Fifteenth Centuries* (Garden City, N.Y., 1954); Marc Bloch, *Feudal Society* (Chicago, 1964); E. P. Thompson, *The Making of the English Working Class* (London, 1963); and Emmanuel Le Roy Ladurie, *Montaillou: The Promised Land of Error* (New York, 1978).

18. Representative works from the first wave are Charles Tilly, *The Vendée* (Cambridge, Mass., 1964); Stephan Thernstrom, *Poverty and Progress: Social Mobility in a Nineteenth-Century City* (Cambridge, Mass., 1964); and Lawrence Stone, *Crisis of the Aristocracy, 1558–1641* (Oxford, 1967).

19. Clifford Geertz, "Religion as a Cultural System," in *Interpretation of Cultures*, 91.

20. Clifford Geertz, " 'From the Native's Point of View': On the Nature of Anthropological Understanding," in *Local Knowledge: Further Essays in Interpretive Anthropology* (New York, 1983), 56. This essay originally appeared in the *Bulletin of the American Academy of Arts and Sciences* in 1974.

21. Geertz, "From the Native's Point of View," 58.

22. Geertz has written four essays that use the term "cultural system" in the title: "Religion as a Cultural System" and "Ideology as a Cultural System," in *Interpretation of Cultures*; and "Common Sense as a Cultural System" and "Art as a Cultural System," in *Local Knowledge*.

23. Clifford Geertz, "Ethos, World View, and the Analysis of Sacred Symbols," in *Interpretation of Cultures*, 127.

24. Ibid., 130.

25. Clifford Geertz, "Person, Time, and Conduct in Bali," in *Interpretation of Cultures*, 404.

26. Louis B. Namier, *The Structure of Politics at the Accession of George III* (London, 1929); Emmanuel Le Roy Ladurie, *Le carnaval de Romans: De la Chandeleur au mercredi des Cendres, 1579–1580* (Paris, 1979); Huizinga, *Waning of the Middle Ages*; Burckhardt, *Civilization of the Renaissance*; and Robert Darnton, "Workers Revolt: The Great Cat Massacre of the Rue Saint-Séverin," in *The Great Cat Massacre and Other Episodes in French Cultural History* (New York, 1984), 75–106.

27. On the use of academic languages of judgment to understand the preoccupations of different disciplines, see Clifford Geertz, "The Way We Think Now: Ethnography of Modern Thought," in *Local Knowledge*, 157–58.

28. In fact, his early monographs on Indonesian modernization, cited in note 15, might have been of direct assistance. But they were so similar in style to studies already

being done by social historians that they were not much noticed. It was the later, more synchronic essays that captured historians' imaginations.

29. On the French case, see Peter Burke, *The French Historical Revolution: The Annales School, 1929–89* (Stanford, 1990).

30. The invocation of "historyland" is of course a reference to the immortal Bernard Cohn's "History and Anthropology: The State of Play," in *An Anthropologist Among the Historians and Other Essays* (Delhi, 1990), 18–49.

31. Geertz, "Religion as a Cultural System," 92.

32. Ibid., 92–93.

33. Clifford Geertz, "The Growth of Culture and the Evolution of Mind," in *Interpretation of Cultures*, 66–69; quote from 69.

34. Ibid., 68.       35. Ibid., 75.

36. Ibid., 80. Geertz quotes this phrase from D. O. Hebb and W. R. Thompson, "The Social Significance of Animal Studies," in *Handbook of Social Psychology*, ed. Gardner Linszey (Reading, Mass., 1954), 532–61.

37. Ibid.       38. Ibid.

39. Geertz, "Religion as a Cultural System," 104.

40. I have made attempts at such revisions in "Three Temporalities: Toward an Eventful Sociology," in McDonald, *The Historic Turn*, 245–80, and "A Theory of Structure: Duality, Agency, and Transformation," *American Journal of Sociology* 98, no. 1 (1992): 1–29. So has Marshall Sahlins, e.g., in *Historical Metaphors and Mythical Realities* (Ann Arbor, 1981), and *Islands of History* (Chicago, 1985). The work of classical social theory that most fully embodies what I regard as a historian's appreciation of contingency is Max Weber's *The Protestant Ethic and the Spirit of Capitalism* (New York, 1958). But even here the possibility of contingency gives way to teleology; once capitalism is established, it becomes, in Weber's memorable phrase, an "iron cage" (181).

41. Clifford Geertz's most recent book, *After the Fact: Two Countries, Four Decades, One Anthropologist* (Cambridge, Mass., 1995), is much more concerned with issues of diversity, power, struggle, and social transformation than were either *The Interpretation of Cultures* or *Local Knowledge*. A kind of poetic autobiographical meditation on changes in anthropology and the world over the course of Geertz's career, it takes up these issues obliquely in the course of the narrative rather than addressing them head on. But as I read it, the book is actually quite compatible with the critiques and revisions of his earlier theories that I spell out here.

42. Geertz, "Religion as a Cultural System," 93.

43. Ibid.

44. See the example of Robert Venturi, Denise Scott Brown, and Steven Izenour, *Learning from Las Vegas: The Forgotten Symbolism of Architectural Form* (Cambridge, Mass., 1977).

45. See Thomas Dublin, *Women at Work: The Transformation of Work and Community in Lowell, Massachusetts, 1826–60* (New York, 1979).

46. Here my arguments are very close to and have been strongly influenced by those of Marshall Sahlins: "The worldly circumstances of human action are under no inevitable obligation to conform to the categories by which certain people perceive them. In the event they do not, the received categories are potentially revalued in practice, functionally redefined"; Sahlins, *Historical Metaphors and Mythical Realities*, 67.

47. Geertz, "Religion as a Cultural System," 99.

48. For such analyses, see, e.g., Geertz, "Religion as a Cultural System," "Ethos, World View," "Person, Time, and Conduct in Bali," and "Deep Play," all in *Interpretation of Cultures*; Geertz, "Found in Translation: On the Social History of the Moral Imagina-

tion," "From the Native's Point of View," and "Common Sense as a Cultural System," in *Local Knowledge*; Clifford Geertz, *The Religion of Java* (Glencoe, Ill., 1960); and Clifford Geertz, *Islam Observed: Religious Development in Morocco and Indonesia* (New Haven, 1968).

49. Max Weber, "The Types of Legitimate Domination" and "Charisma and Its Transformations," in *Economy and Society: An Outline of Interpretive Sociology*, 2 vols., ed. Guenther Roth and Claus Wittich (Berkeley, 1978), 1:241–54, 2:1111–56. See also Weber, *The Protestant Ethic*. Emile Durkheim's *Elementary Forms of the Religious Life*, trans. Karen Fields (New York, 1995) also has extremely interesting things to say about the role of emotion in social life. For an attempt to use some of Durkheim's insights in the analysis of cultural transformation, see William H. Sewell Jr., "Historical Events as Structural Transformations: Inventing Revolution at the Bastille," *Theory and Society* 25, no. 6 (1996): 841–81.

50. Three examples among many are Annette Wiener, *Women of Value, Men of Renown: New Perspectives in Trobriand Exchange* (Austin, Tex., 1976); Lila Abu-Lughod, *Veiled Sentiments: Honor and Poetry in a Bedouin Society* (Berkeley, 1986); and Emily Martin, *The Woman in the Body: A Cultural Analysis of Reproduction* (Boston, 1987).

51. The best known manifesto of reflexive anthropology is Clifford and Marcus, *Writing Culture*. See also George E. Marcus, *Anthropology as Cultural Critique: An Experimental Moment in the Human Sciences* (Chicago, 1986). The pioneering anthropologist of colonialism is Bernard Cohn, *Anthropologist Among the Historians*, and *Colonialism and Its Forms of Knowledge: The British in India* (Princeton, 1996).

52. Perhaps the most celebrated examples are Thompson, *Making of the English Working Class*, and Eugene Genovese, *Roll, Jordan, Roll: The World the Slaves Made* (New York, 1974).

53. On "history from below" and anthropology, see Renato Rosaldo, "Celebrating Thompson's Heroes: Social Analysis in History and Anthropology," in *E. P. Thompson*, 103–24.

54. On the place of Lyon in the development of workers' revolts, see William H. Sewell Jr., *Work and Revolution in France: The Language of Labor from the Old Regime to 1848* (Cambridge, 1980), esp. 206–7. On Sherpa religion, see Sherry B. Ortner, *High Religion: A Cultural and Political History of Sherpa Buddhism* (Princeton, 1989).

55. Clifford Geertz, "The Impact of the Concept of Culture on the Concept of Man," in *Interpretation of Cultures*, 53.

56. Ibid.

57. Clifford Geertz, "Thick Description: Toward an Interpretive Theory of Culture," in *Interpretation of Cultures*, 9.

# NATALIE ZEMON DAVIS

## Religion and Capitalism Once Again? Jewish Merchant Culture in the Seventeenth Century

### I

*The Jew rises before us unmistakably as more of a business-man than his neighbor. . . .*
*He recognizes, in the true capitalist spirit, the supremacy of gain over all other aims.*
*I know of no better illustration than the* Memoirs of Glückel von Hameln, *a*
*mine of information, by the way, about Jewish life and thought in the early capitalistic*
*age. . . . In very truth, money is the be-all and end-all with her, as with the other*
*people of whom she has anything to say. . . . What was specifically Jewish was the*
*naïveté and directness with which money was made the pivot of life; it was a matter*
*of course. . . .*

    *It is well known that the religion of the Christians stood in the way of their*
*economic activities. It is equally well known that the Jews were never faced with this*
*hindrance. . . . A beautiful illustration of the way religion and business were fused in*
*the mind of pious Jews may be found in the delightful* Memoirs of Glückel von
Hameln. *"Praise be to God, who gives and takes, the faithful God, who always made*
*good our losses," she says.*[1]

THUS THE HISTORICAL SOCIOLOGIST WERNER SOMBART
spoke of the origins of capitalism in the early modern period and used the autobiography of a seventeenth-century merchant woman of Hamburg to illustrate his point.[2] *Die Juden und das Wirtschaftsleben* (The Jews and Economic Life) of 1911 was Sombart's answer to Max Weber's *Die protestantische Ethik und der Geist des Kapitalismus* of 1904–1905, a debate begun by Sombart himself in 1902, when he published *Der moderne Kapitalismus.*[3] Like Weber, Sombart saw modern capitalism as distinctive to the West. Like Weber, he sought a "spirit of capitalism" informing that economic change. And like Weber, he opened his study with social description showing the predominance of a certain group in business enterprise, and then moved on to the religious mechanisms and religious qualities that accounted for that predominance.

But their differences were important. If they both agreed that rational calculation was essential to the spirit of capitalism, they diverged in regard to motives and sources. Sombart thought an unlimited appetite for gain and for money itself fueled capitalistic action, while Weber considered "ruthless acquisition" the standard

56

characteristic of *pre*capitalistic economies. For Weber, self-denial was the mechanism that led to the accumulation of profits. He quoted Benjamin Franklin as his supreme example:

After industry and frugality, nothing contributes more to the raising of the young man in the world than punctuality and justice in all his dealings. . . . The sound of your hammer at five in the morning, or eight at night, heard by a creditor, makes him easy six months longer. . . . Beware of thinking all your own what you possess, and of living accordingly. . . . To prevent this, keep an exact account both of your expenses and your income. . . . Remember. . . . money can beget money.[4]

The two sociologists also stressed different arenas for the playing out of rational calculation, Weber being especially interested in the organization and discipline of free labor in industrial capitalism, Sombart in the development of credit instruments, the financial support of modern states, and international commerce, including luxury trade, and colonies. And finally, Weber viewed the Puritans with their predestinarian theology, their ascetic self-regulation, and their this-worldly callings as the major "culture-bearers" of the spirit of capitalism, while Sombart assigned that role to the Jews. For Sombart, the Puritan aptitude for business came from characteristics similar to (or derived from) the Jews: "Puritanism *is* Judaism." He even thought there was a racial underlay to the Jewish genius for business: it was ancient and hereditary among a people who "for some twenty centuries . . . have kept themselves ethnically pure."[5]

Apart from his views on "the race question," Sombart offered two sources for the Jewish aptitude for capitalist action. There were, to start with, the mental and practical consequences of the Jews being dispersed over many areas of Europe, where they lived as relative outsiders, with the legal status of strangers rather than the deep roots of citizenship. This prompted skills of "speedy adaptation" to different circumstances and loosened their moral ties to the non-Jews with whom they were in economic contact so much of the time.[6]

Further, and especially important, Sombart claimed Judaism was a thoroughly rational religion, hostile to mysticism. Its adherents were called upon to live strictly according to the Law, in this world not the next: "Holiness is the rationalization of life," the Jewish source of "this-worldly asceticism."[7] The covenant between the Lord and his people made the contract the central form of religious perception and action for the Jews. Reward and punishments to humans for keeping or breaking the contract were meted out in this world, and wealth was one of the rewards. Even the Jewish liturgy showed businesslike qualities, as the honor of reading from, holding high, and rolling up the Torah scroll was sold to the highest bidder.

Sombart backed this argument up with citations from the Scriptures, the rabbis, the Law, and the memoirs of "Glückel of Hameln," just published in German translation from the Yiddish.[8] Her autobiography was the only such personal text he cited along the way; it played a role in his argument similar to that of Franklin's *Advice to a Young Tradesman* for Weber.

Sombart's *Die Juden* aroused much commentary at the time and over the next decades. To Weber, Sombart was wrong on several grounds, including his racial theories. The Jews' status as outsiders, so central to Sombart's argument, led them into the risky "pariah capitalism" of government loans rather than into the self-denying rationality of the "bourgeois organization of labor."[9] The distinguished economic historian Lujo Brentano took issue with both sociologists. Descended himself from Italian Catholics who had moved to Frankfurt in the seventeenth century, Brentano said Weber had neglected the innovative role of the Catholic merchants of the Italian Renaissance and the teaching of the late Schoolmen on callings and trade. As for Sombart's description of the economic activities of the Jews and the teachings of their rabbis, it was inaccurate and arbitrary, "a deplorable publication."[10]

Nonetheless, Jewish scholars and specialists in Jewish history found Sombart's book at least worthy of examination. To dismiss their interest in Sombart as a sign of Jewish self-hatred—"of the self-deprecatory posture of German Jewry"—ignores what seemed fresh about the text to contemporaries.[11] In its pages Jewish traders, bankers, and entrepreneurs were the major actors in the transformation of European society into modernity, rather than playing only supporting roles or being limited to the confines of Jewish history (as in, say, Heinrich Graetz's magisterial *Geschichte der Juden*, whose eleventh volume appeared posthumously the same year as Sombart's book).[12]

Moreover, Sombart kept his text uncannily free of normative statements that would disclose his strong aversion to the capitalistic calculation allegedly invented by the Jews. Initially a Marxist, Sombart was increasingly inspired by a Nietzschean hope for a "German" form of entrepreneurial modernity over a rational and commercial "Jewish" form of modernity.[13] Such views he expressed vigorously in an anti-Semitic political pamphlet of 1912, *Die Zukunft der Juden* (The Future of the Jews), but in his scholarly tome he was descriptive rather than prescriptive—an example of the "value-free" style that he and Weber were insisting on within the German Sociological Society. Sombart characterized the woman he called Glückel von Hameln as "distinguished" and her book as "splendid," even while claiming that she put money above everything else. Her life "rich in experience" reminded him of Goethe's mother.[14] Moses Hoffmann, rabbi and historian of medieval Jewish economic history, found in his 1912 review that *Die Juden und das Wirtschaftsleben* was "unusual in its impartiality."[15]

Finally, Sombart's racial chapters were written in a tone of excited speculation, with occasional citation of a Jewish thinker willing to entertain the concept of a "Jewish race" shaped by heredity.[16] Readers in 1911–1912 could not foresee where those views would lead in Nazi times or that Sombart would write in defense of National Socialist principles in the 1930s. Reviewing *Die Juden* for the *Revue des études juives* in 1911, Raphael-Georges Lévy commented that Sombart had "avoided all debate over the superiority or inferiority of any race."[17]

Both Lévy and Hoffmann were unconvinced that Jews had any long-term traits as a "race" or as a "people." What economic skills and activities Jews undertook at any given period were a result of "milieu," of historical circumstance. For Hoffmann, Sombart was most sorely lacking in his treatment of Jewish religious sensibility and moral teaching. The sociologist had missed the strong mystical strain in Jewish religious history and had ignored the force of rabbinical teachings reproving wealth and worldliness. Talmudic flexibility had given the Jews mechanisms by which to adjust to economies where lending, buying, and selling were all that was permitted to them, but it had not led to the invention of capitalism.

Especially interesting is the reaction of Mordecai Epstein, the translator of *Die Juden und das Wirtschaftsleben* into English in 1913. Epstein was a young economic historian who, encouraged by Sidney Webb, had written his Heidelberg dissertation on the early history of the Levant Company. In 1906–1907 he had attended Sombart's lectures and seminars in Berlin, had been part of the group of students dining with Sombart after class, and had been charmed by his energy, learning, and humor. The professor's early political thought intrigued Epstein as well, for his first translation of Sombart was *Socialism and the Social Movement* (1909), a work that went back to 1896, when Sombart still believed in the possibilities of a modern evolutionary socialism.[18] Sombart's many books were controversial, Epstein said in his preface to *The Jews and Modern Capitalism*, but had "contributed much that is valuable to economic thought." For this translation, he had, with the author's agreement, shortened certain sections, including the one on "modern race theory."[19] In fact, Epstein cut many pages from the chapters on race, while retaining paragraphs where Sombart stressed the limits of contemporary knowledge about racial traits and where Sombart contrasted "anti-Semitic pamphlet[s]" (to quote him directly) with his own "reasoned" discussion of how "the Jew's inherent 'Nomadism' or 'Saharaism' . . . was always kept alive through selection or adaptation."

Thus, Sombart's work was presented to English and American readers by a practicing economic historian and in a form that mitigated some of its most troubling claims. Epstein repeated his qualified endorsement a few years later in reviewing and then translating Sombart's *Der Bourgeois* of 1913.[20] Here Sombart had elaborated on his division of the bourgeois temperament into its heroic and calculating forms. All European peoples were capable of capitalism, but "biologically" the Germanic peoples had special talents for entrepreneurship, while the Florentines and the Scottish now shared with the Jews special talents for trading. But the Jews still won the capitalism prize over the centuries. The teachings of the scholastics may have encouraged entrepreneurship and wealth, but Judaism went much further with its unreserved acceptance of riches, rationalization of life, and double code for dealing with Jew and non-Jew. A decade later, Epstein would take a view of Jewish religious teaching very different from Sombart's.[21] At the opening of World War I, he found Sombart's theories on the biological and religious factors behind capitalistic development clearly speculative, but still "exceedingly suggestive and stimulating."

Whether one agreed with it or not, Sombart's wide-ranging *Die Juden* defined the issues in research in Jewish economic history for many years to come.[22] A poignant example is the seminar conducted in Lyon in 1941 on "The Jews in Economic Life." Given clandestinely by the French economist Louis Rosenstock-Franck, it was part of a study project of the Central Consistory of France for scholars excluded from their posts by the Vichy Statut des Juifs of October 1940 and now living without employ in the nonoccupied zone of France. Rosenstock-Franck thought it fitting "to study and—if you permit the expression—to unmask the first important effort at systematizing the influence of the Jews on economic life," that is, Sombart's *Les Juifs et la vie économique,* known to French readers through the 1923 translation of S. Jankélévitch.

Was Sombart an anti-Semite in the book, a Nazi before the letter? Rosenstock-Franck asked his listeners. There was nothing hostile simply in affirming a Jewish role in economic life, though Sombart's claims about the importance of the Jews remained to be verified.

But Sombart, whether he wished to or not, served anti-Semitism when, having proved that the Jews created various economic instruments, he maintained that they used them for personal ends that were repugnant to national communities, to the social world around them, and to Christian mentality.

Still, his book had in it some "big ideas" to consider: the possible accord between Jewish religion and the requirements of capitalist civilization and, especially interesting, the "individualist, anational, or supernational character of Jewish economic action." These last traits, so objectionable to Sombart, might at least guarantee that Hitler, Mussolini, and Stalin would be unlikely to find a great Jewish financier—a twentieth-century "Court Jew"—to do their bidding.[23]

## II

My report on Jewish merchant culture in the seventeenth century will in part follow the path opened by earlier critics of Sombart. I will examine Sombart's views about Jewish mentalities through the Yiddish autobiography of the Hamburg merchant-woman who has been known as Glückel of Hameln and one other allied text: the biography of Zevi Hirsch Ashkenazi, a teacher and rabbi in Hamburg and adjacent Altona in the late seventeenth and early eighteenth century, written in Hebrew by his son Jacob Emden.[24] More important, this evidence will push me to question the pursuit of economics and religion in the terms and with the stakes that Weber and Sombart set in the early twentieth century and that were lucidly restated by R. H. Tawney in his 1930 foreword to the first English edition of Weber's *Protestant Ethic*. Then an important early work of Clifford Geertz on Indonesia will illustrate the movement from a relatively spent mode of analysis to one that is rich in potentiality for understanding economics as a cultural activity. Geertz's subsequent study of Morocco fulfills that potentiality through an ethnographic examination of the bazaar, showing among other things new ways to connect economic behavior with religion—here Judaism and Islam.

But first some introduction to our sources, beginning with the merchant woman. Her name was not Glückel of Hameln or Glückel von Hameln, as it appears on printed title pages in the twentieth century, but Glikl bas Judah Leib, Glikl daughter of Judah Leib.[25] She was born in Hamburg in 1646–1647 into a family of traders. The Sephardic community of Jews, with its international bankers and merchants, had been established in that Lutheran Hanseatic town since the early seventeenth century. The Ashkenazic community, to which Glikl's parents belonged, lived in the city on a more precarious basis until the very end of the century, when for a large annual payment they were given a regular status. By that date, too, many of them had risen from middle-level traders to substantial international merchants.

Glikl was married at twelve to the young trader Haim ben Joseph (known to Christian recordkeepers alternately as Haim Hamel and Haim Goldschmidt), the early age of marriage not uncommon among Jews of central Europe. The couple brought fourteen children into the world, twelve of whom lived long enough to marry and, in all but one case, have children of their own. Meanwhile Haim traded in gold, silver, pearls, jewels, and money, attending the fairs at Leipzig and Frankfurt and arranging sales across Europe from Moscow to London. For a time he supplied silver to the Jewish mint-master of Stettin in Pomerania, though that turned out to be an ill-fated venture. Glikl participated in all the business decisions, drew up the partnership contracts, and helped with accounts and local pledges. We started out young and "without great wealth," said Glikl, but eventually the couple could draw on much credit in Hamburg and elsewhere.

Then, in January 1689, Haim fell on his way to a business appointment in the Christian part of town and died soon after. Glikl was left with eight "orphans" still at home to raise, dower, and marry. In the next years, she carried on the Jewish strategy (born of considerations of business and of safety) of marrying some of her children close to home and some of them in distant cities: Berlin, Amsterdam, Metz, and elsewhere. The family business she took on herself, setting up a shop for manufacturing hose, buying and selling pearls and other jewelry, importing wares from Holland, attending the fairs of Braunschweig and Leipzig, and lending money and honoring bills of exchange across Europe. Unlike Haim, she did not have partners or agents outside the family: her elder sons or a brother accompanied her to fairs, since a respectable woman could not travel alone. At her height she was able to marshal 20,000 reichstaler in cash from Jews and non-Jews in a morning on the Hamburg Exchange and go off to Vienna with 50,000 reichstaler-worth of jewelry to sell. If this put her well below the great bankers, it was still quite substantial, and she and her son Nathan were part of the credit networks upon which "Court Jews" like the Oppenheimers at Vienna depended for their imperial loans.

As a businesswoman, Glikl was not unusual among the German Jews. Her grandmother and mother were both involved in loans, crafts, and trade, and Glikl described other resourceful matrons, such as Esther, "a pious honorable woman, who . . . always went to the fairs."[26] And traveling around to fairs did not detract from a Jewish widow's reputation, especially when she made as much money as Glikl did. If anything, it brought added invitations for marriage.

For more than a decade Glikl turned down all such proposals. Then, in 1699, her daughter and son-in-law suggested a match with the recently widowed Hirsch Levy, a wealthy merchant-banker and leader of the Jewish community of Metz, just within the border of the kingdom of France. Letter in hand, Glikl reflected on the uncertainties of her state as she neared the age of fifty-four. One of her children had put heavy drains on her future through his commercial follies. And what other worries she had:

I still had a big business to manage, my credit was large with Jews and non-Jews both, and it all gave me nothing but grief. In the heat of summer and the rain and snow of winter I went to the fairs; every day I went to the market; even in winter I stood in my stall. And since little was left of what I once possessed, I was morose and tried only to sustain my honor so as not, God forbid, to become the charge of my children.

Glikl also feared that as she was less able to take the strain of fairs and to check on all her bales and goods, her business might founder and she "might, God forbid, become bankrupt and my creditors take a loss through me, thus shaming me, my children, and my pious husband, who lay under the sod."[27]

So she accepted the match, made an advantageous arrangement for her dowry and for the support of her last unmarried child, and moved into the splendidly appointed household of Hirsch Levy—or Cerf Levy, as he was called in France. The city on the Moselle was a frontier town, its population kept busy provisioning Louis XIV's troops, producing craft products, and redistributing grains from the region around Metz. Some five percent of the population were Ashkenazic Jews, who had been allowed to reside in the city even after its Protestants had departed in the wake of the revocation of the Edict of Nantes. The royal intendant wrote of their usefulness in 1699, the very year of Glikl's marriage. The Jews provided the king's troops with much-needed grains and horses. They constituted "a kind of republic and neutral nation," able to travel easily and inexpensively, to acquire accurate price information, and to move merchandise across borders because of their connections with fellow Jews.[28] Had not Cerf Levy and his partner brought six thousand sacks of grain to Metz during the threatened famine the year before? Apart from this, the Jews were bankers, making big loans to officers and *seigneurs* and petty loans to butchers and peasants (we find Glikl's daughter Esther Goldschmidt cosigning with her husband Moses Schwabe a large loan to a financial officer,[29] but most Jewish women were involved in making small loans) and dealers in gold, jewelry, currency, and secondhand goods.

And then, just as Glikl was getting accustomed to a house in which she had seen "more gold and silver than in any wealthy man's in all of Ashkenaz," Hirsch Levy went bankrupt.[30] He was honest and trustworthy in his enormous business, said Glikl, but his creditors devoured him. The Jewish *Gemeinde* (as the community organization was called) thought there had been some "disorder" in Levy's affairs, but blamed his fall especially on the greed of Christians who had lent to him at exorbitant interest. All during 1702 notaries were busy drawing up contracts whereby Jewish and Christian creditors consolidated their claims against Hirsch, and finally there was a settlement in which they received about half of what they were owed.

Instead of living in opulence and independence, Glikl bas Judah Leib and Hirsch ben Isaac had to be helped by their children. Glikl may have resumed some jewelry trading, but Hirsch was reduced to giving advice to his son Samuel, urging him to be satisfied with his role as Rabbi of Alsace and not take on the mint of the Duke of Lorraine, outside France. Samuel ignored him, and Hirsch's premonition was borne out: Louis XIV, concerned about currency smuggled into France, forbade Samuel Levy and his partners to reenter the kingdom unless they broke with the Lorraine mint.[31]

Samuel ben Hirsch stayed in Lorraine and his father died brokenhearted in 1712, leaving Glikl less than a third of her marriage portion. As she neared seventy, Glikl finally moved in with her daughter and wealthy son-in-law. From their house she saw her grandson marry well and her stepson Samuel build a house like a "palace" in Lorraine only to go into bankruptcy a few years later and be accused of staging it fraudulently. She died at seventy-eight in 1724.

Zevi Hirsch Ashkenazi, the other figure in our test of Sombart, came to know Glikl's Hamburg well.[32] He had been born in Moravia in 1660 of a lineage of learned rabbis and had begun to write commentaries on the Torah as a boy. Trained in Budapest, Salonika, and Belgrade, he had sat at the feet of both Ashkenazic and Sephardic masters and sustained relations—both friendly and conflictual, but always close—with both Jewish communities throughout his life. This was an unusual crossing of boundaries, since rabbis ordinarily confined themselves to what they called their own "Jewish Nation." He was to learn many of the languages of the Mediterranean and Europe along the way: the somewhat differing Hebrew of the Sephards and Ashkenaz and their vernaculars (Ladino, Yiddish), German, Spanish, Italian, Turkish, and Arabic.

The fortunes of war sent Zevi Hirsch from Budapest, where his first wife and daughter died in the imperial siege of that city in 1680, to Sarajevo and then to Berlin, where he met and married Sarah bas Mechullam, daughter of the head rabbi of Hamburg and the adjacent towns of Altona and Wandsbek. By 1690 the couple was in Hamburg/Altona. Over the next twenty-four years Sarah gave birth to at least twelve children, ten of them still alive decades later—another astonishing record like that of Glikl and Haim.

As teacher in Altona and then as head rabbi of the Ashkenazic communities in Hamburg, Altona, and Wandsbek, Zevi Hirsch had diverse connections with business, money, and credit. Many rabbis were also in trade, but not Zevi Hirsch. Provided with a house and a school building, he received a small annual salary of 60 reichstaler a year and payments from the sale of kosher wines from France and Italy, whose arrival he supervised to make sure there was no contamination. Beyond that, he refused the gifts that notable merchants urged upon him and that rabbis almost always accepted. He did care about supporting his growing family, so his son Jacob reported, and fell into melancholy when a trading partner assigned him by the Jewish *Gemeinde* lost all their money and fled. But above all he wanted to remain independent. Finally, some wealthy supporters (including one of Glikl's kin) took what money Zevi Hirsch had, invested it in jewelry for him, and maintained the rabbi and his family with the profits.

Zevi Hirsch was also a celebrated judge, arbitrating disputes, evaluating charitable projects, and writing and ultimately publishing responses (*responsa*) to queries from Jews all over Ashkenaz and Sephardy, from London to Lvov. Whether he was determining the presence of heresy, the rightfulness of a divorce decree, or the legitimacy of a Torah scroll, he liked to see himself as "fearing no man," no matter how powerful, and as "father and protector of the poor." Some of his *responsa* were directly on economic matters, as when he said that those who lent at interest were transgressors of the Torah.[33]

Other times, riches and business were among the threads in a complex tangle of conflict. Such was the case in 1709, when a conjuncture of three different issues led to Zevi Hirsch's resignation as rabbi. Throughout, Zevi Hirsch was pitted against Baer Cohen, a merchant who had come to Hamburg/Altona poor and had become very rich. Cohen was also devoted to Talmud study, and somewhat generous to those in need. But he had terrorized the members of the Jewish *Gemeinde* by his tactics against those whom he disliked, spreading false rumors about them to harm their credit with Jews and non-Jews and abruptly cutting off business relations with them. He was also arbitrary in his imposition of interest rates, raising or lowering them as it suited his fancy.

According to Jacob Emden, Baer Cohen's hatred for his father was aroused when Zevi Hirsch reproached Baer for these immoral economic practices. According to Glikl, Zevi Hirsch crossed Baer Cohen by holding the merchant to a pledge made to his first wife on her deathbed that he would marry his wife's young niece, whom they had raised. Baer finally found other rabbis to release him from a promised union with "an orphan he had brought up as his own child." According to the rabbinical tradition, it was a fine point of religious law that set Baer Cohen against Zevi Hirsch Ashkenazi. The rabbi was asked whether a chicken without a heart was kosher. Yes, answered Zevi Hirsch, in a famous judgment: the wife had dropped or lost the heart or she could not recognize it; there was no such thing as a chicken without a heart; thus it was kosher. An outcry was heard about this decision from rabbis near and far, including from one Moses Rothenberg, whom Baer Cohen and his allies were backing for rabbi of Altona. Unwilling to be co-rabbi with such a man, Zevi Hirsch resigned and a year later moved with his brood to Amsterdam.[34]

His four years in Amsterdam, from 1710 to 1714, resembled those at Hamburg/Altona except that his rabbinical salary from the Ashkenazic community was higher and he judged even more commercial cases than before. Then he had a serious falling out with the Sephardic leaders of the city, who had initially welcomed him. One Nehemiah Hayon had arrived from the Levant and Berlin, and Zevi Hirsch claimed his writings gave support to the false Messiah Sabbatai Zevi.[35] (Sabbatai Zevi had been proclaimed the Messiah in December 1665, and then had disappointed most of his many Jewish followers across Europe by converting to Islam. Decades later, a small number still believed he was the Jewish savior under a Muslim guise. Rabbis like Zevi Hirsch were ever on the lookout for Sabbatian heresies, visions, and prophecies hidden in seemingly innocent works.) When a Sephardic commission found, to the contrary, that Hayon's writings were just good mystical Kabbalah, Zevi Hirsch disagreed and refused to apologize, fearing "desecration of the name of God" if he made a false retraction.[36]

Again he picked up his household and left Amsterdam. After more wandering—including a visit to London, where he was received in the streets "like a king" by both Sephards and Ashkenaz—he ended up in southern Poland. There he was lodged, nourished, and cared for with his whole family by the pious Israel Rubinowicz, general manager of the vast estates, villages, and towns of the Sieniawski family. He died rabbi of Lvov in 1718.[37]

### III

The autobiographical/biographical texts being used here have certain common sources, even while their authors had divergent learning. Glikl began to write her Yiddish memoirs in 1689 to help her fight the "melancholy thoughts" that followed the sudden loss of her first husband and then added to them during her years of widowhood and remarriage in Metz. Though her experience keeping business accounts may have encouraged her skills of self-observation, her autobiography was not a spinoff from a ledger or *livre de raison*, as was often the case in Christian Italy and France. Rather, Jewish life history was fostered by the centuries-old "ethical will," an exposition of moral lessons and personal wisdom passed on to one's children along with instructions for one's burial and the disposition of one's goods.[38] This connection helps us understand the moral tension in

Glikl's text, a tension heightened by her insertion of folktales at several junctures to illustrate or comment on the story of her life. The cultural resources she drew upon for the writing were primarily the vernacular ones open to Jewish women and to "men who are like women" in not knowing Hebrew very well: Yiddish books that brought her excerpts from Scripture and from rabbinic commentary, moral teachings, prayers, all kinds of stories, and German news accounts and popular books. Her debates with herself in her book are informed not by the style of Talmudic analysis of cases like the chicken without a heart, but by the oral tradition, female and male, that always begins "that reminds me of a story."

Jacob Emden was born in Hamburg/Altona in 1697, the fourth child and first son of Zevi Hirsch and Sarah.[39] Educated by his father and by his own travels and experience, Jacob had wide learning, interests, and language skills (German, Dutch, and Latin, along with Hebrew and Yiddish). His religious associations throughout Europe were primarily with Ashkenazic rabbis and communities, however, and he acquired his name "Emden" after his few years (1728–33) as rabbi in that north German town. Mostly he lived as a scholar and writer, settling with his first and then second and third wives and children in Altona until his death in 1776, publishing his writings from a printing press in his own house. Like his father he went about unmasking hidden Sabbatians, along with composing other works on Jewish law and liturgy. Like his father, he spoke out against wrongful business practices and made enemies of those he offended. In his prayer book *Siddur*, after quoting from an ancient Sage "one must not teach one's son to sell spices," he went on, "we could add moneylending to this prohibition in our own day for the brigandage of these people is causing all kinds of trouble."[40]

Like his father he refused to accept gifts, while complaining vociferously about fathers-in-law and brothers-in-law who cheated him of his due and about debtors to his late father from whom he could not collect. Ultimately, for ten or twelve years after 1730, Emden did accept the patronage of the Norden family, "known throughout Ashkenaz for their wealth, their good name, and their generosity toward the needy," and went into the jewelry trade with goods supplied by them. After this the demands of a growing family pushed him into other shortlived commercial efforts: clocks from England, tea, lottery tickets, even small loans secured by pawns (an enterprise begun by his first wife). Everything came to naught; profits "went up in smoke." Either he was unlucky in the market or incompetent or had been tricked and defrauded. If only his second wife, from a merchant family, had been good at trade: "my worries would have been over; I could have devoted myself to my dear studies and thought only of the Torah!"[41]

Emden began to write his autobiography when he was in his forties, to tell his children of God's gifts to him, to recount his many woes, and to defend his innocence against his enemies and detractors. Like Glikl, he wanted his children to know where they came from, and like her, he began with an account of his ancestors, branching into a full biography of his celebrated father Zevi Hirsch Ashkenazi, based on letters, papers, and memories. The complexity in his writing came not from a mixture of life-story with folktale, but from the juxtaposition of biography and autobiography, his own life repeating his father's but also diverging from it and allowing him to state grievances against his honored progenitor.

Let us examine these texts first in terms of money and gain, the "be-all and end-all," "the pivot of life" for Jews in Sombart's view. Reichstaler, the German coin of account, appear frequently in Glikl's pages as a marker for riches: the amount of reichstaler in a dowry given to a daughter, son, or grandson; the amount of reichstaler that a father, future in-law, or former business partner was worth; the amount of money lost at a fair or by the improvident deals of a son. Sometimes she used other signs for affluence: the house of a Jewish banker "like a palace," or the lavish hospitality and high-ranking non-Jewish guests at a wedding. More often it was money. How could it be otherwise when German Jews ordinarily could not build or own a house, but merely leased one in a crowded Jewish quarter or ghetto, and rarely had estates or landed titles? Twice Glikl introduced political connections to indicate both wealth and status: once in describing Haim's former business partner, Judah Berlin, who "stands so high in the esteem of the Prince Elector [of Brandenburg] and does so much business with him that if God, may his name be praised, does not turn against him, he will be the richest man in all Ashkenaz when he dies"; once in characterizing as "Court Jew" (Hofjud) her in-law Solomon Samson, banker and provisioner to the Margrave of Baiersdorf.[42] But how many Jews had such office?

Reichstaler provided a simple and practical form in which to circulate news rapidly about the marriage pool and credit across the widely dispersed Ashkenazic communities of Europe. In fact, money represented more than riches for Glikl. It was a shorthand not only for the gold ornaments and silver she saw in Hirsch Levy's house but also for prestige rankings within the *Gemeinde*. Reichstaler were counters in her intense marriage negotiations with her fellow Jews. At least as important as wealth were the proposed partner's reliability and temperament, the expectations that the future in-laws would receive and train a young son during the first years of marriage, and the promise for a congenial intimacy that would produce ample progeny. It is especially interesting that, as a symbolic marker, money was reserved by Glikl for the children of Israel. Other markers were used to denote the riches, power, and prestige of "the people of the nations," as Glikl called the non-Jews.

In his theory of capitalism, Werner Sombart was heir to the concepts of Georg Simmel, in which money always brought with it a single homogeneous meaning, flattening quality and difference and thus (supposedly) facilitating rational calculation. In a recent book Viviana Zelizer has urged us, on the contrary, to recognize the multiple meanings of money and the varied messages it carries with it. Glikl's memoirs are a perfect example of that multivalence.[43]

In addition, Glikl rarely praised wealth by itself, but ordinarily coupled it with honor, wealth and honor, "*oysher un koved*," to quote her Yiddish. "My mother married off her daughters in *oysher un koved*"; "[my sister's father-in-law] died in Berlin in *oysher un koved*."[44] The esteem in which one was held was shown in many ways: by the hospitality with which one was greeted in visits to Jewish communities, say, in Berlin or Metz; by one's place at the dining table. A man was honored by being selected as an officer of the *Gemeinde* and an agent in negotiating with Christian governors; a rabbi by invitations to teach from several communities.

For Jews more generally, *koved* was especially connected with uprightness and honesty in business. Haim and Glikl were constantly seeking and praising Jewish business partners who were *erlikher, redlikher*, and it was a point of honor for Glikl that she left Hamburg "owing not a single reichstaler to Jew or non-Jew."[45] (Not technically a point of truth, for she departed with her exit taxes unpaid to both the Jewish *Gemeinde* and the Hamburg government—but these evidently did not have the same importance to her as business debts.)

Glikl's fear of commercial failure was very much a matter of shame and disgrace. In relation to non-Jews, bankruptcy was all the worse because it could reflect on other Jews as well as bringing *Hillul ha-Shem*, the desecration of God's name. Thinking back on her life in the immediate wake of the bankruptcy of her second husband in Metz, she wrote, "I should not have thought of marrying again for I could not hope to meet another Haim Hamel." Instead, "I fell into the hands of [Hirsch Levy] and had to live the very shame against which I had hoped to protect myself."[46]

In his *Parfait Négociant* (The Perfect Merchant) of 1679, Jacques Savary, author of the French Commercial Ordinance of 1673, talked of commerce as both "useful and honorable." Business failure brought shame and disgrace, even when it was due to misfortune rather than to overstocking of merchandise or reckless loans or other imprudent actions and get-rich-quick schemes. This was as it should be because the public had to have faith in merchants and entrepreneurs: there is "nothing of which merchants must be more jealous than their honor." Savary instructed bankrupt merchants to put on a modest countenance and use gentle words in facing their creditors. Nor was this just advice. Thomas Luckett has shown how important honorable reputation was to the merchants of Paris in the eighteenth century and how shameful bankruptcy.[47]

In these examples, Christian merchants were making a claim against traditional noble disdain for the mercenary nature of their trade. The Jewish merchants were affirming their honor against a Christian world that rarely accorded them more than Shylock's raw sense of injury against Antonio's rudeness. Little recognized by Christian contemporaries in the early modern period, the intense Jewish sense of *koved* was completely missed by Sombart and has not been given its due by students of Jewish commercial culture. More generally, we have here an element to add to the history of early modern credit. Craig Muldrew has pointed out that neighborly sentiment, backed by Christian moral teaching, served to guarantee the extensive credit relations in seventeenth-century English communities, quite apart from the threat of litigation.[48] The Jewish and Christian examples show how honor and shame played a similar role in sustaining the credit relations of merchants.

If Glikl insisted that honor counted as much as riches in a good life, she sometimes went much further in expressing doubts to her children about the value of wealth. It is an issue she debated with herself throughout her memoirs. On one page, she says admiringly of an uncle who died young, "Had he lived he would have become immensely rich; in his hands, you should pardon the expression, dung turned to gold." On another page, she asks, "Who knows if it is good to live in great riches . . . and spend our time in this transient world in nothing but pleasure?" A Jewish merchant can rise in the world, but he or she can also fall. What of Haim's brother Abraham, "as full of Torah as a pomegranate is of seeds," who had become rich in Hannover after his study years in Poland and then been ruined by the trickery of his partners? If she told her children that Haim had recouped his losses from an unjust lawsuit against him by ample sales at the fairs because "the dear Lord saw our innocence," she also declared that wicked persons often arrived at great wealth.[49]

Thus, one could not always understand the Lord's ways in regard to worldly riches. Best to remember Job's admission, "Naked were we born and naked we must depart." Glikl told her children the story of how Alexander the Great learned about the limits of material desire. He had found his way to the Garden of Eden, but was not admitted because he was not righteous. Instead he was thrown a human eye and told to balance it on the scales against all his gold and silver. The eye was always heavier than the gold and silver. Then, at Aristotle's bidding, Alexander threw a little dirt on the eye, and it immediately lost its weight. Aristotle explained that the human eye is insatiable while it is in a living person, but when the person dies, a little earth is sufficient.[50]

The autobiography of Glikl bas Judah Leib expresses not Sombart's "supremacy of gain," but deep ambivalence about the unending pursuit of gain. In the life of Zevi Hirsch Ashkenazi, as described by his son, there was even more tension in regard to wealth. Reichstaler and other coinages are mentioned in connection with dowries, salaries, and debts, but they are not as significant as markers in Zevi Hirsch's life as they are in Glikl's. Here learning and rabbinical lineage rather than money bear the freight of multiple meanings.

It is especially Zevi Hirsch's role as judge that calls riches into question. He is "the Just," in one of his son's favorite appellations. As he was strict in the fulfillment of the laws of diet and purity, denouncing the slovenly practices of those in charge of Passover matzoh and ritual slaughter, so he was strict in denouncing wrongful economic practices. In arbitrating disputes, "he made no exception for person and gave no favor for riches, for money was to his eyes 'like stones and dust of gold' " (the reference is to Job 28, where the riches of the earth are contrasted with God's unfathomable wisdom). He condemned loans at fixed rates of interest, and urged instead loans based on pawns "to be practiced according to the law of love and grace."[51]

As for Zevi Hirsch's enemies, they were rich on ill-gotten gains and immoral action: Baer Cohen, his opponent in Hamburg, the lying destroyer of other people's credit; Moses Rothenberg, his competitor for the rabbinate at Altona, who had thrown another rabbi into a Christian prison for inability to pay a debt, thereby causing the good man's death on a Sabbath; Aaron Gokkes and his two associates at Amsterdam, leaders of a corrupt faction among the Ashkenaz, "who had amassed a great fortune without respect for the law." Failing to bribe Zevi Hirsch to support them against the "men who cared for justice and peace," Gokkes and his accomplices tried to evict him from his rabbinate.[52]

But God kept a watch on these rich wrongdoers. He let Baer Cohen and his son maintain their prosperity, but the grandchildren of Baer Cohen were reduced to begging as Jacob Emden wrote his account. Moses Rothenberg had suffered bankruptcy, even though he had won the Altona rabbinate. The three Ashkenaz of Amsterdam lost their positions in the congregation, and two of them died horribly, one being strangled, the other breaking his neck in a fall from a carriage.

Nonetheless, there is no absolute condemnation of wealth in the life of Zevi Hirsch. "The quest for goods" was allowable by the Talmud, and there was nothing wrong in Zevi Hirsch requiring the Ashkenazic community of Amsterdam to raise the salary assigned to his post if he were to come there with his large household. The previous rabbi had supplemented his annual salary with many gifts from local families, which the Just would refuse to accept. As presented by his son, Zevi Hirsch stands for independent moderation in regard to wealth, a wish to live by the clarity of contracted salary rather than the ambiguous obligations of gifts. He was fastidious even about permitted income: deeming impure the kosher wine imported into Hamburg/Altona one year because of its contact with soldiers, he had all the barrels dumped rather than taking his allowed payment through a sale to non-Jews. Beyond his family's needs, he gave away the excess, donating, for instance, the traditional payments made by litigants for rabbinical judgments back to the Amsterdam community.

If God sometimes punished wealthy evildoers, he could on occasion give material reward to the good. One of the fruits attributed to Zevi Hirsch's rabbinate in Hamburg/Altona was community prosperity (a view perhaps originating with the father himself, since the son was born only in the middle of those years):

As long as the glory of my father dwelled in [Hamburg/Altona/Wandsbek], blessing dwelled there too. The members of the *Gemeinde* did good business and everything they undertook succeeded. Rich people became numerous and the communities grew in size, honor and riches. Truly, there was money in abundance. . . . The three communities surpassed all the others in Ashkenaz until the day my father, of pious memory, departed. Then they began to have serious trouble.[53]

Great wealth was acceptable to Zevi Hirsch, at least in other men, but only so long as it was rightfully obtained and suitably combined with piety, love of Torah, and charity. One such man was "the very rich" Hirsch Hannover, who visited Zevi Hirsch to talk of points of law and begged him unsuccessfully to accept payment for one hour of study each day. Another such was Israel Rubinowicz, the manager of the Sieniawski estates, who maintained Zevi Hirsch and his family in his last years in a spacious house near Częstochowa. Zevi Hirsch finally allowed himself to receive such gifts because Rubinowicz was "a man of great rectitude and God-fearing . . . who wished to make of his house a tabernacle for the service of the Torah."[54]

Rubinowicz, like Glikl and her fellow merchants, cared also about honor. "I esteem my lady's favor more than money," he wrote to Elisabeth Sieniawska in the wake of an unsatisfactory jewelry purchase, where he offered to take the loss. "However poor I may be, even if I lose everything, I will remember to preserve my honor."[55] This returns us to Zevi Hirsch's concern for honor and "good name," a concern maintained consistently through his shifting evaluations of wealth. Indeed, defense of good name is a central project of Emden's whole biography/autobiography. Intensifying "good name" for the individual, the family, and the Jewish people was its profound connection with *Hillul ha-Shem*, fear of desecrating or profaning the name of the Lord. The vigor of Hirsch's pursuit of Sabbatian heresy, his refusal to apologize to a suspect, and his other campaigns were fired by *Hillul ha-Shem*.

Zevi Hirsch Ashkenazi's silver seal shows how honor linked together the different features of Jewish sensibility: it had a carved handle with two lions (the lions of Judah) supporting tablets of the Law on which were engraved the letters for *shem tov*, "good name." On the seal itself was a deer—the referent of Hebrew *zevi* and Yiddish *hirsch*—within a crown next to the letters for *keter Torah*, the "crown of Torah." A passage of Mishnah is here evoked: "R. Simeon said, 'There are three Crowns: the Crown of Torah, the Crown of Priesthood, and the Crown of Royalty; but the Crown of good name exceeds them all.' "[56]

## IV

Multiple meanings of money, ambivalence and widely ranging attitudes toward wealth, the prestige of riches surpassed by rabbinical glory, an all-important sense of honor and good name in dealing with Jews and non-Jews— the cases of Glikl and Zevi Hirsch do not yield quintessential "Jewish" traits or "the spirit of capitalism" by Sombartian definitions. Once again Jewish honor is defended against his claims. Weber and Tawney would surely urge us to explicate further the relation between the rabbi and the pious ethical merchant, between rabbinical holiness and community prosperity, but such analysis would not lead us to the "rational calculation" that was their goal.

Let us come back to "the origins of capitalism" in a moment, after we consider two other features of seventeenth-century Jewish culture suggested by these writings. The first is the proximity of, the porousness between, family matters and commercial matters. Haim returned from fairs with marriage proposals, and dowry news was awaited as eagerly as news of the Danzig pearl trade. Glikl's many trips for negotiating marriages or weddings also brought commercial profits: precious stones sold at Amsterdam after one daughter's wedding, at Vienna after a son's; a fair at Naumburg fitted in after a betrothal agreement in Bayreuth; children's dowry money lent out at interest until it had to be paid. (Jacob Emden lent out part of the dowry money from his second wife to a Hamburg Christian, with the debtor's furniture as security, but with his usual bad luck, the debt was not repaid and another creditor seized the furniture before Emden got to the house.) Glikl's scheduling is not just Benjamin-Franklinesque time-saving; it is interconnected experience.

The porous boundary existed also in the quarrels that rent and held together the Jewish communities. Family and business intertwined with struggles for religious prestige and about the meaning of the Law. We have seen this already in the Zevi Hirsch Ashkenazi/Baer Cohen affair. Let us now examine another such interweaving in a set of events involving Glikl's children and the learned Zevi Hirsch, as recounted in part by Jacob Emden.[57] After Haim's death, Glikl married her daughter Freudchen to Mordecai ben Moses, the son of the Hamburg merchant and learned Talmudist, who invested Zevi Hirsch's money in the jewelry trade for him—one of the "good merchants." By the late 1690s, Mordecai and Freudchen moved to London, where Mordecai began to trade in diamonds. In 1706 the rabbi of the small Ashkenazic community in London privately divorced one Ascher Ensel Cohen from his wife. Heavily in debt and an obsessive gambler, Ensel was going to leave for the West Indies to avoid his creditors. The divorce was supposedly to go into effect only if he did not return. (In fact, the divorce was a bankruptcy strategy—used by contemporary Christians and Jews both—to protect what assets the husband had by bestowing them on his wife.)

When news of the divorce leaked out, Mordecai ben Moses challenged it as invalid, for it had been pronounced without consultation and written secretly in one sitting by a Sephardic scribe. Everyone knew that an Ashkenazic scribe often required ten tries until a bill of divorce was free of irregularity, especially when issued to a Cohen, that is, to a descendant of the High Priest Aaron. (Mordecai's suspicions were sound. The Sephardic scribe had been selected because the son-in-law of the Ashkenazic scribe had lost his money at cards with Ensel, and it was feared that the aggrieved father-in-law would not cooperate with this dubious project.) The rabbi was incensed; was it not ancient tradition that no Jew dare speak against a divorce that has been duly pronounced? Mordecai was excommunicated with a total ban: no Ashkenaz could associate with him, his sons could not attend school, and Freudchen was denied the right to have her newly born daughter given a name in the synagogue.

The affair instantly went out on the Jewish networks, stimulating responses from rabbis in several cities and in Hebrew printed pamphlets with titles like *Oracle* and *The True Story of a Rabbi*. It was even talked of on the London Stock Exchange.[58] Mordecai ben Moses turned to the esteemed Zevi Hirsch Ashkenazi. Friend to Mordecai's father, Zevi Hirsch was also kin to the angry rabbi, but the Just "feared no man." He sent a long opinion from Hamburg/Altona that vindicated Mordecai completely and was circulated under the title *An Important Event*. Rabbis from Amsterdam and Rotterdam also insisted that Mordecai had been punished much too severely. Mordecai then founded a synagogue with a prayer quorum (*minyan*) in his own house and built his own cemetery. He went on to become a leader in the diamond trade with Madras.[59]

This story does not fit the model—originated by Max Weber and elaborated by Raymond de Roover in his study of the Medici bank[60]—of the separation of business strategy and accounting from domestic strategy and accounting as a necessary and inevitable step toward rational advanced enterprise. Almost the opposite seems to be the case here. Crossed-over strands of action and communication networks buzzing with diamond prices, bills of divorces, bans, bankruptcies, and rabbinical admonition seem to heighten the energy of enterprise, religion, and family life all at once.

Is this perhaps a distinctive Jewish style? Only comparative research could answer this question. Family matters and business matters intersect in the Christian world, surely. What may make the entanglement more frequent in the Jewish case is the character of the population and of partnership. The German-Jewish commercial families spread across Europe knew each other, and the web of in-laws was extensive. Their partnerships were usually among circles of kin or at least familiars; large sums of money were raised quickly, not through a relatively anonymous trading company or governmental rent-charge, but through, say, a discussion after a prayer service. Especially important, disputes of all kinds came before rabbis for arbitration and judgment, including economic matters when the actors were Jews. (Jews sometimes haled each other before Christian courts, a scandalous action decried by both Glikl and Jacob Emden.)[61] Thus, the weaving of family, economics, and religion into a single public narrative was facilitated by the character and practice of Jewish law.

The second example of Jewish commercial culture—the uses of secrecy—is a more highly developed variant on a European pattern. Stephanie Jed has written some insightful pages on secrecy and the writing of merchants in the Christian world of fifteenth-century Florence. She has argued that the keeping of secret account books gave merchants a sense of protection for their family interests and was also part of the process by which "a conceptual distinction [was maintained] between public and private space."[62] With account books in the Ashkenazic-Jewish community, the stakes were a little different. Written in Yiddish in Hebrew characters, they could rarely be read by Christians. Glikl's accounts in Hamburg she would have kept in Yiddish, and, except for a moment when Haim contemplated calling a former partner before a Christian court (to Glikl's horror), she would probably never have thought of making or having someone make translations in German script. In France after the bankruptcy laws of 1673, all merchants were required to keep properly signed books, the Jewish merchants of Metz being ordered to keep them in French as well as in Yiddish. Glikl's son-in-law, Moses Schwabe, was fined in 1717 when he failed to do so.[63]

Correspondence between Ashkenazic Jews was usually in Yiddish as well. Transactions with non-Jews would have to be recorded in at least one copy in the local vernacular—German, French, or English—as would any document, such as a marriage contract, that the family wanted registered with the secular government. In Metz, Glikl's family and other Jewish families of her day had marriage agreements drawn up in Hebrew *ketubbahs* and in notarized French contracts, while their wills ordinarily remained in Hebrew. In the eighteenth century, the hundreds of letters that the Prager firm (specializing in colonial goods) exchanged between its London and Amsterdam offices and with Jewish traders as far away as Petersburg were all in Yiddish, while a smaller correspondence with non-Jews was in English, Dutch, French, or Italian.[64]

Thus, the sense of inside space created by account books and other records in Hebrew characters was more than a family space; it was a larger Jewish space. Within it, Jewish traders established shifting partnerships with each other and had heated fights before rabbinical courts. We can see the affective and practical advantages of that larger secrecy in Jewish autobiographies like Glikl's, unpublished as they usually were until the late eighteenth century and even more surely concealed from the eyes of outsiders.[65] She could talk with frankness and finally forgiveness of the business follies of her son Leib. She could talk with frankness and vehemence of business quarrels with her fellow Jews. Young Judah Berlin, despite all the good she and Haim had done him, withheld 1,500 reichstaler from their joint business and then refused to return their merchandise when Haim politely dissolved the contract. Haim lost his suit against Judah in a case that aroused intense partisanship in several Jewish communities. Eventually the two men lived in peace, and Judah, later banker and provider of jewels to the court of Prussia, received Glikl and her children warmly in Berlin. Other false partners and agents were described with more indignation: "the real Herod of my whole family," she said of one; and of another, "a puffed-up, fat, overstuffed, arrogant, wicked man."[66]

Not that everything could be recorded fully, even for the insiders. Glikl complained of the treatment of her sons after Haim's death. Mordecai was being hard pressed in connection with goods he had purchased from a local merchant. Needing credit, he and his brothers submitted bills of exchange to a non-Jewish merchant at the Hamburg Börse, who then asked a Jewish merchant for an estimate of their reliability. When the young men came back for the money, the non-Jewish merchant refused to honor their bills. Even while calling on God to avenge Mordecai, Glikl did not name any of the merchants in the text she left for her children. We can easily guess that the Jewish merchant was the influential Baer Cohen, up to his usual tricks. Of him she said merely, "I cannot blame the man I have in mind because I do not know his thoughts. Humans judge by what the eyes see, but God by the heart."[67]

An advantage of Yiddish secrecy was that it allowed Jews to stage their own social dramas quite apart from the criteria of the Christian world around them and to invest trading relations with meanings that went well beyond reichstaler. Hebrew, the Holy Tongue, brought a similar benefit to accounts of rabbinical quarrels and to *responsa* about chicken hearts, Sephardic versus Ashkenazic Torah scrolls, and golems (all three matters concerning boundaries, which were pronounced upon by Zevi Hirsch), even though in printed form, these were sometimes read by Christian Hebraists. Jewish religious controversy divided communities from Safed to London, but also created a common and absorbing theater for them. Jewish business produced profits and losses, but it also generated a treasury of good stories told at the time and for many years afterward.

If we want to consider the "economic functionality" of these various traits in the early modern period, I would talk not of their contribution to rational calculation, but of elements that make business an *interesting* activity, arousing energy and intensity. Here was a payoff more durable and less dangerous than usury. Such elements facilitate extensive credit networks, even while allowing people to air their doubts about each other, or perhaps we should say *just because* they allow closely linked participants to air their doubts about each other. They also make possible the information flow and rapid movement of goods noted by the Metz intendant in 1699.

### V

Weber and Sombart were pioneers in developing a historical theory of the role of "culture" in stimulating or shaping change in economic behavior and institutions. They had much to go on—the work of Karl Marx and Georg Simmel's *Philosophy of Money* among others—but they were the ones who set out the task for historians. Their case was modern capitalism, to whose "spirit" they gave a single definition. (Sombart's heroic German capitalism was still a hope for the future.) They both assumed that there was *one* historical path by which to arrive at patterns of behavior and institutions informed by "rational" calculation of profits.

The initial historical criticism of their views in the 1920s did not fully dislodge either the one-path model or the single definition of genuine modern capitalism or the limiting of "culture" to religious matters. Following Brentano's earlier criticism, André Sayous showed how Catholic merchants of the Italian Renaissance were full-fledged capitalists and thus opened the door to many later studies of scholastic teaching on just price, letters of exchange, and the market; but it could still be argued that the Catholic Mediterranean was a culture bearer for a time and then the initiative passed to the Protestant North. R. H. Tawney's *Religion and the Rise of Capitalism* of 1926 clarified the interplay between "economic and social change" and "religion," and added the social teachings and sermons of the Puritans as a central source.[68] With the publication of H. M. Robertson's *Aspects of the Rise of Economic Individualism* in 1933, accounting was added to religion as a process capable of forming business mentality in its own right, though it was assumed that double-entry bookkeeping was the sole route to true capitalism.[69]

In the international atmosphere and conflicts that followed World War II, comparative studies of "modernization" broadened the perspective further. Alexander Gerschenkron's models of modernization in different settings—English, French, German, Russian—undermined the notion of one right path, even though his title was *Economic Backwardness*. S. N. Eisenstadt edited a collection of essays in 1968 on *The Protestant Ethic and Modernization*, in which it was observed that non-Western countries like Japan could have their own equivalent of the "calling" and "this-worldly asceticism" without benefit of Puritanism.[70] But the pursuit of rational calculation still remained the primary goal and "who got to industrialization first?" or "who got to electrification first?" remained the major kind of question for historical reflection, even though the difference in time from one country's "modernization" to the next might be only a few decades.

Other approaches were emerging. Nothing illustrates better the tension between the one-path evolutionary study and a new way to explore economies and culture than an early book by Clifford Geertz, *Peddlers and Princes: Social Change and Economic Modernization in Two Indonesian Towns* (1963). Geertz had done his fieldwork in the 1950s, just before and just after receiving his doctorate at Harvard in 1956. He had been part of an excited young interdisciplinary team that was sweeping anthropology into the study of large-scale industrializing societies rather than smaller preindustrial communities and into the production of results useful for the direction of social and economic change. (The team projects were sponsored by the Ford and Rockefeller Foundations.) Geertz's thesis and subsequent book, *The Religion of Java* (1960), opened with the grateful hope that "in some way this book may contribute to the realization of [my informants'] aspiration to build a strong, stable, prosperous, and democratic 'New Indonesia'" and ended with a chapter on religion, social conflict, and integration. But primarily it was a rich description of the various forms of religious life and belief. *Peddlers and Princes* came closer to fulfilling the social science and policy goals of the initial project.[71]

Max Weber's perspectives provided some of Geertz's questions for *Peddlers and Princes* (Talcott Parsons, who chaired Geertz's Harvard department, had been translator of the 1930 edition of *The Protestant Ethic*), as did the writings of economists on "takeoff" and "the dynamics of development" in postwar and newly independent societies. What could be shown about such theories by a close ethnographic study of two Indonesian towns poised, or perhaps caught, between past and future, between the "traditional" and the "modern"?

The Javanese town of Modjokuto was organized around the bazaar, a busy and communicative world of small traders, whose daily bargaining gave free play to economic rationality unhampered by "peasant traditionalism." Geertz thought Weber had underestimated the ethos of the bazaar economy, seeing it merely as a setting for "absolute unscrupulousness in the pursuit of selfish interests" rather than as a place where proficient traders followed known rules for negotiation.[72] But Modjokuto was deficient in generating permanent institutions that could extend and transform the economy beyond the bazaar. A few entrepreneurs had created business firms in connection with stores or factories; most of them were Reformist Muslims, whose focus on doctrine and morality made them Javanese versions of Max Weber's Protestants. But their accomplishment was precarious, always in danger of being eroded by the informality and individualism of the bazaar.

The Balinese town of Tabanan was organized around agriculture and rural crafts. Here, in a situation quite unlikely under Weberian (or Sombartian) expectations, the leaders in economic change were the Hinduized aristocrats, displaced from political power but sustaining much prestige in a society accepting traditional ideas of caste and deference. Organizational life was highly developed, every task arousing collective enterprise and the "quack-quack" (in the Balinese term) of many voices, quite in contrast with the one-on-one haggling of the Modjokuto bazaar. The industrial firms created by the Tabanan aristocrats were strong and were in a position to encourage change in the whole urban economy. But here too there were deficiencies: oligarchical structures brought rigidity and collective habits carried with them customary moral concerns, thereby "interfer[ing] with the free play of economic rationality and form[ing] serious obstacles to further growth."[73]

Though Geertz's analysis still used the language of "lacks" and precise changes that "must" be made ("the mentalities of the peddler and the prince must both be abandoned, and in their place must come that of the professional manager"),[74] the breadth, abundance, and nuance of his observation led him to question constricting historical formulations about the study of economic life:

The Weberian tradition is without doubt correct in insisting that economic change is inevitably part and parcel of broader changes occurring throughout society, not an isolated and independent sequence of events. Where it is less certainly correct is in assuming an essential uniformity of the relationship between economic and non-economic changes from case to case. From a narrowly economic point of view development takes the same general form always and everywhere; it consists of a progressively more rational employment of scarce means toward the achievement of specified material ends. But from a sociological point of view it is not clear that such a basic and obvious similarity of form exists, that the changes in religious outlook, class structure, family organization, and so on are identical from one developing society to another.[75]

He went on to attack "highly dichotomous generalized concepts" and "holistic types." Not everything is possible, but flexible and detailed studies will show a wider range of trajectories for change.

In the next years, Geertz subordinated these concerns to the ethnographic quest for webs of meaning and conceptual structures in precise settings. These could still be explored in connection with economic acts, though the link would now be shared conceptual statements ("The cockfight . . . is fundamentally a dramatization of status concerns," as he says in his celebrated 1972 essay)[76] rather than functional actions (furthering or impeding economic change). *Peddlers and Princes* has a bit of both, as in its portrait, say, of Balinese musical-instrument makers, organized in patrilineal kin groups and drowning out the sound of each other's hammers as they vie to make larger and larger gongs. Here kin rivalry is dramatized in work sounds, and traditional structures support economic innovation.

Then, in a publication of 1979, an economic institution moved once again to the center of Geertz's interest: the Moroccan *suq*, or bazaar.[77] A little-understood institution, the bazaar had been treated with reserve by most anthropologists, who preferred the alleged solidarity of non-market exchange to the agonistic higgling of the *suq* traders. Economists thought the bazaar useful insofar as this higgling allowed integrating prices to emerge, but judged it to be clearly a "backward" form, better effaced and replaced by modern commercial methods as soon as possible.

Geertz's goal was to discover the central intentions, actions, and relationships in bazaar exchange and to reveal the "meaning and order" (to cite the book's title) in the shouts, whispers, vigorous gestures, cups of tea, and seemingly random moving about through crowded lanes of men (for the North African bazaar was primarily an affair of men) dressed in anything from silk robes to cotton rags. His case was the town of Sefrou, an age-old major stop on the caravan route between the Mediterranean and Fez to the north and the Sahara and beyond to the south. In the twentieth century during the French Protectorate, the bazaar had expanded to include a European sector, and then Sefrou had become the center of an important regional market: a "hub," as Geertz puts it, rather than a "way-station."

Geertz traces this history, including the role of the Jewish traders of Sefrou in initiating the various changes until the departure of many of them after mid-century to France and Israel. In particular, he gives a close analytical description, drawn from visits to Sefrou in the 1960s, of all the actors, origins, trades, places, codes, customs, language forms and expressions, social relations, organizations, and religious sensibilities that make up the events of the bazaar. Religion had its role to play, through organizations and devotional styles—different for Muslims and Jews—which gave festive expression to the division of labor and allowed trade and piety to flourish side by side. The economic drama that emerges is a ceaseless quest for information on the part of all participants—about products, people, and their trustworthiness—with clientage connections essential to the information flow. The accompanying exchange is, if anything, "hypercommercial," but it flows through a world in which the homogenization and impersonality considered essential to modernity are not present. Instead there is a fine division of labor, a specific identification of people by their origins (geographical and, in the case of the Jews, religious), a lack of standardization in goods and services, and a strong preference for personal contract and witnessing.

Geertz insists that this is not an archaic holdover but a twentieth-century form. It is "still more in the world economy than of it," but it has changed with the times and continues to respond to the shifting demands of national movements and of the Moroccan state. Rather than urge the destruction of the bazaar, as most development theorists would do, Geertz reflects on "the reconstruction of the bazaar as a communications system, the creation of institutional forms within which the individual [*suq* trader's] access to relevant information would be improved."[78]

Geertz's evidence from Indonesia and Morocco; S. D. Goitein's evidence on medieval Jewish traders in the Arab world from the Cairo Geniza documents;[79] the seventeenth-century Ashkenazic evidence presented here; Yannick Lemarchand's demonstration of the viability of *two* forms of accounting in early modern France;[80] recent studies of gifts, exchange, and credit in early modern Europe and trade diasporas worldwide—all point to an approach that is ethnographic and comparative and that does not limit itself to the definitions of culture and economy and the paths for economic change laid down by Weber and Sombart.

An ethnographic/comparative approach also gives us the chance to study the culture of a group—here, of European Jews—without so readily falling into ahistorical reification. Rather than seeing a single Jewish Merchant emerging from the text (as he does in seventeenth-century Christian stereotypical and often anti-Semitic engravings), the historian can savor the difference between the storytelling Jewish woman from Hamburg who made a fortune at the fairs and her rabbi who dumped unkosher wine into the Alster; between the Sephardic Jews who exported Mediterranean coral to India and the Ashkenazim who had to be satisfied with importing diamonds; between Haim ben Joseph, who never missed his Torah reading for the day, no matter how busy he was running about Hamburg buying and selling gold, and Glikl bas Judah Leib, who fit in her Yiddish morality books whenever she had the time to pick them up. Understanding those differences is the business of the historian.

# Notes

This paper was presented as the R. H. Tawney Lecture to the meeting of the Economic History Society in Edinburgh in March 1995. I am immensely grateful to the members of the Society and especially to Maxine Berg for comments and advice. I also want to thank participants in the Shelby Cullom Davis Center for Historical Studies at Princeton University for their comments on an early version of this paper in September 1994.

1. Werner Sombart, *Die Juden und das Wirtschaftsleben* (Leipzig, 1911), 155, 157, 260. Werner Sombart, *The Jews and Modern Capitalism*, trans. Mordecai Epstein (1913), with a new introduction by Samuel Z. Klausner (New Brunswick, N.J., 1982), 131–33, 222. I use Epstein's translation in this paper, with slight modifications when it is not a complete rendering of the German.

2. Studies of Werner Sombart include Arthur Mitzman, *Sociology and Estrangement: Three Sociologists of Imperial Germany* (New York, 1973), part 3; Jeffrey Herf, *Reactionary Modernism: Technology, Culture, and Politics in Weimar and the Third Reich* (Cambridge, 1984), chap. 6; Werner Krause, *Werner Sombart's Weg vom Kathedersozialismus zum Faschismus* (Berlin, 1962); and Nicolaus Sombart, *Nachdenken über Deutschland. Vom Historismus zur Psychoanalyse* (Munich, 1987), 14–21.

3. Recent assessments of Max Weber's thesis, with material relevant to Sombart's views, are Gordon Marshall, *In Search of the Spirit of Capitalism: An Essay on Max Weber's Protestant Ethic Thesis* (London, 1982), and Hartmut Lehmann and Guenther Roth, eds., *Weber's "Protestant Ethic": Origins, Evidence, Contexts* (Washington, D.C., 1993).

4. Benjamin Franklin quoted in Max Weber, *The Protestant Ethic and the Spirit of Capitalism*, trans. Talcott Parsons, with a foreword by R. H. Tawney (1930; reprint, New York, 1958), 49–50.

5. Sombart, *Juden*, 293, 346; *Jews*, 249, 288.

6. Sombart, *Juden*, chap. 10; *Jews*, chap. 10.

7. Sombart, *Juden*, 265–66; *Jews*, 225–26.

8. *Die Memoiren der Glückel von Hameln*, trans. Bertha Pappenheim (Vienna, 1910). Sombart cites this edition (*Juden*, 450 n. 146), describing it accurately as "Privatdruck." That he got access to a limited edition so promptly illustrates his connections to circles of Jewish scholarship.

9. Weber, *Protestant Ethic*, 30–31, 165–66, 185 n. 2, 270–71. On Weber's reservations about racial science and his preference for sociocultural explanations, see Harry Liebersohn, "Weber's Historical Concept of National Identity," in Lehmann and Roth, *Weber's "Protestant Ethic,"* 126–31.

10. Lujo Brentano, *Die Anfänge des modernen Kapitalismus* (Munich, 1916), 127–34, 159 ff. On Brentano, see Guenther Roth, "Weber the Would-Be Englishman," in Lehmann and Roth, *Weber's "Protestant Ethic,"* 104–6.

11. Paul R. Mendes-Flohr, "Werner Sombart's: The Jews and Modern Capitalism: An Analysis of Its Ideological Premises," *Year Book of the Leo Baeck Institute*, 21 (1976): 94.

12. Heinrich H. Graetz (1817–1891), *Geschichte der Juden von den ältesten Zeiten bis auf die Gegenwart*, 11 vols. (Leipzig, 1897–1911). The tenth and eleventh volumes were devoted to the period 1618–1848 and describe Jewish settlements in different parts of Europe and, very briefly, across the Atlantic. The status of the Jews in different Christian and non-Jewish polities and religious movements within the Jewish community are the

central elements of the historical narrative. In 1912, a Hebrew translation of excerpts from Sombart's *Juden* was published by early Zionist circles in Kiev. Jewish readers would have their hearts lifted, said the introduction, by learning from sound historical evidence the many activities of the Jews; Samuel Klausner, introduction to Sombart, *Jews*, c–ci. See also the thoughtful essay by Giacomo Todeschini, "Une Polemica Dimenticata: Sombart e *Die Juden und das Wirtschaftleben* nella Discussione Storiografica," *Societá e Storia* 35 (1987): 139–60.

13. Sombart, *Juden*, xii (reference to Friedrich Nietzsche). To present-day readers, Sombart's "Puritanism is Judaism" may call to mind phrases in an early work of Karl Marx, "On the Jewish Question" (1844): "Money has become a world power and the practical spirit of the Jew has become the practical spirit of the Christian people"; Karl Marx, *Early Texts*, ed. and trans. David McLellan (Oxford, 1971), 85–114. The works are alike in their hostility to "money," that is, in Sombart's case, the rational calculation of capitalism, in Marx's case, the "haggling" of trade and the power of money "to confound and exchange all things" (as he said, quoting Goethe and Shakespeare, in another essay written in 1844 and included in *Early Texts*, 178–83). There are several differences. Sombart was writing a sweeping economic history against Weber's views that Puritanism was the source of capitalism; Marx was writing an essay insisting on the distinction between the state and civil society against Bruno Bauer's view that "the Jewish question" would be solved if Jews would just convert and live in a de-Christianized liberal state (a path that Marx's father had tried to follow). Sombart made the Jews the carriers of rational capitalism because of their religion, their historical situation, and their "race." Marx gave a wider role to the Jews, making them representative of the "principle of civil society," namely, "practical need, egoism." The role of the Jews was determined not by religion ("Let us look for the secret of the Jew not in his religion"), not by "race," but by history, which made haggling and money their way of satisfying practical need and selfishness. Sombart, who was moving from an earlier total rejection of capitalism to a distinction between a bad calculating Jewish capitalism and a good heroic German capitalism, wanted to liberate society only from the former. Marx, who was moving from his earlier idealistic Hegelianism to materialism, wanted to liberate civil society from fulfilling practical need by money and capitalism. Thus, "the social emancipation of the Jew implies the emancipation of society from Judaism." For an insightful study on these matters in Marx, see Dennis K. Fischman, *Political Discourse in Exile: Karl Marx and the Jewish Question* (Amherst, Mass., 1991).

14. Sombart, *Juden*, 155; *Jews*, 131. Harry Liebersohn, "Value-Freedom in the German Sociological Association," in *Fate and Utopia in German Sociology, 1870–1923* (Cambridge, Mass., 1988), 109–20.

15. Moses Hoffmann, *Judentum und Kapitalismus. Eine Kritische Würdigung von Werner Sombarts "Die Juden und das Wirstchaftsleben"* (Berlin, 1912), 3. Interestingly enough, Sombart's book was attacked by those who did not think it anti-Semitic enough: F. Roderich Stoltheim, *Die Juden im Handel und das Geheimnis ihres Erfolges. Zugleich eine Antwort und Ergänzung zu Sombarts Buch: "Die Juden und das Wirtschaftsleben"* (Steglitz, Germ., 1913).

16. Sombart, *Juden*, 346–53, 470–72; *Jews*, 288–92, 396–97.

17. Raphael-Georges Lévy, "Le rôle des Juifs dans la vie économique," *Revue des études juives*, 62 (1911): 162. See also the evidence assembled by Klausner on the strength and limits of Sombart's attachment to the principles of National Socialism; introduction to Sombart, *Jews*, cii–cv.

18. Mordecai (later Mortimer) Epstein (1880–1946), *The English Levant Company: Its Founda-*

*tion and Its History to 1640* (London, 1908), prefatory note. Another edition was printed the same year under the title *The Early History of the Levant Company* (London, 1908). Werner Sombart, *Socialism and the Social Movement*, trans. M. Epstein (London, 1909), translator's introduction.

19. Werner Sombart, *The Jews and Modern Capitalism*, trans. M. Epstein, with introduction by Bert Hoselitz (New York, 1951), translator's introductory note, London, 21 April 1913 (not included in the 1982 edition).

20. M. Epstein, review of *Der Bourgeois* by Werner Sombart, *The Economic Journal*, 24, no. 95 (1914): 403–6. Werner Sombart, *The Quintessence of Capitalism: A Study of the History and Psychology of the Modern Business Man*, ed. and trans. M. Epstein (New York, 1915).

21. Writing for *The Jewish Chronicle* in 1920–1924 under the pen name Benammi, Epstein spoke of Judaism as a religion of love and righteousness: the Pentateuch insisted on honesty, and those who made cruel bargains went against Jewish ideals. During the Middle Ages, "the common people preferred to deal with a Jew rather than with a Lombard. The Lombard was a harsh creditor; the Jew had a soft spot in his heart for a man in distress"; Mortimer Epstein, *Aspects of Jewish Life and Thought (The Letters of Benammi)* (New York, 1922), vi, 19–22, 154–60; Mortimer Epstein, *Essays on Jewish Life and Thought (The Letters of Benammi: Second Series)* (London, 1924), vi, 64–69.

22. For the impact of Sombart's definition of the issues on a young Jewish historian of Poland in the early years of the twentieth century, see Jacob Litman, *The Economic Role of Jews in Medieval Poland: The Contribution of Yitzhak Schipper* (Lanham, Md., 1984), 42–50. In recent decades, Sombart's formulation of the questions is still important in Léon Poliakov, *Les banchieri Juifs et le Saint-Siège du 13e au 17e siècle* (Paris, 1965), 2, 222–23, 266–69, 291–305; and Hillel Levine, *Economic Origins of Antisemitism: Poland and Its Jews in the Early Modern Period* (New Haven, 1991), 22–26, 78–79, 108–35. The point here is not whether these authors agree with Sombart, but whether they take seriously his statement of the historical question about the origins of capitalism. In his *Economic History of the Jews in England*, Harold Pollins specifically eschews such questions of "grand theory" in favor of "factual foundations" and "middle range theories" (Rutherford, N.J., 1982), 9. Max Weber is included in Pollins's bibliography, but not Sombart. Similarly, Péter Hanák states that he will not "enter into the hoary discussion about the presumed 'economic talents' and intellectual virtues of the Jewish people" in his interesting study of Jews in the Hungarian economy in the eighteenth and nineteenth centuries. He considers only structural and situational issues and does not draw upon cultural material in his analysis; Péter Hanák, "Jews and the Modernization of Commerce in Hungary, 1760–1848," in Michael K. Silber, ed., *Jews in the Hungarian Economy, 1760–1945: Studies Dedicated to Moshe Carmilly-Weinberger on his Eightieth Birthday* (Jerusalem, 1992), 23–29. Derek Penslar puts the Sombart thesis in a wider framework in his excellent essay "The Origins of Jewish Political Economy," *Jewish Social Studies* 3 (1997): 27–60.

23. Louis Rosenstock-Franck, "Les Juifs et la vie économique" (seminar presentations, Lyon, 1941), preserved in the Archives du Consistoire central, Fonds Moch 63, library of the Alliance Israélite universelle, Paris. Rosenstock-Franck did not refer in these seminar presentations to Sombart's *Deutscher Sozialismus* of 1934, in which the German sociologist spelled out his own program for National Socialism. Louis Rosenstock-Franck was a graduate of the Ecole polytechnique, who had published books on *L'économie corporative fasciste en doctrine et en fait* (1934) and *L'expérience Roosevelt et le milieu social américain* (1937). In 1942, he seems to have been in Washington D.C. writing pamphlets on the French economy for the Brookings Institute. He returned to France after the war.

24. The Yiddish manuscript of Glikl bas Judah Leib's autobiography was first edited and published by David Kaufmann under the title *Die Memoiren der Glückel von Hameln, 1645–1719* (Frankfurt am Main, 1896). All future references to this text will be abbreviated as GM. The most complete English translation is *The Life of Glückel of Hameln, 1646–1724, Written by Herself*, trans. Beth-Zion Abrahams (London, 1962). All future references to this text will be abbreviated as GL. Jacob Emden's Hebrew biography of Zevi Hirsch Ashkenazi together with his own autobiography, the *Megillat Sefer*, was first printed from a manuscript at Oxford in 1896. I am using the French translation: *Mémoires de Jacob Emden, ou l'anti Sabbataï Zewi*, trans. Maurice-Ruben Hayoun (Paris, 1992). All future references to this text will be abbreviated as JM. Translations of Glikl's text have been aided by the Abrahams text, but have been checked by me and modified when necessary from the Yiddish edition. All translations from the French edition of Emden's *Mémoires* are mine.

25. I have given extensive treatment to the life, writing, and milieux of Glikl bas Judah Leib, as well as bibliography about her, Hamburg, and Metz in Natalie Zemon Davis, *Women on the Margins: Three Seventeenth-Century Lives* (Cambridge, Mass., 1995).

26. GM, 30; GL, 17.

27. GM, 273–74; GL, 150.

28. Marc Antoine Turgot, *Mémoire redigé pour l'instruction du Dauphin* (1700), cited in *Les Juifs lorrains. Du ghetto à la nation, 1721–1871* (Metz, 1990), 43, catalog no. 123.

29. Archives départementales de la Moselle, 3E3705, no. 83; 3E3706, no. 196.

30. GM, 300; GL, 163.

31. This episode is treated more fully in Natalie Zemon Davis, "Riches and Dangers; Glikl bas Judah Leib on Court Jews," in Vivian B. Mann and Richard I. Cohen, eds., *From Court Jews to the Rothschilds: Art, Patronage, and Power, 1600–1800* (Munich, 1996), 45–57, 125.

32. In addition to the biography of Jacob Emden, information about Zevi Hirsch Ashkenazi can be found in the excellent introduction by Hayoun to JM; in David Kaufmann, "Rabbi Zevi Ashkenazi and his Family in London," *Transactions of the Jewish Historical Society of England*, 3 (1896–1898): 102–25; and in the *Encylopaedia Judaica*, 16 vols. (Jerusalem, 1971–1972), 3:733–35.

33. JM, 77, 84, 109.

34. JM, 95–102. GM, 257–62; GL, 142–44. *Encyclopaedia Judaica*, 3:734. Zevi Hirsch Ashkenazi, *Sefer She'elot u-Teshovot Chakham Zevi* (Amsterdam, 1712; reprint, New York, 1960), nos. 74, 76, 77.

35. On Nehemiah Hayon and the *Oz le-Elohim* of 1713, see *Encylopaedia Judaica*, 7:1499–1503, and Gershom Scholem, *Sabbatai Sevi, The Mystical Messiah*, trans. R. F. Zwi Werblowsky (Princeton, 1973), 901–3.

36. JM, 117.

37. JM, 119. Israel Rubinowicz's career as estate manager for one of the greatest houses in Poland is described in detail by M. J. Rosman, *The Lords' Jews: Magnate-Jewish Relations in the Polish-Lithuanian Commonwealth during the Eighteenth Century* (Cambridge, Mass., 1990). On his patronage of Zevi Hirsch Ashkenazi, see 154–55.

38. On ethical wills, see Israel Abrahams, ed., *Hebrew Ethical Wills* (Philadelphia, 1976), foreword by Judah Goldin. I have given further analysis and bibliography on Jewish autobiographical writing in the early modern period in Davis, *Women on the Margins*, 19–22, and in Natalie Zemon Davis, "Fame and Secrecy; Leon Modena's *Life* as an Early Modern Autobiography," in Leon Modena, *The Autobiography of a Seventeenth-Century Venetian Rabbi: Leon Modena's "Life of Judah"*, trans. Mark R. Cohen (Prince-

ton, 1988), 50–70. Also see Abraham Yagel, *A Valley of Vision: The Heavenly Journey of Abraham ben Hananiah Yagel*, ed. and trans. David Ruderman (Philadelphia, 1990), introduction.

39. On Jacob Emden, see Hayoun's introduction to JM; *Encyclopaedia Judaica*, 6:721–24; and David Kaufmann, "Zu R. Jakob Emdens Selbstbiographie," in *Gesammelte Schriften* (Frankfurt am Main, 1915), 3:138–49.

40. JM, 330.

41. JM, 283, 310.

42. GM, 121, 255; GL, 67, 141.

43. Georg Simmel, *The Philosophy of Money* (1900), trans. T. Bottomore and D. Frisby (London, 1978). Viviana A. Zelizer, *The Social Meaning of Money: Pin Money, Paychecks, Poor Relief, and Other Currencies* (Basic Books, 1994). See also Marc Shell, *Money, Language, and Thought: Literary and Philosophic Economies from the Medieval to the Modern Era* (Berkeley, 1982).

44. GM, 170, 175; GL, 92, 95.     45. GM, 277; GL, 152.

46. GM, 276–77; GL 151–52.

47. Jacques Savary, *Le Parfait Negociant ou Instruction Generale pour ce qui regarde le commerce des Marchandises de France et des Pays Etrangers* (Paris, 1736, revised from the edition of 1679), part 2, book 4, chaps. 1–3. Thomas Luckett, "Credit and Commercial Society in France, 1740–1789" (Ph.D. diss., Princeton University, 1992), chaps. 2–3.

48. Craig Muldrew, "Interpreting the Market: The Ethics of Credit and Community Relations in Early Modern England," *Social History*, 18, no. 2 (1993): 163–83. Further on the importance of credit, see Jacob M. Price, "Transaction Costs: A Note on Merchant Credit and the Organization of Private Trade," in James D. Tracy, ed., *The Political Economy of Merchant Empires: State Power and World Trade, 1350–1750* (Cambridge, 1991), 276–97.

49. GM, 13, 32, 62, 120; GL, 7, 18, 34, 67.

50. GM, 14, 303–5; GL, 8, 165–66. Alexander the Great plays an important role in Jewish tradition, tales about him going back to Josephus and the Talmud and carried on in many medieval Hebrew collections; Micha Joseph Bin Gorion, *Mimekor Yisrael: Classical Jewish Folktales*, trans. I. M. Lask, abridged ed. and annotated by Dan Ben-Amos (Bloomington, 1990), 89–104 (see esp. the tale of Alexander and the human eye: no. 48, "Tribute from Eden").

51. JM, 85, 109.     52. JM, 107.

53. JM, 94–95.     54. JM, 81–82, 132.

55. Rosman, *Lords' Jews*, 152.

56. The seal is in the Einhorn Collection in Tel Aviv and is reproduced and explicated in *Encylopaedia Judaica*, 3:734.

57. JM, 117–19, 183–85; Kaufmann, "Rabbi Zevi Ashkenazi," 102–25.

58. The story about Mordecai circulated sufficiently in the Hebrew press that it finally became known to Christian observers and polemicists: Johann Jacob Schudt, *Jüdische Merckwürdigkeiten*, 4 vols. (Frankfurt, 1715–1718), 4:135–37.

59. Gedalia Yogev, *Diamonds and Coral: Anglo-Dutch Jews and Eighteenth-Century Trade* (Leicester, 1978), 152–58.

60. Raymond de Roover, *The Rise and Decline of the Medici Bank, 1397–1494* (Cambridge, Mass., 1963).

61. GM, 320; GL, 176; JM, 116–17.

62. Stephanie Jed, *Chaste Thinking: The Rape of Lucretia and the Birth of Humanism* (Bloomington, 1989), chap. 3, 86.

63. Claude Dupouÿ, *Le droit des faillites en France avant le Code de Commerce* (Paris, 1960), 191–92, discussing the ordinance of 1673. *Factum pour Mayeur Tresnel et Olry Abraham Cahen, Juifs de Metz … Creanciers de Ruben Schaube … Contre le même Ruben Schaube, Juif, cy-devant Banquier à Metz* (1717), Bibliothèque nationale de France, nouv. acq. fr. 22705, no. 28, p. 39.

64. Yogev, *Diamonds*, 183–85.

65. I have discussed the significance of secrecy for Jewish communication and the sense of self in Davis, "Fame and Secrecy," cited in note 38.

66. GM 119, 161; GL, 66, 87.      67. GM, 124; GL, 69.

68. André Sayous, preface to Werner Sombart, *L'apogée du capitalisme*, trans. S. Jankélévitch (Paris, 1931), 1:i–lxxvi. Henri Hauser, "L'oeuvre scientifique de quelques économistes étrangers. VII. Werner Sombart," *Revue d'économie politique*, 49 (1935): 1233–55. R. H. Tawney, *Religion and the Rise of Capitalism* (based on the Holland Memorial Lectures of 1922) (London, 1926); new edition and new preface (London, 1937).

69. H. M. Robertson, *The Rise of Economic Individualism* (Cambridge, 1933). The study of the history of accounting went back to the late nineteenth century, but Robertson was one of the first to bring it to bear on the debate about the historical origins of capitalism. For a bibliography of the field, see Ernest Stevelinck, ed., *La comptabilité à travers les âges*, with an introduction by Raymond de Roover (Brussells, 1970). Here again, the hero of the story in this very useful book is double-entry bookkeeping.

70. Alexander Gerschenkron, *Economic Backwardness in Historical Perspective: A Book of Essays* (Cambridge, Mass., 1962); S. N. Eisenstadt, ed., *The Protestant Ethic and Modernization: A Comparative View* (New York, 1968).

71. Clifford Geertz, *Peddlers and Princes: Social Change and Economic Modernization in Two Indonesian Towns* (Chicago, 1963), vii–viii. Clifford Geertz, *The Religion of Java* (London, 1960), ix–x, 383–86. Clifford Geertz, *After the Fact: Two Countries, Four Decades, One Anthropologist* (Cambridge, Mass., 1995), 99–108.

72. Geertz, *Peddlers*, 34 and 34 n. 5.

73. Ibid., 140.      74. Ibid.      75. Ibid., 145.

76. Clifford Geertz, "Deep Play: Notes on the Balinese Cockfight," in *The Interpretation of Cultures* (New York, 1973), 437.

77. Clifford Geertz, "Suq: the bazaar economy in Sefrou," in Clifford Geertz, Hildred Geertz, and Lawrence Rosen, *Meaning and Order in Moroccan Society* (Cambridge, 1979), 123–313.

78. Geertz, "Suq," 234.

79. S. D. Goitein, *A Mediterranean Society: The Jewish Communities of the Arab World as Portrayed in the Documents of the Cairo Geniza*, vol. 1, *The Economic Foundations* (Berkeley, 1967). See also Giacomo Todeschini, "Familles juives et chrétiennes en Italie à la fin du Moyen Âge: Deux modèles de développement économique," *Annales: Economies, sociétés, civilisations ESC* 45, no. 4 (1990): 787–817; Barry Supple, "A Business Elite: German-Jewish Financiers in Nineteenth-Century New York," *The Business History Review*, 31, no. 2 (1957): 143–78.

80. Yannick Lemarchand, "Style mercantile ou mode des finances. Le choix d'un modèle comptable dans la France d'Ancien Régime," *Annales: Histoire, sciences sociales* 50, no. 1 (1995): 159–82. Lemarchand shows that receipt/expense accounts were used in mining and metallurgical enterprises, where the capital came from nobles or financiers, while double-entry bookkeeping was used in textile enterprises, connected with merchant capital. A major study of the forms of accounting in Jewish milieux is much to be desired.

# GEORGE E. MARCUS

## The Uses of Complicity in the Changing Mise-en-Scène of Anthropological Fieldwork

Rapport: *Report, talk. Reference, relationship; connexion, correspondence, conformity. A state in which mesmeric action can be exercised by one person on another.*

Collaboration: *United labour, co-operation; especially in literary, artistic, or scientific work.*

Collaborate: *To work in conjunction with another.*

Complicity: *The being an accomplice; partnership in an evil action. State of being complex or involved.*

Complice: *One associated in any affair with another, the latter being regarded as the principal.*[1]

In what is perhaps his most broadly influential essay, "Deep Play: Notes on the Balinese Cockfight," Clifford Geertz opens with a tale of fieldwork in which the rapport that is so much sought after by anthropologists among the peoples they study is achieved through a circumstance of complicity.[2] In 1958, Geertz and his wife moved to a remote Balinese village to take up, in the tradition of Bronislaw Malinowski, the sort of participant observation that has given distinction to the ethnographic method. Unfortunately, their initial efforts to fit in were met with marked inattention and studied indifference: "people seemed to look right through us with a gaze focused several yards behind us on some more actual stone or tree."[3] However, their status changed dramatically about ten days after their arrival, when they attended a cockfight that was raided by the police. Geertz and his wife ran from the invading police along with the rest of the village, and when they were finally discovered by a policeman and questioned about their presence, they were passionately defended by the village chief, who said they belonged in the village and did not know anything about any cockfight. From the next morning on, their situation in the village was completely different: they were no longer invisible, and they had indeed achieved the kind of relationship that would allow them to do their work and eventually produce the account of a cultural artifact that follows this opening tale of fieldwork—an account that became a widely assimilated exemplar of a style of interpretive analysis in which deep meanings are derived from the close observation of a society's most quotidian events. Geertz concludes his anecdote by saying,

Getting caught, or almost caught, in a vice raid is perhaps not a very generalizable recipe for achieving that mysterious necessity of anthropological field work, rapport, but for me it worked very well. It led to a sudden and unusually complete acceptance into a society extremely difficult for outsiders to penetrate. It gave me the kind of immediate, inside-view grasp of an aspect of "peasant mentality" that anthropologists not fortunate enough to flee headlong with their subjects from armed authorities normally do not get.[4]

In Geertz's anecdote I am primarily interested in the ironic entanglement of complicity with rapport that he draws. Indeed, for anthropologists trained from the 1950s through the 1980s, rapport has been the powerful shorthand concept used to stand for the threshold level of relations with fieldwork subjects that is necessary for those subjects to act effectively as informants for anthropologists—who, once that rapport is established, are then able to pursue their scientific, "outsider" inquiries on the "inside."

The range of definitions given in the *OED* for the word *rapport*—from "talk" to "relationship" to "conformity" to the unusual meaning of "a state in which mesmeric action can be exercised by one person on another"—aptly conveys the mix of senses of this key figure within the ideology of anthropological practice. Of course, behind this figure are the immensely complex stories, debates, views, and critiques that surround the relationships that anthropological fieldwork imposes. Since the 1960s, this probing of fieldwork relationships has moved from informal, ethos-building professional talk—a regulative ideal—to a more formal articulation found in both reflections on fieldwork and essays on anthropology's distinctive method, discussions in which Geertz himself has been a seminal, though ambivalent, voice.[5]

Until recently, much of this discussion has assumed the essential desirability and achievability of rapport—it remains the favored condensed view and disciplinary emblem of the ideal condition of fieldwork—even while the path to rapport seems always to have been fraught with difficulties, uncertainties, happenstance, ethical ambiguity, fear, and self-doubt. However, there are now signs of the displacement of this foundational commonplace of fieldwork, given the changing mise-en-scène in which anthropological research is now frequently being constituted. It is probably a healthy sign that no replacement figure, as such, is emerging to take rapport's place. Rather, a deep reassessment of the nature of fieldwork is beginning to occur as a result of defining the different conditions in which it must be designed and conceptualized.

Purely as a means of lending perspective to and representing the set of changes that are affecting anthropological practice and the way that it is thought about, I have chosen in this essay to emphasize the concept of complicity. Indeed, many fieldwork stories of achieving rapport are in some way entangled with acts of complicity, as in Geertz's epochal anecdote. But while complicity has a certain kinship of meaning with rapport, it is also its "evil twin," so to speak. (In this regard, I appreciate the *OED*'s definitions of complicity as including both the "state of being complex or involved" and "partnership in an evil action.") In no way am I promoting complicity as a candidate for a new shorthand or common-place of disciplinary practice in our changed circumstances—its "dark" connotations certainly don't lend it to that use. Rather, a focus on the term will serve as a device for tracing a certain critique, or at least complexation, of the valorized understanding of fieldwork relationships from within the reigning figure of rapport to an alternative conception of fieldwork relationships in which the figure of rapport has lost much of its power as a regulative ideal.

In the following section, then, I want to explore the ways in which Geertz dealt with the issue of complicity within rapport, since his representations of fieldwork represent for me the most subtle understandings of the traditional ideology of fieldwork practice at its apogee. Following that, I want to address two directions that critiques of ethnographic authority and rhetoric took in the 1980s, producing an unprecedentedly reflexive and critical perspective on fieldwork relations (a perspective that Geertz unquestionably helped to inspire and from which he interestingly has distanced himself).[6]

One of these directions displaces rapport with an ideal of collaboration that both preserves the traditional, enclosed mise-en-scène of fieldwork and avoids paying explicit attention to the issue of complicity that Geertz himself saw as so entangled with the very achievement of rapport. The other direction, aptly expressed in Renato Rosaldo's notion of "imperialist nostalgia,"[7] directly confronts complicity in fieldwork relationships within the broader historical context of colonialism in which the traditional mise-en-scène of ethnography has always been situated; but it fails to go beyond the ethical implications of that context to consider the cognitive ones.

Finally, I want to offer a conception of complicity that is largely free of the primary connotations of rapport. In so doing, I want to move beyond the predominant and troublesome ethical implications associated with complicity in past views of anthropological practice to an understanding of the fieldwork relationship that entails a substantially different vision of the contemporary mise-en-scène of anthropological research. Complicity here retains its ethical issues, but it does so in a way that forces a rethinking of the space and positioning of the anthropologist-informant relationship that is at the heart of fieldwork as it has been commonly conceived.

The larger stake of the discussion that I want to develop is indeed the current level of self-conscious awareness and response of anthropologists to the changing circumstances in which they now work—what I have referred to earlier as the mise-en-scène of fieldwork. Of course there have recently been many theoretical and direct conceptual discussions of these changing circumstances—the talk of transcultural processes, global-local relations, and deterritorialized cultures[8]—but it is not clear what, if anything, these discussions have meant for the deeply ingrained and reassuring ideologies of fieldwork practice. Until these macrochanges are understood at the heart of anthropology's distinctive method, in terms of the commonplaces and powerful figures by which anthropologists have conceived fieldwork as an ideology of professional culture, it is quite likely that the traditional conception in use of the mise-en-scène and the central relationship of anthropologist to informant will remain immune from the more radical implications of the new theoretical visions and discussions of anthropology's changing objects of study. A consideration of these changes within anthropology's sacred domain, so to speak, is precisely what I intend to initiate by tracing complicity as at first an integral but underplayed dimension of rapport that has eventually become an independent means of understanding how certain deep assumptions and commonplaces about fieldwork might finally be modified in line with otherwise clear perceptions among anthropologists about how their objects and contexts of study are changing.

### Geertz and Complicity

> But what is, to me anyway, most interesting about . . . these attempts to produce highly "author-saturated," supersaturated even, anthropological texts in which the self the text creates and the self that creates the text are represented as being very near to identical, is the strong note of disquiet that suffuses them. There is very little confidence here and a fair amount of outright malaise. The imagery is not of scientific hope, compensating inner weakness, à la Malinowski, or of bear-hug intimacy dispelling self-rejection, à la Read, neither of which is very much believed in. It is of estrangement, hypocrisy, helplessness, domination, disillusion. Being There is not just practically difficult. There is something disruptive about it altogether.[9]

As we have seen in the cockfight anecdote, for Geertz a certain *kind* of complicity generates rapport. In a manner characteristic of his signature style as a writer and thinker, in this passage Geertz seems to make light of a figure or commonplace of his discipline—rapport—while remaining passionately committed to *his* version of it—a version that actually strengthens the figure in the shadow of his playful, trenchant critique of it. He may disdain his discipline's too-easily assimilated shoptalk—about, for example, the figure of rapport—but finally he improves upon that talk and, in a committed way, preserves the traditional sense of the craft that the figure of rapport stands for. In "Deep Play," the ethnographer's powerful and exemplary analytic magic that follows the tale of complicity breaking into rapport is a testament to this.

In the cockfight anecdote, complicity makes the outsider the desired anthropological insider. It is a circumstantial, fortuitous complicity that, by precipitating a momentary bond of solidarity, gains Geertz admission to the inside of Balinese relations (the means to ethnographic authority) and converts the Balinese village into a proper mise-en-scène of fieldwork—a physically and symbolically enclosed world, a culture for the ethnographer to live within and figure out. Very pragmatically, Geertz realizes that he can benefit from this complicity only by presenting himself as a naïf, a person subject to events and looked out for by others (and this vulnerability of finding himself on the side of the village against the state and its agents, rather than representing himself as someone officially there through the auspices of the state, suggests both a shrewd and an ambiguous innocence about the historic era in which anthropological fieldwork was then being done).[10]

So complicity in this particular famous tale of fieldwork is rather neat and simple; it is an uncomplicated complicity that "breaks the ice" and provides the anthropologist the coveted fictional acceptance that will allow him to create the counter-"mesmerism" of rapport whereby he is no longer invisible, as before, but will be indulged as a person. But in a lesser-known paper on fieldwork, Geertz tells another more complex, yet complementary, story from the field in which he considers how complicity, internal to the development of relations with informants once he has gotten "inside," is deeply entangled with the motivated fiction of sustaining rapport itself.[11] This paper tells how a kind of complicity is necessary for sustaining the working relationships of fieldwork, without which its very mise-en-scène—let alone rapport—would not be possible in the anthropologist's imaginary. This paper, "Thinking as a Moral Act: Ethical Dimensions of Anthropological Fieldwork in the New States," reveals Geertz's astute foresight of the possible development of a hyperreflexivity upon the conditions of anthropological knowledge—a subject that, after a complicated treatment in this paper, he turns away from in favor of accepting the fictions of fieldwork relations so that ethnographic interpretation and the historic anthropological project to which he is committed can continue (that is, the project of U.S. cultural anthropology in the line of, for example, Johann Herder, Franz Boas, Margaret Mead, and Ruth Benedict, among many others).

In "Thinking as a Moral Act," Geertz describes a complicity of mutual interest between anthropologist and informant, subtly but clearly understood by each, that makes rapport possible—indeed that constitutes, even constructs, it. Geertz calls this key rapport-defining act of complicity an "anthropological irony" of fictions that each side accepts:

One is placed, in this sort of work, among necessitous men hoping for radical improvements in their conditions of life that do not seem exactly imminent; moreover, one is a type benefactor of just the sort of improvements they are looking for, also obliged to ask them for charity—and what is almost worse, having them give it. This ought to be a humbling, thus elevating, experience; but most often it is simply a disorienting one. All the familiar rationalizations having to do with science, progress, philanthropy, enlightenment, and selfless purity of dedication ring false, and one is left, ethically disarmed, to grapple with a human relationship which must be justified over and over again in the most immediate of terms.[12]

What I am pointing to . . . is an enormous pressure on both the investigator and his subjects to regard these goals as near when they are in fact far, assured when they are merely wished for, and achieved when they are at best approximated. This pressure springs from the inherent moral asymmetry of the fieldwork situation.[13]

To recognize the moral tension, the ethical ambiguity, implicit in the encounter of anthropologist and informant, and to still be able to dissipate it through one's actions and one's attitudes, is what encounter demands of both parties if it is to be authentic, if it is to actually happen. And to discover that is to discover also something very complicated and not altogether clear about the nature of sincerity and insincerity, genuineness and hypocrisy, honesty and self-deception.[14]

Here again, as in the cockfight anecdote, the broader context of implication— that of colonialism and neocolonialism—that has so exercised the subsequent critics of ethnography is submerged in Geertz's account, implied but not explicitly noted. The anthropology of the 1950s and 1960s was part of the great mission of development in the new states—in the midst of which Geertz was a very American as well as an anthropological writer, accepting this mission with a certain resignation that did not particularly define a politics of fieldwork. That politics instead emerged in terms of the always slightly absurd but very human predicaments of a well-meaning outsider thrust among people with very different life chances. According to the presumptions of the development mission, themselves based on Western notions of liberal decency, the outsider was in some sense the model of a desired future.[15]

In Geertz's writings on his fieldwork of the 1960s and 1970s, we see first a virtual outline and summary of the major moves of later critique—built on the reflexive study of the conditions of anthropological knowledge not only in terms of its traditional mise-en-scène of fieldwork but also in terms of the broader historic contexts that Geertz tended to elide—and then a hesitation and a pulling back for the sake of sustaining a distanced practice of interpretation. Finally, as Geertz argues in his paper "Thinking as a Moral Act,"

I don't know much about what goes on in laboratories; but in anthropological fieldwork, detachment is neither a natural gift nor a manufactured talent. It is a partial achievement laboriously earned and precariously maintained. What little disinterestedness one manages to attain comes not from failing to have emotions or neglecting to perceive them in others, nor yet from sealing oneself into a moral vacuum. It comes from a personal subjection to a vocational ethic . . . to combine two fundamental orientations toward reality—the engaged and the analytic—into a single attitude. It is this attitude, not moral blankness, which we call detachment or disinterestedness. And whatever small degree of it one manages to attain comes not by adopting an I-am-a-camera ideology or by enfolding oneself in layers of methodological armor, but simply by trying to do, in such an equivocal situation, the scientific work one has come to do.[16]

Indeed, the Balinese cockfight essay itself enacts Geertz's position on critical self-knowledge in anthropological practice. Once the incident described in the opening reflexive fieldwork anecdote has authoritatively secured the standard and idealized condition of rapport, or "mesmeric" possibility, the work of interpretation proceeds by the participant who is still a detached observer, famously able to read Balinese culture "like a text." Geertz's shrewd perception of the complicit heart of the otherwise soporific, too-easy professional invocation of rapport, followed by his pulling back from further reflexive examination and its implications, probably has disturbed his critics more than if he had not bothered to make this move into reflexivity at all.

The fact that he *did* and that he then pulled back from looking too closely at the conditions of the production of anthropological knowledge—a topic that he brilliantly introduced at a time of maximum positivist hopes and confidence in the social sciences—is not a sign of the ambivalence or hesitation that are otherwise so much a part of Geertz's expository style of delivering insight. Rather it is a sign of his commitment to the frame of reference in which anthropology could be done: the frame that the figure of rapport guaranteed and that Geertz played with, could see the critique of, but would not go beyond for the sake of a historic anthropological project that he had done so much to renew in the 1960s and 1970s and that defined for him a "vocational ethic." His concern—expressed in the passage with which this section opens and which first appeared in his 1988 book *Works and Lives* as a sideways commentary on that decade's seminal critique of anthropological knowledge—was over the malaise that an unfettered reflexivity, following his own opening, might lead to. And has it?

### The Collaborative Ideal

*This possibility suggests an alternate textual strategy, a utopia of plural authorship that accords to collaborators not merely the status of independent enunciators but that of writers. As a form of authority it must still be considered utopian for two reasons. First, the few recent experiments with multiple-author works appear to require, as an instigating force, the research interest of the ethnographer who in the end assumes an executive, editorial position. The authoritative stance of "giving voice" to the other is not fully transcended. Second, the very idea of plural authorship challenges a deep Western identification of any text's order with the intention of a single author. . . . Nonetheless, there are signs of movement in this domain. Anthropologists will increasingly have to share their texts, and sometimes their title pages, with those indigenous collaborators, for the term informants is no longer adequate, if it ever was.*[17]

One strong direction of the critique of anthropological rhetoric, representation, and authority that occurred during the 1980s reconceived the figure of rapport in terms of collaboration. Associated with the writing of James Clifford and loosely derived from Mikhail Bakhtin's notions of polyphony and dialogism as an alternative to the monologic authority of modes of voicing in the novel, the vision of a collaborative relationship between anthropologist and informant as authors of ethnography in the field has provided a strong reimagining of the regulative ideal of rapport in the ideology of anthropological practice. As presented by Clifford in a scholarly style of historical literary criticism, the collaborative ideal is less a methodological prescription or figure or fieldwork in a changing mise-en-scène than a rereading, an excavation, of certain overlooked dimensions of past ethnography. Its power, then, is in its suggestiveness of a more pleasing, post-1960s practice of thoroughly participatory fieldwork—and it is developed in a way that suggests that anthropologists need only consciously activate what was always there, an obscured dimension of classic fieldwork that was previously concealed by the monologic authority of the conventions of ethnographic writing.

Collaboration ("co-operation" in dialogue) thus replaces rapport ("relationship" or "connexion," with its connotation of a means or instrumentality for fulfilling the ends primarily of one of the partners—the initiating one—of the relationship). Theoretically, collaboration creates a figure for a much more complex understanding of fieldwork, but in Clifford's writing, which looks back at the ethnographic tradition through its classics and classics-in-the-making, this replacement figure is also very much forged in the traditional mise-en-scène of fieldwork—and in fact reinforces that traditional setting, giving it a needed new face, so to speak. The scene of fieldwork and the object of study are still essentially coterminous, together establishing a culture situated in place and to be learned about by one's presence *inside* it in sustained interaction. The collaborative ideal entails the notions that knowledge creation in fieldwork always involves negotiating a boundary between cultures and that the result is never reducible to a form of knowledge that can be packaged in the monologic voice of the ethnographer alone. But still, the polyphony implied in the idea of collaboration preserves the idea of the representation of a bounded culture, however nonreductive, as the object of study and reinforces the same habits of work that rapport valorized. The independent voices in collaboration still emerge within a distinctively other form of life. Perhaps because of the way this ideal was developed in the critique of anthropology—by excavating from *within* the tradition of ethnography—it inherited the limits of the mise-en-scène that had preceded it.

Of course, neither collaboration nor the idea of dialogism on which it is based necessarily implies the harmony of "united labour" in a scientific, literary, or artistic endeavor, as the *OED* definition suggests, and Clifford does not develop the idea with this connotation. The positive *OED* sense remains a potentiality, but more often than not, collaboration is conflicted, based on misrecognitions, coercions, and precisely the sort of ironies/complicities that Geertz cataloged so well in his writing on fieldwork. Clifford differs from Geertz only in finally not being personally tied to the scientific vocation of anthropology; thus, he can indulge a reflexivity that transforms the commonplace ideal of the fieldwork relation. Indeed, to recognize and legitimate as partners one's subjects of study and to generate only polyphonic texts would indeed make something radically different of ethnography; but it wouldn't significantly change the traditional frame of study.

Collaboration does evoke the reflexive space and suggests new conventions for the normalized discussion of the complexities, ambiguities, and nuances of the anthropologist-subject relationship central to fieldwork. Yet Clifford's articulation of the ambiguities of this relationship still remains rather mute as to the different senses of complicity that surround, motivate, and make this relationship possible. In particular, the broader colonial context as it operates in collaboration, while a part of Clifford's discussion, is not strongly developed.[18]

In relation to the particular sense of complicity that I want to develop below, which corresponds to a break with the traditional mise-en-scène of fieldwork, Clifford's discussion of collaboration can even be seen as evasive. It goes somewhat further than Geertz's in recognizing how the broader context of the anthropological project is registered in fieldwork, but it recognizes this context *only* in terms of the long-standing question of anthropology's relationship to colonialism. What is missing in the evocation of the ideal of collaboration is the much more complicated and contemporary sense of the broader context of anthropology operating in a so-called postmodern world of discontinuous cultural formations and multiple sites of cultural production. This context is certainly shaped in part by a history of colonialism, but it cannot be fully represented by that venerable bête noire, which has long served as the broader context in commonplace professional ideology, ambivalently cradling the traditional mise-en-scène of fieldwork.[19]

In the imagining of collaboration as fieldwork, then, complicity has not been a very important component, either in its ethical sense or in its cognitive potential for reconfiguring the fieldwork scene itself. But by fully opening a reflexive space that went beyond Geertz's own self-limited explorations of the regulative idea of rapport, the figure of collaboration created the necessary ground for going further. The explicit dimension of complicity remained to be powerfully articulated—and again, with regard to colonialism as the broader context—as part of the 1980s critique of anthropology by Renato Rosaldo, perhaps the spoiler of all of fieldwork's other fictions.

### Imperialist Nostalgia and Complicity

*Processes of drastic change often are the enabling condition of ethnographic field research, and herein resides the complicity of missionary, constabulary, officer, and ethnographer. Just as Jones received visits from American constabulary officers during his field research, Michelle Rosaldo and I often used the missionary airplane for transportation in the Ilongot region. Jones did not police and we did not evangelize, but we all bore witness, and we participated, as relatively minor players, in the transformation taking place before our eyes.*[20]

Moving in another direction from the possibilities foreseen by Geertz, Renato Rosaldo takes the critique of the traditional mise-en-scène to its limit and finally makes explicit the broader context of anthropology in the scene of fieldwork. This is where complicity potentially has its greatest power as a figure. Rosaldo's work has developed very much within the specific compass of interpretive anthropology that Geertz established in the 1960s and 1970s. As such, his essay "Imperialist Nostalgia" constitutes an appropriate expression of the evolution of Geertz's thinking on fieldwork, now in its most politicized form. Among the critiques of the 1980s, this essay is the most recognizable successor to Geertz's own writing.

The trenchant insight of this essay—indeed, another exemplar of anthropological irony, as Geertz called complicity in fieldwork—is that the key ideological sentiment that has allowed anthropologists to distance themselves from other foreign agents in the field is precisely the sentiment that both denies and constructs their own agency in that very same transformative process. As Rosaldo says, "My concern resides with a particular kind of nostalgia, often found under imperialism, where people mourn the passing of what they themselves have transformed. . . . When the so-called civilizing process destabilizes forms of life, the agents of change experience transformations of other cultures as if they were personal losses."[21] Here, Rosaldo captures and indicts the characteristic rhetoric of ethics that pervades ethnography, at the same time pinpointing the primary relation of complicity in fieldwork—not with the informant or the people, but with the agents of change. This is the politicizing complicity from which Geertz backed off, and about which the alternative view of collaboration was not blunt enough.

This politicization at the limits of the figure of rapport is achieved by placing a primary emphasis on what was the play of complicity in Geertz. Rather than simply being the ironic means to a rapport that cements the working bond between fieldworker and informant, complicity becomes the defining element of the relationship between the anthropologist and the broader colonial context. In so doing, the problem of the broader outside context—again, thought of as colonialism— is finally brought squarely to the inside of the fieldwork relation, something that the collaborative ideal achieved only intermittently or indirectly.

So where has Rosaldo's argument about "imperialist nostalgia" brought us in our tracing of the entanglements of complicity with the powerful regulative ideal of rapport? To the verge of talking primarily about complicity rather than rapport as constructing the primary fieldwork relation, and as such, to the brink of reconceiving the stubbornly held mise-en-scène of fieldwork to better accommodate

a different kind of ethnographic project that is now emerging and being professionally normalized in anthropology.

In Geertz's writing, rapport requires that the anthropologist be complicit with
the inside of a community or group of subjects. While not effacing the "insideness"
essential to the fieldwork mise-en-scène, Rosaldo understands every apparent inside move the fieldworker makes as primarily complicit with the broader external
context of colonialism. But, like Geertz's earlier politically muted critique of
fieldwork and Clifford's contemporaneous critique of monologic authority in anthropological practice, Rosaldo's essay is still located within rapport and its mise-
en-scène, though at its outer limit. As such, the recognition of the sort of complicity
that brings the outside into the scene of fieldwork with the very arrival of the
anthropologist—who can no longer protect herself with the nostalgia that preserves her difference from other agents of change—remains for Rosaldo a *moral*
lesson, one for which there is little further response from within the traditional
ideology of rapport. For Rosaldo, anthropology of the old sort either is over, is
paralyzed by moralizing insight, or continues to be practiced as a tragic occupation, done in the full awareness of the pitfalls of its powerful rhetorics of self-
justification.

With Rosaldo, then, we come to an impasse. The kind of sustained reflexivity
that Geertz feared, turned away from, and has more lately confirmed for himself
as leading to malaise has now been taken to its limit within the traditional project
of anthropology, revealing the implication of complicity that has always shadowed
the positive figure of rapport. But is this really the end?

### Complicity and the Multisited Spaces
### of Contemporary Ethnography

*There exists a very strong, but one-sided and thus untrustworthy idea that in order to
better understand a foreign culture, one must enter into it, forgetting one's own, and view
the world through the eyes of this foreign culture. . . . of course, the possibility of seeing
the world through its eyes is a necessary part of the process of understanding it; but if
this were the only aspect it would merely be duplication and would not entail anything
enriching. Creative understanding does not renounce itself, its own place and time, its
own culture; and it forgets nothing. In order to understand, it is immensely important
for the person who understands to be located outside the object of his or her creative
understanding—in time, in space, in culture. In the realm of culture, outsidedness is a
most powerful factor in understanding. We raise new questions for a foreign culture, ones
that it did not raise for itself; we seek answers to our own questions in it; and the foreign
culture responds to us by revealing to us its new aspects and new semantic depths.*[22]

The transformation of complicity that I want to trace, from its place in
the shadows of the more positive and less ethically ambiguous notion of rapport
to its emergence as a primary figure in the ideology of fieldwork, is occasioned by

the changing conditions of fieldwork itself and of its objects of study. These changing conditions are effectively stimulating the traditional mise-en-scène of fieldwork to be turned inside out within the professional ideology, and it is the figure of complicity that focuses this change.

Discontinuity in cultural formations—their multiple and heterogeneous sites of production—has begun to force changes in the assumptions and notions that have constructed the traditional mise-en-scène of fieldwork. Anthropologists, of course, continue to work intensively and locally with particular subjects—the substance of ethnographic analysis requires this—but they no longer do so with the sense that the cultural object of study is fully accessible within a particular site, or without the sense that a site of fieldwork anywhere is integrally and intimately tied to sites of possible fieldwork elsewhere. The intellectual environment surrounding contemporary ethnographic study makes it seem incomplete and even trivial if it does not encompass within its own research design a full mapping of a cultural formation, the contours of which cannot be presumed but are themselves a key discovery of ethnographic inquiry. The sense of the object of study being "here and there" has begun to wreak productive havoc on the "being there" of classic ethnographic authority.[23]

However complicity was implicated in the achievement of rapport in the critical versions of Geertz, Clifford, and Rosaldo, all three sustain the sense that the symbolic and literal domain of fieldwork exists inside another form of life—entailing crossing a boundary into it and exploring a cultural logic of enclosed difference (however fraught with difficulty the translation process is).

Once released from this mise-en-scène, complicity looks quite different. The focus on a particular site of fieldwork remains, but now one is after a distinctly different sort of knowledge, one for which metaphors of insideness or the crossing of cultural boundaries are no longer appropriate.

In any particular location certain practices, anxieties, and ambivalences are present as specific responses to the intimate functioning of nonlocal agencies and causes—and for which there are no convincing common-sense understandings.[24] The basic condition that defines the altered mise-en-scène for which complicity rather than rapport is a more appropriate figure is an awareness of existential doubleness on the part of *both* anthropologist and subject; this derives from having a sense of being *here* where major transformations are under way that are tied to things happening simultaneously *elsewhere*, but not having a certainty or authoritative representation of what those connections are. Indeed, there are so many plausible explanations for the changes, no single one of which inspires more authority than another, that the individual subject is left to account for the connections—the behind-the-scenes structure—and to read into his or her own narrative the locally felt agency and effects of great and little events happening elsewhere.

Social actors are confronted with the same kind of impasses that academics uncomfortably experience these days, and this affinity suggests the particular salience of the figure of complicity. But for the subjects of ethnography, these impasses are pragmatic problems that, for everyday life to proceed at all, require responses ranging from evasions and displacements to halfhearted investments in old theories or exotic constructions and idiosyncratic visions of the way the world works. In terms of the traditional mise-en-scène of fieldwork, most anthropologists have always understood themselves as being both inside and outside the sites in which they have been participant observers. That is, they have never naively thought that they could simply "go native" and in fact are critical of those among them who are so naive. Rather, they understand well that they always remain marginal, fictive natives at best. Still, they have always operated on the faith, necessary for the kind of knowledge that they produce, that they could be relatively more insiders than outsiders if only by mastering the skills of translation, sensitivity, and learned cultural competencies—in short, that they could achieve rapport.

In contrast, while it begins from the same inside-outside boundary positioning, investment in the figure of complicity does not posit the same faith in being able to probe the "inside" of a culture (nor does it presuppose that the subject herself is even on the "inside" of a culture, given that contemporary local knowledge is never only about being local). The idea of complicity forces the recognition of ethnographers as ever-present markers of "outsideness." Never stirring from the boundary, their presence makes possible certain kinds of access that the idea of rapport and the faith in being able to get inside (by fiction à la Geertz, by utopian collaboration à la Clifford, or by self-deception à la Rosaldo) does not. It is only in an anthropologist-informant situation in which the outsideness is never elided and is indeed the basis of an affinity between ethnographer and subject that the reigning traditional ideology of fieldwork can shift to reflect the changing conditions of research.

What ethnographers in this changed mise-en-scène want from subjects is not so much local knowledge as an articulation of the forms of anxiety that are generated by the awareness of being affected by what is elsewhere without knowing what the particular connections to that elsewhere might be. The ethnographer on the scene in this sense makes that elsewhere *present*.[25] It is not that this effect of fieldwork is currently unrecognized in anthropology, but it is always referenced in terms of an ethical discourse, and this frame does not get at what the more generative sense of the idea of complicity seeks to document.

This version of complicity tries to get at a form of local knowledge that is about the kind of difference that is not accessible by working out internal cultural logics. It is about difference that arises from the anxieties of knowing that one is somehow tied into what is happening elsewhere, but, as noted, without those connections being clear or precisely articulated through available internal cultural models. In effect, subjects are participating in discourses that are thoroughly localized but that are not their own. Douglas Holmes, whose research is discussed later, uses the term "illicit discourse" to describe this phenomenon, in which fragments of local discourses have their origins elsewhere without the relationship to that elsewhere being clear. This uncertainty creates anxiety, wonder, and insecurity, in different registers, both in the ethnographer and in her subjects.

This recognition of a common predicament is the primary motivation for thinking about the changed conception of fieldwork relationships in terms of complicity. It would be possible to understand our emphasis on the figure of complicity as the achievement of a different kind of rapport, but it would be a mistake to identify it with the precise construction of that figure in the traditional mode. The investment in the figure of complicity rests on highlighting this contemporary external determination of local discourses, marked and set off by the fieldworker's presence but free of the figures of rapport and collaboration that have traditionally characterized fieldwork. Free of these, complicity between an ethnographer whose outsideness is always prominent and a subject who is sensitive to the outside helps to materialize other dimensions that the dialogue of traditional fieldwork, conceived as taking place inside rapport, cannot get at as well. Only thus we do we escape the tendency to see change as a disruption of what was there before—a disruption of a world in which the anthropologist might have been more comfortable and on the "prior-ness" of which he or she can still rely in exercising the assumptions of the traditional mise-en-scène of fieldwork, even in a site undergoing massive and long-term changes. In such cases, the formative expressions of anxiety that construct cultures in change and boundaries between cultures are likely to be either missed or rationalized in terms of prior cultural logics. Only when an outsider begins to relate to a subject also concerned with outsideness in everyday life can these expressions be given focal importance in a localized fieldwork that, in turn, inevitably pushes the entire research program of the single ethnographic project into the challenges and promises of a multisited space and trajectory—a trajectory that encourages the ethnographer literally to move to other sites that are powerfully registered in the local knowledge of an originating locus of fieldwork. This is what the notion of complicity as an aid in the rethinking of fieldwork potentially offers.

According to its *OED* definitions, *complicity*, compared to *rapport* and *collaboration*, carries a heavier load of ethical meaning and implication. However, this ethical sense is very different when complicity is evoked as a critical probe of the traditional figure of rapport in the writing of Geertz, Clifford, and Rosaldo—among others—than when it becomes the central figure used to explore the mise-en-scène of fieldwork in new circumstances. The usual ethical questioning of the fieldwork relationship relies heavily on exploring the dynamics of the assumed unequal power relations between ethnographer and subject, always weighted *structurally* on the side of the ethnographer, who is implicated in Western colonialism (which, as I noted earlier, has stereotypically defined the broader context of classic anthropological fieldwork). When the politicized nature of fieldwork has been highlighted in the past, it has been developed by calling anthropology to account for its colonial, and now postcolonial, complicities.[26]

This predictable construction of the ethical issues involved in fieldwork has become far too limited a means of addressing current changing views of the mise-en-scène of fieldwork in the broader context of multisited research. With theoretical metanarratives and frames of world-systems processes now under prominent debate and reformulation, a broader contextual framing for any location of fieldwork is less available to ethnographers. The shifting boundaries of the ethnographic project, as described above, are moving speculatively into this broader frame itself, treating it ethnographically through the multisited trajectory of research. This is partly because of the noted inadequacy and loss of authority of both older and new formulations of metanarratives—like colonialism (or postcolonialism), Marxist political economy, and globalization (an as-yet poorly theorized, but apparently necessary, concept in wide currency)—and partly because of the changing nature of the kind of material sought from and offered by fieldwork subjects who think in terms of their connections beyond the local. This need to deal more directly with the broader context of focused research without the aid of adequate frames created by other kinds of scholarship leads to a much less determined and available context than does the history of colonialism, for example, in considering the politics and ethical implications of contemporary fieldwork. Likewise, as the figure frequently evoked in past critiques of fieldwork to probe the ethical problems of a too-innocent figure of rapport, complicity specifically plays to and constructs a different and more complex sense of the substance of the ethnographer-subject relationship.

The changing contextualization for assessing the ethical implication of complicity as the normal characterization of contemporary fieldwork relationships is reflected in the shifting power valences of these relationships, as the fieldworker moves from site to site, and the often ethically ambiguous management by the fieldworker of the accumulation of these developing relationships in specific situations. Of course, ethnographers have often been faced with such ethical issues within the villages and communities in which they have worked, but in multisited research, the broader context is in a sense entirely of the ethnographer's and his informants' own making, rather than attributable to more abstract and already morally loaded forces such as capitalism and colonialism. So, within the boundaries of a single project, the ethnographer may be dealing intimately and equivalently with subjects of very different class circumstances—with elites and subalterns, for instance—who may not even be known directly to one another or have a sense of the often indirect effects that they have on each other's lives.

The ethical issues in multisited research are raised by the ethnographer's movement among different kinds of affiliations within a configuration of sites evolving in a particular research project. The inequality of power relations, weighted in favor of the anthropologist, can no longer be presumed in this world of multisited ethnography. The fieldworker often deals with subjects who share his own broadly middle-class identity and fears, in which case unspoken power issues in the relationship become far more ambiguous than they would have been in past anthropological research; alternatively, he may deal with persons in much stronger power and class positions than his own, in which case both the terms and limits of the ethnographic engagement are managed principally by them. Here, where the ethnographer occupies a marked subordinate relationship to informants, the issues of use and being used, of ingratiation, and of trading information about others elsewhere become matters of normal ethical concern, where they were largely unconsidered in previous discussions.

As I have remarked elsewhere, the anthropologist, by virtue of these changing circumstances of research, is always on the verge of activism, of negotiating some kind of involvement beyond the distanced role of ethnographer, according to personal commitments that may or may not predate the project.[27] To what extent and on what terms can such activism be indulged within the activity of ethnography, and what are the consequences of avoiding it or denying it altogether for the continued achievement of the "disinterestedness" that Geertz argued for in the traditional mise-en-scène of research? These are the questions that define the much more complicated ethical compass of contemporary fieldwork for which the past understanding of ethnography (in the throes of more abstract world historical forces) can no longer serve as an adequate frame of assessment.[28]

What complicity stands for as a central figure of fieldwork within this multisited context of research, and particularly as characterizing those relationships that work effectively to generate the kind of knowledge engaged with the outside that I evoked earlier, is an affinity, marking equivalence, between fieldworker and informant. This affinity arises from their mutual curiosity and anxiety about their relationship to a "third"—not so much the abstract contextualizing world system but the specific sites elsewhere that affect their interactions and make them complicit (in relation to the influence of that "third") in creating the bond that makes their fieldwork relationship effective. This special sense of complicity does not entail the sort of evading fictions that Geertz described as anthropological irony, in which anthropologist and informant pretend to forget who and where they otherwise are in the world in order to create the special relationship of fieldwork rapport. Nor is this the covered-up complicity of fieldwork between the anthropologist and imperialism, as is described in Rosaldo's essay. Rather, complicity here rests in the acknowledged fascination between anthropologist and informant regarding the outside "world" that the anthropologist is specifically materializing through the travels and trajectory of her multisited agenda. This is the *OED* sense of complicity that goes beyond the sense of "partnership in an evil action" to the sense of being "complex or involved," primarily through the complex relationships to a third.

The shared imagination between anthropologist and informant that creates a space beyond the immediate confines of the local is also what projects the traditional site-specific mise-en-scène of fieldwork outward toward other sides. The loaded and more commonly acknowledged ethical implication of complicity glides here into its cognitive implication for the design and purview of fieldwork, turning the traditional mise-en-scène inside out. It will be recalled that for Rosaldo, the recognition of fieldwork as complicity was a stopping point for ethnography, a possibly paralyzing insight revealing how anthropology in its most self-justifying rhetoric participates in the broader context of an "evil partnership" with colonialism. In contrast, complicity as a defining element of multisited research is both more generative and more ambiguous morally; it demands a mapping onto and entry of the ethnographic project into a broader context that is neither so morally nor so cognitively determined as it appeared in previous critiques of rapport.

In conclusion, I want to offer a brief consideration of the developing research project of Douglas Holmes, in discussion with whom I worked out a number of the ideas presented in this paper concerning the value of recasting the mise-en-scène of fieldwork in terms of the figure of complicity. Holmes's project traces and examines in situ the discourses of the contemporary European right, frequently placing him in disturbing relation to his subjects. It is thus a dramatic example of the politics of fieldwork in multisited space, where the risk of complicity in its full negatively moral sense of "evil partnership" is alive at several levels. Certainly not many of the several other arenas of research in which multisited agendas are emerging are as charged.[29] Here there is the challenge of the fieldworker treating with a modicum of sympathy subjects whom, as a citizen, he would certainly otherwise oppose and revile. The doctrine of relativism, long considered a partial inoculation of the anthropologist against ethically questionable positions in far-off places, does not work as well in fieldwork among fascists and Nazis—the complicities of fieldwork relationships establishing strong affinities between ethnographer and subject in relation to a shared world or arena of discourse will not allow for a distancing relativism in the field. For Holmes, this problem is captured in his attempt to understand ethnographically the circulation of illicit discourse in contemporary Europe.

### Illicit Discourse

Holmes's project examines how cultural struggles are shaping European politics in the post-cold-war era. In explaining the background of his research, he writes: "The project has a prehistory that stretches back to the mid-1980s and the Friuli region of northeast Italy—the terrain of Carlo Ginzburg's studies of sixteenth-century agrarian cults and inquisitorial persecutions."[30] Elsewhere he writes, "While pursuing an ethnographic portrayal of this domain, I encountered for the first time what appeared to be a rough antipolitics that seemed to subvert the formation of an independent political outlook and identity. In subsequent years these marginal sensibilities and aspirations insinuated themselves into the heart of European political discourse."[31]More recently, Holmes has made fieldwork sites of the European Parliament in Strasbourg and the offices of the openly racist and neofascist British National Party in the East End of London. From his work in Strasbourg, he has published a 1991 interview with Bruno Gollnisch, professor of Japanese law and literature at the University of Lyons, who was elected to the European Parliament as a member of the Technical Group of the European Right, the chairman of which is Jean-Marie Le Pen; and from his London fieldwork he has produced an interview with Richard Edmonds, who is the national organizer of the British National Party.[32]

Holmes's project is to piece together the manifestations, resemblances, and appeals of certain related discourses that have made themselves present in settings like Friuli, Strasbourg, and East London, among others. For the most part, he is not guided by a map of transnational and transcultural "flows" or "scapes"—the cartographic or diagrammatic imagery is inapt for the discontinuous spaces in which he works. The lines of relationship between the discourses in these different sites are not at all charted, and this uncertainty or even mystery as to the genealogies in the spread of right-wing discourses is in part what makes them formidable to both analysts and those who wish to oppose them. What Holmes brings to the enterprise is an ethnographic ear for the perversions of discourse in different settings that mark and define the changing social character of the right. What is challenging about these discourses for the ethnographer is that they are not alien or marked off from respectable ranges of opinion but in fact have deep connections with them. They deserve to be listened to closely before being exoticized as a figment of the politically extreme or being ethically condemned too precipitously. This calculated and imposed naïveté, necessary for fieldwork to be conducted at all, is potentially the source of greatest strength and special insight of ethnographic analysis, leading to both the "complex or involved" sense of complicity as well as exposure to complicity's other sense, of "being an accomplice, partnership in an evil action."

The working conceptual frame for Holmes's multisited fieldwork—what conceptually defines the affinities among sites whose connections are not otherwise preestablished—lies in his notion of "illicit discourse," which he describes as follows:

An illicit discourse aims at reestablishing the boundaries, terms, and idioms of political struggle. The resulting political practice is deconstructive. Its authority is often parasitic, drawing strength from the corruption, ineptitude, obsolescence, and lost relevance of the established political dogmas and agendas. *Its practitioners negotiate and map the points of contra-*

*diction and fatigue of particular positions.* They scavenge the detritus of decaying politics, probing areas of deceit and deception. By doing so they invoke displaced histories and reveal deformed moralities. They strive to introduce the unvoiced and unspeakable into public debate. Established political forces resist these "illicitudes," defining those who articulate them as racists, terrorists, bigots or as some form of essentialized pariah (italics mine).[33]

Different senses of the notion of complicity abound in Holmes's fieldwork. But the particular sense that is relevant to my argument here, and to other multisited research projects, concerns not the heightened ethical question of dealing with the odious from the necessarily open and cordial demeanor of the fieldworker wanting access, but the more subtle issue of the *cognitive/intellectual* affinity between the ethnographer and the purveyor of illicit discourse in different locations (as keyed by the statement that I have italicized in the quotation in the previous paragraph). Despite their very different values and commitments, the ethnographer and his subjects in this project are nevertheless broadly engaged in a pursuit of knowledge with resemblances in form and context that they can recognize. This constitutes the most provocative and potentially troubling sense of complicity in the fieldwork relationship.

What particularly struck Holmes in his fieldwork was the agile appropriation by people marked as objectionable of all sorts of registers of familiar discourse. He was being neither beguiled nor fooled by his informants—he was not complicit with them in this very direct normative sense. Rather, he was simply surprised by what was available in their discourse—its range of overlap and continuities with familiar and otherwise unobjectionable positions. When a researcher is dealing with extremes on either end of the political spectrum, the anthropological assumption is often that one is dealing with the cultlike, the exotic, and the enclosed (and, to some degree, anthropologists might be attracted to subjects in new terrains where they can analogically reproduce their traditional gaze). Extremists are supposed to be like exotic others, living within their own cosmologies and self-enclosed senses of the real. In such a construction, fieldwork complicity with them is highly artificial and not as troubling—it becomes, again, simply complicity to facilitate professional rapport. But when Holmes actually deals with as sophisticated and subtle a speaker as Gollnisch or as cunning a one as Edmonds, what is disrupted in the classic anthropological view is the notion that these speakers are "other"— that they have an "inside" that is distinctly *not* the fieldworker's.

While Holmes does not share his subjects' beliefs—nor does he fear being seduced in this way—he is complicit in many respects with their discourse and critical imaginary of what shapes political cultures in contemporary Europe. They share a taste for deconstructive logics and for, in short, understanding changes in terms of the infectious dynamics of illicit discourse. However differently they normatively view its operation, they share the same speculative wonder about it. By the fluid, appropriative capacity of right-wing discourse, Holmes finds himself being brought closer to his informants, who are accomplished ideologues/theorists/storytellers. His informants are as responsible for this connection (if not more so) as is Holmes—who, as fieldworker, would otherwise be thought of as the frame setter—and in this way, illicit discourse as experienced in fieldwork is particularly infectious.

Complicity not only raises difficult ethical questions here, but, in so doing, it also provides an opening to more general questions posed in "honest" intellectual partnership with fascists. What marks distinctive difference in the mise-en-scène of multisited fieldwork more generally is this unexpected affinity/complicity— more cognitive than ethical—between the fieldworker and the (in Holmes's case) vile informant. Because they are not the usual subjects, the anthropologist looks for other connections that triangulate him and them, and this is what pushes the ethnography elsewhere—in search of other connections, other sites. Finally, Holmes does not fear moral complicity in his fieldwork relationships in any obvious way; rather, he is constantly in danger of becoming an accomplice in the mutual making of illicit discourse because of the commonalities of reference, analytic imaginary, and curiosity that fieldworker and subjects so productively share— each for their very different purposes.[34]

### A Concluding Note

After a strong critical reflection in the 1980s upon the historical project of cultural anthropology as a discipline, articulated through an assessment of its rhetorical traditions, we are now in the midst of a rethinking of the ideology of its distinctive method of fieldwork. Much is at stake in this, since it touches upon the core activity that continues to define the discipline's collective self-identity through every anthropologist's defining experience. The figure of rapport has always been acknowledged as being too simplistic to stand for the actual complexities of fieldwork, but it has had—and continues to have—great influence as a regulative ideal in professional culture. As were many other issues concerning anthropology's contemporary practice, the more troubling figure of complicity shadowing that of rapport was explored in Clifford Geertz's landmark essays of the 1960s and 1970s, written with his signature turn-of-phrase style of deep insight combined with considerable ambivalence. He significantly furthered the anthropological tradition with renewed intellectual power while pragmatically managing the doubt that comes with any exertion of an acute critical capacity. The exercise undertaken in this paper, of amplifying the implication of this shadow figure of complicity for the changing circumstances of anthropological fieldwork without proposing it as a new regulative ideal, is offered in the continuing spirit of Geertz's own seminal balancing of ethnography's possibilities and problems at another, very different moment in the history of anthropology.

# Notes

1. *Oxford English Dictionary*, 1971 compact ed., s.v. "rapport," "collaboration," "collaborate," "complicity," "complice."
2. The most common source of this essay ("Deep Play: Notes on the Balinese Cockfight") is Clifford Geertz, *The Interpretation of Cultures* (New York, 1973), 412–53, but it was first published in *Daedalus* 101 (Winter 1972): 1–37, and as an undergraduate at Yale, I first heard Geertz deliver a verson of it at a colloquium in the mid-1960s. This essay was remarkable for its elegant condensation of virtually all of the major styles and moves that were to make interpretation within the context of ethnography such an attractive research program throughout the 1970s and 1980s, not only in anthropology but also especially in social history and in the new historicist trend in literary criticism, among other methods and disciplines. Segments of "Deep Play" could be easily appropriated as models for different tasks of cultural analysis as these were becoming prominent in a variety of fields. For example, the opening anecdote on which I focus served as a model of the kind of fieldwork story that gets the writer into the material. The rhetorical technique of opening with such a story was to become a major (and now perhaps, dully repetitive) strategy of both writing and analysis in ethnographic, historical, and literary scholarship.
3. Geertz, "Deep Play," 412.
4. Ibid., 416.
5. By now, the literature of fieldwork accounts as well as the critical literature on fieldwork itself are both vast and diverse. For recent assessments in line with the argument here, see Akhil Gupta and James Ferguson, eds., *Culture, Power, Place: Explorations in Critical Anthropology* (Durham, N.C., 1997); Akhil Gupta and James Ferguson, eds., *The Concept of Fieldwork in Anthropology* (Berkeley, 1997); George E. Marcus, ed., *Critical Anthropology Now: Unexpected Contexts, Shifting Constituencies, New Agendas* (Santa Fe, 1997); and George E. Marcus, "Ethnography in/of the World System: The Emergence of Multi-Sited Ethnography," *Annual Review of Anthropology* 24 (1995): 95–117.
6. Standard references for these critiques include James Clifford and George E. Marcus, eds., *Writing Culture: The Poetics and Politics of Ethnography* (Berkeley, 1986); George E. Marcus and Michael Fischer, *Anthropology as Cultural Critique: An Experimental Moment in the Human Sciences* (Chicago, 1986); James Clifford, *The Predicament of Culture* (Cambridge, Mass., 1988); and Renato Rosaldo, *Culture and Truth: The Remaking of Social Analysis* (Boston, 1989).
7. Renato Rosaldo, "Imperialist Nostalgia," in *Culture and Truth*, 68–87.
8. See, for example, Arjun Appadurai, *Modernity at Large: Cultural Dimensions of Globalization* (Minneapolis, 1996), and Susan Harding and Fred Myers, eds., *Further Inflections: Toward Ethnographies of the Future*, theme issue of *Cultural Anthropology* 9, no. 3 (1994).
9. Clifford Geertz, *Works and Lives: The Anthropologist as Author* (Stanford, 1988), 97.
10. We can compare the relative inattention of Geertz to broader complicities of presence (characteristic of the scholarly zeitgeist of the development era of the 1950s and 1960s) to Renato Rosaldo's explicit reflection on his own circumstantial complicity with the historic forces of colonialism (characteristic of a post-1970s zeitgeist in which tales like that of the cockfight incident can no longer be told innocently).
11. Clifford Geertz, "Thinking as a Moral Act: Ethical Dimensions of Anthropological

Fieldwork in the New States," *Antioch Review* 28, no. 2 (1968): 139–58. Again, compare the ironies of fieldwork fictions in this essay of the development era, in which scholarly distance not only remains possible but is considered the most desirable outcome, to James Clifford's reassessment of Marcel Griaule in the field: James Clifford, "Power and Dialogue in Ethnography: Marcel Griaule's Initiation," in *Observers Observed: Essays on Ethnographic Fieldwork*, ed. George Stocking (Madison, 1983), 121–56, one of the key works that placed anthropological fieldwork intimately in colonial context. The way to knowledge for Griaule is through a certain humbling, which puts the desirability of the return to the anthropological "vocation" in doubt.

12. Geertz, "Thinking as a Moral Act," 150–51.

13. Ibid., 151.     14. Ibid., 154–55.

15. In Clifford Geertz's recently published, memoirlike *After the Fact* (Cambridge, Mass., 1995), written with the hindsight knowledge of the murderous turbulence that was to sweep through Indonesia following his years of fieldwork, there is this same matter-of-fact noting of the broader historic dramas and contexts of moments of anthropological fieldwork. These are conveyed with a weary resignation, in which striking insights are encompassed in turns of phrase full of the kind of detachment and wryness that has angered his younger critics.

16. Geertz, "Thinking as a Moral Act," 156.

17. James Clifford, "On Ethnographic Authority," *Predicament of Culture*, 51.

18. Again, Clifford's essay on Marcel Griaule is probably his most explicit and strongest piece on the colonial context and shaping of fieldwork relations. Interestingly, neither Clifford nor the *OED* points to the very common and darker connotation of the term *collaboration* that arose with its special use during World War II (as in *collaborating* with Nazis in occupied countries). In this sense, the connection of the term with *complicity* is of course most prominent.

19. This more complicated and contemporary broader context has begun to be constructed as a rhetorical, theoretical, and ethnographic exercise—for example, in the "Public Culture" project as reflected in the journal of that name and in the recent volume, cited above, by Appadurai, *Modernity at Large*. Also important for thinking about the scene of fieldwork in the different broader context of global political economy is the formulation of and debate about the notion of "reflexive modernization"; see Ulrich Beck, Anthony Giddens, and Scott Lash, *Reflexive Modernization: Politics, Tradition, and Aesthetics in the Modern Social Order* (Stanford, 1994). It should be noted that Clifford's more recent work is a strong move beyond his earlier concentration on the historical context and conventions of the ethnographic mise-en-scène; see his *Routes: Travel and Translation in the Late Twentieth Century* (Cambridge, Mass., 1997).

20. Rosaldo, "Imperialist Nostalgia," 87.

21. Ibid., 69–70.

22. From Mikhail Bakhtin, *Speech Genres and Other Essays*, quoted in Paul Willeman, *Looks and Frictions: Essays in Cultural Studies and Film Theory* (Bloomington, Ind., 1994), 199.

23. In addition to the general discussions on the emergence of multisited ethnography, referenced in note 4, see, for a very specific example, the excellent description by Sherry Ortner of the materialization of this multisited space in her fieldwork among the now dispersed members of her high school class; Sherry B. Ortner, "Ethnography Among the Newark: The Class of '58 of Weequahic High School," *Michigan Quarterly Review* 32, no. 3 (1993).

24. Discussions about reflexive modernization (see note 19) are for me the most searching theoretical discussions available of this mode of being.

25. Geertz saw this clearly, but he argued that the anthropologist and the informant, joined in the complicity of "anthropological irony," blunted these insights in a calculated way through the achievement of rapport by mutual, self-interested, and pragmatic fictions. The sense of complicity that I evoke here is quite different; it is based precisely on the anthropologist and his subject *not* engaging in the fictions that achieve rapport.

26. Under the powerful stimulus of postcolonial studies that have emerged through the writings of scholars such as Edward Said, Gayatri Spivak, Homi Bhabha, and those of the Subaltern Studies group, an important body of work in anthropology has developed reassessing both colonialism and its legacies. In reflecting new exchanges between anthropology and history as well (especially those that have come out of the University of Michigan and the University of Chicago), it has made ethnography's traditional broader context of colonialism itself a complex object of study. While this work overlaps somewhat with the as-yet halting attempts to provide large, systematic perspectives on what is meant by the term *globalization*, its program still remains within a frame that I believe takes a more conservative position on challenging the regulative ideology of ethnographic practice. As such, the ethical critique of fieldwork in this body of scholarship, although immensely enriched, is still expressed restrictively in terms of anthropology's complicity with colonialism and its legacies—categories that do not encompass the diversity of fieldwork relationships that have been created in anthropology's contemporary forays into, for example, science studies, media studies, and political economy.

27. Marcus, "Ethnography in/of the World System," 113–14.

28. The more complex ethical compass of multisited research can be read into Emily Martin's pioneering *Flexible Bodies: The Role of Immunity in American Culture from the Days of Polio to the Age of AIDS* (Boston, 1994). While the explicit discussions of complicities operating in this research are not that developed or rich in Martin's book, she does map very well the special kind of moral economy that emerges from doing multisited fieldwork.

29. Multisited projects are beginning to emerge prominently in the forays of anthropological research into media studies, the study of science and technology (an outgrowth of the diverse interests of the prominent subfield of medical anthropology), the study of environmental and indigenous social movements, the study of development through the activity of NGOs (nongovernmental organizations), the study of art worlds, and the study of diasporas. I myself learned the methodological issues of multisited research through my long-term study of dynastic families and fortunes, and the worlds that they make for others; George E. Marcus, *Lives in Trust: The Fortunes of Dynastic Families in Late-Twentieth-Century America* (Boulder, 1992). While none of these arenas have generated projects with ethical issues of complicity quite as stark as the ones Douglas Holmes has encountered in his fieldwork among the European right, each does place anthropologist and local subject in uncomfortable, but interesting, relationships of mutual complicity in relation to an imagined world of outside sites of activity in which they have very different interests.

30. Douglas R. Holmes, *Cultural Disenchantments: Worker Peasantries in Northeast Italy* (Princeton, 1989).

31. Douglas R. Holmes, "Illicit Discourse," in George E. Marcus, ed., *Perilous States: Conversations on Culture, Politics, and Nation*, Late Editions 1 (Chicago, 1993), 255.

32. The Bruno Gollnisch interview forms the body of Holmes's "Illicit Discourse," and

the Richard Edmonds interview appears in "Tactical Thuggery: National Socialism in the East End of London," in George E. Marcus, ed., *The Paranoid Style at Century's End*, Late Editions 6 (forthcoming).

33. Holmes, "Illicit Discourse," 258.

34. As a citizen, experiencing events largely from a distance and through the available media of journalism, one is inoculated against the heterogeneous seductions of the odious—but not as an ethnographer. For example, an Italian reader of Holmes's Gollnisch interview was not at all impressed with Gollnisch's discourse, which he found easy to see through and situate. This reader responded from an activist political position on the left, whose own discourse has a long history of being shaped by an embedded dialectic of distanced relationship to the changing guises of the European right. But close-up, from the necessary openness of ethnography, Gollnisch is seductive, at least for a moment. This persuasiveness of the moment makes illicit discourse effective in its own political project just as it pulls the ethnographer in as well, making him an accomplice even as it does so in the name of the latter's own distinctive scholarly project, conceived in a tradition of disinterested fieldwork.

# LILA ABU-LUGHOD

## The Interpretation of Culture(s)
## after Television

IF I WERE TO OPEN, AS CLIFFORD GEERTZ did one of his most celebrated (not to mention controversial) essays, with a story about how I began my recent fieldwork in a village, there would be telling differences.[1] I would confess that rather than walking anonymously around the Upper Egyptian village with the feeling that people were looking through us as if we were "gusts of wind," my spouse and I were immediately recognized and firmly placed—in a social network of Canadian, American, and French scholars, journalists, and archaeologists whom the villagers had known. On the west bank of the Nile and a ferry ride from Luxor, the hamlet was in and among the Pharaonic temples that for over a century archaeologists had been unearthing and tourists—now in air-conditioned buses, on donkeys, or riding bicycles—had been admiring.

When I arrived in the spring of 1990, the friendly welcome I received was also due to intense curiosity. Here, finally, was "the wife." My husband had preceded me there, following the trail of an American writer who in 1978 had published a popular life story of a village youth. This was a story that had (too) closely echoed earlier accounts by Jesuits and Orientalists of "the Egyptian peasant," a timeless creature of habit and violence.[2] My husband had sought out a few individuals whom a friend of ours from Cairo, a folklorist writing a dissertation on Upper Egyptian funeral laments, had told him about and to whom she had sent greetings. He had made a special point of meeting Zaynab, whose household had been our friend's haven.[3]

I, in turn, found Zaynab serious and gracious. Her weathered face and unkempt hair, peeking out from her patterned black head shawl, betrayed exposure to the sun and the pressures of being a mother of six (at that time) whose husband had migrated to the city. She asked for news of the folklorist "Leez," as she would do every time I arrived in the village over the next five years, whether from Cairo or the United States. I was forced to exaggerate my knowledge of Liz even as I tried to distance myself from other foreigners I did not know and whose morals and behavior in the village could not be guaranteed. I played on my half-Palestinian identity to distinguish myself. But in the end, Zaynab knew I was from the world of the foreigners she had met, and she took advantage of our time together to improve her understanding of fellowships, dissertations, the cost of living in the

United States, research, and books, among other more troubling aspects of Euro-American life. I was a message bearer and informant as well as a researcher.

In my story of rapport, moreover, instead of a dramatic police raid on an illegal cockfight that people passionately cared about, I would have to make do with the quiet pleasure of recognition that Zaynab and her children, like most families, evinced when I professed an interest in television. Would I like to watch? They brought out their little televison set. They apologized, as they fiddled with its home-made aerial, that the set was black and white. And they invited me to come watch with them any evening, pitying me for not having access to a television set of my own. Television, not the spontaneous common fear of the police, bonded us. And this bond began to separate me from other foreigners, people who generally, as the villagers knew, did not follow the Egyptian television melodramas they loved.

### Thick Description, Still

Despite the differences my story suggests in the kinds of worlds people now inhabit (more interconnected) and, not unrelated, the kinds of subjects anthropologists find worth studying (mass media), I want to argue that Geertz's call for thick description as the method of ethnography is still compelling.[4] But it needs some creative stretching to fit mass-mediated lives.

Many of the studies of popular culture, and especially television, that I have come across are disappointing. They do not seem to be trying to offer profound insights into the human condition, or even into the social, cultural, and political dynamics of particular communities—goals anthropology has always, perhaps with hubris, set for itself. Is it the object, television, that thwarts us? We are not dealing with intricate rituals or complex kinship systems, or even with histories and structures of conjuncture in colonial moments, all of which have deep traditions in the discipline. Television partakes of the ephemerality of the postmodern and is associated, whether here or there, as Geertz likes to put it, with the kind of ordinary people some call the masses.[5] It is also associated with either commercial entertainment or state propaganda, both always suspect. Does the taint of lowbrow status and the apparent banality of televison rub off on those who study it? Or is it, as Jean Baudrillard might have it, that in a world of simulation and simulacra, of which television is such a conspicuous part, notions like the human condition have become hopelessly obsolete?[6]

I would like to argue something else here: that we are only beginning to find the right point of entry for the ethnographic work—in the field and in our studies—that it would take to draw out the significance of television's existence as a ubiquitous presence in the lives and imaginaries of people in the contemporary world. In a recent review of some studies of "resistance," Sherry Ortner diagnosed their weaknesses as being caused by "ethnographic refusal." This strikes me as an apt diagnosis for media studies as well. If there is one theme that has dominated the study of media, especially television, in the last two decades, it is resistance. And if there is one thing that can be said about these studies, it is that despite their considerable theoretical sophistication they are ethnographically thin.[7]

Ironically, for the last decade in cultural studies, the calls for ethnography as the solution have been insistent. Janice Radway's study of romance readers is hailed as a classic that proves the value of ethnography in analyzing popular culture.[8] Yet researchers seem reluctant to heed the call. Books with promising titles like *Television and Everyday Life* intelligently criticize the finest examples of what are known in the business as reception and audience studies, and propose that more ethnographic (and psychoanalytic) case studies are needed. The author of this particular book argues that "an enquiry into the audience should be an enquiry, not into a set of preconstituted individuals or rigidly defined social groups, but into a set of daily practices and discourses within which the complex act of watching television is placed alongside others, and through which that complex act is itself constituted."[9] Yet the author himself does nothing of the sort. Making appropriate excuses, he defers the practical engagement this would require in order to pursue some (culture-bound) general theorizing about suburbia, modernity, and domesticity. When researchers do pursue ethnography, as one of the most persuasive and subtle advocates of "the ethnographic turn" admits, they use a notion of ethnography that little resembles the anthropological ideal.[10]

What can anthropologists offer when we begin to take television seriously? In her overview of the emergent field of the anthropology of media, Debra Spitulnik claims that anthropologists "have in some way already bypassed many of the debates within media studies . . . because they implicitly theorize media processes, products, and uses as complex parts of social reality, and expect to locate media power and value in a more diffuse, rather than direct and causal, sense."[11] In her "(mild) polemic" on the same subject, Faye Ginsburg locates anthropologists' distinctiveness in their less ethnocentric stance, their attention to the contexts of media texts, and their recognition of "the complex ways in which people are engaged in processes of making and interpreting media works in relation to their cultural, social and historical circumstances."[12]

And indeed, the theoretical arguments by anthropologists for careful ethnography—ethnography that illuminates what Brian Larkin calls "the social space" of television—are promising.[13] In a powerful analysis of the politics and interpretations of a television soap opera that gripped China in 1991, Lisa Rofel argues that ethnography—defined as "attention to the contingent way in which all social categories emerge, become naturalized, and intersect in people's conception of themselves and their world, and further, an emphasis on how these categories are produced through everyday practice"—is necessary to the study of encounters with media because "the moments of immersion in a particular cultural artifact are necessarily enmeshed within other social fields of meaning and power."[14] Drawing more directly on the insights of cultural studies, Purnima Mankekar's study of women television viewers in New Delhi, India, shows how "their interpretations are profoundly influenced by the broader social discourses [primarily those on gender and nationalism] in which they are interpellated; they are shaped by events in the viewers' lives and by the relationships in which those viewers define themselves."[15]

But just how do we trace this enmeshment of television in other social fields?[16] The key, I would argue, is to experiment with ways of placing television more seamlessly within the sort of rich social and cultural context that the sustained anthropological fieldwork that has been our ideal since Bronislaw Malinowski is uniquely able to provide. The special challenge we face in doing so is that the cultural forms transmitted by television have no obvious and simple community and are always only a part—sometimes larger, sometimes smaller—of people's complex lives. Moreover, they are produced deliberately for people, under conditions that vary politically and historically.

Anthropologists are probably best prepared to study what in media studies is narrowly called "reception." But how can we get more than a fragmentary sense of the everyday lives, social connections, and concerns of the people interviewed, or of the diversity of viewing communities? What we often have is only the anecdote or the fragmentary quotation of a decontextualized television watcher. How can we get more than a partial sense of the everyday lives, social connections, concerns, and complexities of the people quoted, not to mention of the much larger group who consume the cultural forms and share the country or community?[17]

As I have argued elsewhere, television's messages are deflected by the way people frame their television experiences and by the way powerful everyday realities inflect and offset those messages.[18] Roger Silverstone's image of the television audience as positioned in multiple spaces and times suggests how daunting the task of fully contextualizing television is. He notes that people "live in different overlapping but not always overdetermining spaces and times: domestic spaces; national spaces; broadcasting and narrowcasting spaces; biographical times; daily times; scheduled, spontaneous but also socio-geological times."[19] Which means we should somehow try to include these various spaces and times in our thick descriptions of people who watch television.[20]

Yet even this is not enough. Anthropologists cannot dispense with "textual" analysis, the equivalent of the symbolic analyses of rituals and myths that have illuminated so much. Even more important, they need to do ethnographies of production. Television programs are produced not just by specialists of a different social status than viewers (like priests and bards), but by professionals of a different class—often urban rather than rural, with national and sometimes transnational identities and social ties—who are working within structures of power and organizations that are tied to and doing the work of national or commercial interests. For a truly thick description, we need to find ways to interrelate these various nodes of the "social life of television."[21]

When I argue that part of the solution to the thinness of studies of popular culture lies in returning to the insights of Geertz's "Thick Description," I do not mean that our goal is necessarily the same as his was—to develop an interpretive theory of culture or to translate cultures—even though I share Geertz's faith that a good analysis demonstrates "the power of the scientific imagination to bring us into touch with the lives of strangers."[22] Rather, I think we need to recall that when Geertz calls for microscopic ethnographic description, he justifies these "protracted descriptions" of distant events as—to borrow a phrase from someone he considers irredeemably wrongheaded—good to think. Thick descriptions of social discourses in particular places have general relevance, he argues, because "they present the sociological mind with bodied stuff on which to feed." With their specific knowledges, anthropologists can think intelligently about, and imaginatively with, the megaconcepts of social science.[23] Or of the humanities, one might now add. Along the same lines, Geertz warns that though anthropologists often study *in* villages, they don't study villages. They confront the same grand realities and big words as other social scientists—but in homely locations and forms.[24]

Extending these ideas, I want to suggest that we can still profit from trying to use careful contextualizations of small facts and events—in this case of television consumption in particular places, including homely villages in Upper Egypt—to help us reflect on some "big words." If television seems banal, then one of Michel Foucault's most memorable phrases should inspire us: "What we have to do with banal facts is to discover—or try to discover—which specific and perhaps original problem is connected with them."[25]

In what follows, I try to show that among the problems that stories about women and television in an Upper Egyptian village can speak to (or be made to speak to, as Geertz reminds us) are those about the nature of "culture" and "cultures" under the conditions of what many would call postcolonial postmodernity. Along the way, I explore a method, a kind of appropriate technology for media studies. In the conclusion, I suggest that the study of television encourages an anthropology that engages not just with the academy and its "big words" but with other social fields of the world in which we work.

### Cultural Texts and "Multisited" Ethnography

In January 1996, when I returned for a short visit to the Upper Egyptian village I had been working in intermittently since 1990, I watched, with friends, some episodes of the current television serial *Mothers in the House of Love*. Set in a retirement home for women, the program's central drama concerned an attempt by the unscrupulous brother-in-law of the widow who ran the place to take it over so he could achieve his dream of building a twenty-two-story hotel. Armed with a newfound purpose, the women residents banded together to defend their threatened home. They forgot their squabbles about which television programs to watch, mobilized their talents to raise the money to buy out his share, and stood up to him.

The serial had been written a few years earlier by Fathiyya al-'Assal, a vibrant and self-confident writer, and one of only a handful of women of her generation writing television dramas in Egypt. Active in the Egyptian leftist party, she had occasionally been jailed and had had numerous story ideas tabled and serials canceled by the television censors—civil servants working for state-owned television—and even by those higher up in the government. Her serials were known for their social concerns, and she considered women's issues critical. She had also done some ethnography in a retirement home to make her script more realistic.

How can we study the encounter between some Upper Egyptian village women and this television serial? With television programs, one is forced to talk not so much about cultures-as-texts as about discrete cultural texts that are produced, circulated, and consumed. Thick description of television therefore requires a multisited ethnography wherein, as George Marcus has put it regarding commodities in a world system, one can "follow the thing."[26] The relevant system here is national. Therefore, I will start with the villagers and their responses to the television serial, using this focus to explore basic structures and meanings in their lives. But I also want to keep tracing the serial back to Cairo, where it was produced in a very different milieu by a leftist intellectual and some urban professionals working with and against a state-controlled medium and with imagined audiences for their work. This approach will, in the end, allow us some insight into the dynamics of "culture"—one of those big words.

I watched several episodes of *Mothers in the House of Love* with my neighbors, who, though intrigued, kept up a running commentary, laughing at ludicrous characters like the compulsive knitter of pullovers. After an episode in which a widow had finally consented to marry an old sweetheart, one person joked, "Now all sixty-year-old women will want to marry." The next day, though, Zaynab commented more realistically on the episode, simply contrasting it to local attitudes: "We say when a girl is past thirty she won't marry. . . . It is shameful. If a woman over thirty does marry, she'll do it quietly, far away, without a wedding celebration."

Zaynab's comment was revealing in so many ways. Directed to me, it posited the difference between the villagers (and Upper Egyptians in general, by extension) and the urban, wealthy Alexandrian women of the television serial as a cultural difference within a moral frame. This construction of difference was partly for the edification of the anthropologist. Zaynab's long years of watching her mother's wealth of funeral laments being carefully noted by our folklorist friend as well as her own regular experiences of being photographed by tourists had no doubt helped her objectify her own culture. Her gifts to me over the years suggested she had learned her lessons well. Her first gift was a crude earthenware casserole dish of the sort locally made and used. The second was a traditional piece of black cloth, offered with the confident announcement that she had got me something I would really like, something rare nowadays. The third was a black shawl, the latest local design for what "traditional" women wore on their heads. Each represented something unique to Upper Egypt and something that those eager to become more sophisticated—like her daughter—would have rejected as old-fashioned.

Yet for Zaynab, a woman very much at home in her social world, a little old before her time and confident as one of the adult women of the village who took her social duties—sick visits and funerals, for example—very seriously, the cultural differences within which she framed her response to the serial were also personally meaningful. Her own experience of marriage was very different from what she saw on television.

Zaynab, like most women in the village, had had an arranged marriage—but, following the lines of closest practical kinship, it was to a maternal, not a paternal, cousin. Zaynab's mother had been a second and younger wife, widowed shortly after she gave birth to her only child. Not close to her husband's patrilineage, she had turned to her own relatives for support, and eventually, for a husband for her daughter. She had inherited from her father some land, on which she and Zaynab later built a two-story mud-brick home. Zaynab's husband had worked on and off in Cairo since he was fourteen, leaving her mostly alone with her mother to raise her children. Secretly, he had married a second wife in Cairo; Zaynab now knew about this and was resigned to the fact that he would probably never return to live in the village.

As the years went by and Zaynab had more children, conceived on her husband's visits home, she had a harder time coping. It was especially difficult when her milk dried up after she gave birth to twins. Not long after that, she and her mother were forced to sell all their livestock because they couldn't take care of them. Then her mother died, leaving Zaynab on her own.

One cannot ignore the possibility that Zaynab had remarked on the episode of the older widow's wedding because it was meaningful to her own personal situation. The idea of remarriage might have been appealing. She was alone, managing a complex household, and her children provided her with her only company most evenings (when they all watched television together). She had no man to help her make decisions about the children's schooling, about what to plant and harvest on which strips of land, and about which domestic livestock to buy or sell. For help with the work in the fields, she had to call on young male relatives or pay for labor. Certainly she had no one for companionship or love. She said about her husband's visits home: "He's like a guest; he doesn't know anything about our lives."

In fact, a recurrent theme in my conversations with Zaynab was the situation of the five or six older women from Switzerland, Germany, and the United States who had married—or had affairs with—village youths they met while on holiday. Some were divorcées with grown children, as Zaynab noted. Using me as an informant about the strange behavior of foreigners, she would ask me how these women could do it. She was puzzled about how their behavior might be acceptable, especially to their children. She was not the only village woman to talk to me about this phenomenon, but I wondered if her curiosity about these older women who had had second lives, second chances at love or sex, might not have had a special resonance, as had the episode about the widow's remarriage. Nevertheless, as a woman whose respectability rested on her marriage, she distanced herself in moral language from what she perceived as a cultural difference between life here, in Upper Egyptian villages, and there, in Alexandria, Cairo, or other cities.

Zaynab could not even begin to recognize that for the Cairene writer of *Mothers in the House of Love*, a progressive activist engaged in arguments with more conservative intellectuals and politicians, this episode about the value of love in the face of social pressure was not meant as a simple portrayal of the middle-class values of Alexandrian society but as a universally applicable revolutionary alternative to enhance women's status and lives.

Another serial of which al-'Assal was proud was about a woman who, rejected by her husband because she is uneducated, goes out and gets herself an education. When her husband then wants to take her back, she refuses, even though they have a son together. Al-'Assal said of this serial, "My point was to emphasize the value of a home as a home. That is to say, a man and woman should only enter on condition that they love one another." Marriage, she contended, should be first and foremost about mutual understanding and love. She contrasted her ideas about companionate marriage to prevailing values that place financial considerations first.[27] Her reference point was urban and middle class, and her views were those of the most progressive and modernist end of a continuum. While the ideal of the bourgeois couple and some version of the idea of companionate marriage have been increasingly idealized and realized by the middle classes in twentieth-century Egypt, al-'Assal's stress on the equality of husband and wife was meant to be more radical than the mainstream middle-class vision.[28] Yet Zaynab's marriage did not even fit the ordinary middle-class ideal; the vocabulary of rights to love and personal happiness was foreign to her.

There are other examples of how the serials both raised relevant issues for village viewers and yet were unassimilable because of fundamental differences of perspective related to social location. In one of the first conversations I had while watching television with Zaynab, she animatedly told me about the program that had just come on the air. This extraordinary weekly show was called *The Confrontation* and consisted of interviews—more like interrogations—of actual criminals serving prison sentences. Imitating the Cairene dialect, Zaynab recounted a memorable interview with a woman drug dealer. When the interviewer asked if she would do it again, the woman had replied, "Of course. As soon as I get out I'll deal in drugs again." Asked why, she replied, "I have to eat." Zaynab added that the woman had become used to a certain way of life and so had to keep it up. Zaynab quoted her again: "They'll jail me and I'll get out and deal. They'll put me in prison, I'll get out and do it again. That's how I make a living."

That Zaynab found this female criminal so compelling seems as significant as the fact that she responded to the television theme of marriage at a late age. The woman drug dealer, trying to make a living, must have represented something intriguing for this person of great integrity, who was insulted by any hint of disrespect. Zaynab's whole life was organized around trying to feed herself and her family—in the larger sense of managing a household and educating, clothing, and raising her children. She farmed three small plots of land (each far apart from the others) as well as raising sheep, a water buffalo, chickens, ducks, and pigeons. She baked bread. Work and economic struggles were the most persistent themes in her conversations with others and the main concerns in her day-to-day life.

The television serial we watched in January (*Mothers in the House of Love*) also treated this theme. But the way women's work and social usefulness were framed made them awkward for someone like Zaynab to assimilate. One of al-'Assal's goals in writing this serial was to show that the perceptions of "old age" and "senility" in women were, at least in part, the results of their not having had any social role. As she put it,

I wanted to create a new role for older women. . . . In the retirement home itself, they started a class for teaching English, because one woman had been an English professor; another woman who had been a silversmith opened a small silver workshop and taught women the skills needed for this work. They participated in the eradication of illiteracy by teaching neighborhood girls to read and write. They also gave classes on household management, and even agriculture. . . . My message is that women can still learn at this age, and we can still benefit from what they have to teach us as well.

The dynamic Cairene writer claimed to speak from her own experience, explaining,

I am sixty years old now. In the past, when a woman was sixty she was supposed to sit at home waiting to die, having already married off her children. I now have four children and eight grandchildren, but because I have my own concerns and ambitions as a writer and a politician, I do not feel that I am getting older. I wanted to communicate this in a serial.

Al-'Assal's socialist feminist message—advocating socially useful roles for women, skills and activities that could take them beyond their place in the family and home, and economic independence that would alleviate the worst effects of male domination—is impressive. Going somewhat against the grain of current conservative sentiments being voiced in the media and Parliament in favor of women's return to the home (at a time when large numbers of women must work out of financial necessity and when professional careers are common), this politically motivated position is underwritten by al-'Assal's own anger. Her father was a wealthy businessman who married twenty women after marrying (and eventually divorcing) her mother, a housewife without the power to object. Al-'Assal was determined to become educated herself and still believes in education as the key for women—and for social progress.

Historically, this is a political position that had its origins at the turn of the century, when elite and some middle-class reformists (both male and female) began advocating women's education. But it was given real support by programs to provide mass education in the 1960s.[29] It was in this era that al-'Assal began her career as a serial writer—when she found that the students she was teaching to read and write would desert the classroom to listen, with the janitor, to the melodramatic serials on the radio. She still tries to work the importance of literacy into many of her plots and proudly told me about one serial called *Moment of Choice*, about a woman of fifty whose husband has run off with another woman, leaving her with no skills or identity. As al-'Assal described it,

It was about how she was able to deal with life, how she refused to ever return to being the wife of so-and-so, how she had to become a person in her own right, how she worked in a publishing house and read and expanded her horizons, and finally how she wrote stories and won a prize for them. The serial ended up on that note, in order to show how she was able to win the prize herself—she was the sole master of the victory.

How might a theme like becoming literate affect Zaynab? Just the year before *Mothers in the House of Love* was broadcast, government-sponsored literacy classes for women had been set up in and around her village. Attending was out of the question for someone as busy as Zaynab. Women went for a variety of reasons, but all those who attended had two things in common: they had no children (or only a few that someone else could watch for a while) and their family situations were such that they could be released from work for a few hours in the afternoon.

When I went to pay a call on Umm Ahmad, another woman I knew and liked, I asked if she was going to the classes. With her eyes bright and a big smile, she said she really wanted to; she was dying to learn to read and she hated it that she couldn't even sign her own name (she had been trying to collect her recently deceased father's pension). "But can I learn?" she asked me dubiously. "No, I'm too old. I've got no brain," she laughed. Then she added, "An old woman—why, they'll talk. They'll say, 'Why does she need to go and learn?'" I asked her who would talk, and she said, "The men. The men will talk."

When her son, a young man in his early thirties and the father of two young children, walked into the room, I teased, "Hey, you should let her go to the literacy classes." He replied, "Fine, that's fine. She can go." Turning to her with a smile, he added, "In fact, I'll get you a book bag." This was an amusing idea, since village women never carry satchels or handbags. If they go to market or visiting, they carry a basket on their heads. Otherwise, what they need is tucked inside their long black overdresses. Only schoolchildren and city people carry bags.

But Umm Ahmad was no downtrodden, superannuated old woman lacking any socially useful role or skills, as al-'Assal might have feared. She was a grand-mother, but a wiry and energetic one—working in the fields, caring for her water buffalo, and selling cheese and butter locally. Her situation was somewhat unusual, but in my experience everyone's story in the village was unique. She had had a bad marriage and returned to live in her father's household. She had only one son who, also unusually, lived with her and worked her father's fields while holding a night job as a guard at a nearby Pharaonic temple. For years she had taken care of her father, who was in poor health and not always lucid. A founder of the ham-let in which they lived, he had been an important figure. Umm Ahmad had been in charge of running her father's household and farming enterprise, especially the livestock, while her son was growing up as well as after he left, desperate for income, to work briefly for a Lebanese-owned chicken-breeding factory near Alexandria.

What significance could a group of wealthy or formerly wealthy women, sitting around a comfortable retirement home and suddenly putting aside their individual troubles and overcoming their sense of helplessness and uselessness, have for Umm Ahmad? What about the modernist feminist ideal of women's rights to education and a meaningful career, or at least socially useful work? What about the idea of winning a prize for writing? Umm Ahmad had to contend with a gender system that constrained women, but this was hardly her main impediment to securing a decent life. Other concerns were more pressing: the cost of farming with more expensive fertilizer, the depressed prices the government paid for crops, the IMF-enforced lifting of subsidies for wheat that made provisioning households with bread a strain for most local families, the higher cost of living in an area where hotels catering to tourists drove up prices, the felt need to get children educated so they might find employment, and the vast inequalities between large landlords and the majority of households.

What possibilities did Umm Ahmad or other village women have for careers that would provide personal fulfillment and the financial independence necessary for a marriage based on equality, when even the finest local men who had become educated might have to content themselves with being foremen at archaeological sites? Or perhaps with waiting for five or six years after graduating from teaching college for a government job as a librarian in the local high school, working a couple of hours a day and making barely enough to pay for cigarettes?

The problem is not just that cultural producers like al-'Assal come from a different social class than these village women who watch her programs, though this is significant. Nor is it a matter of the difference between urban and rural experiences, however considerable. Al-'Assal has actually tried to bridge this kind of difference by writing a serial, broadcast in 1993, about rural Upper Egypt. The serial showed the cruelty and power of large landlords and the powerlessness of peasants who don't seek common cause. But the main theme was revenge (the feud), the metonym by which Upper Egypt has been known to generations of northern Egyptian writers (the violence it signifies now transferred neatly onto Muslim militants whose strongholds are located there).[30]

Al-'Assal wrote this serial out of genuine concern. She even spent months living with a rural family to prepare herself to write the script, just as she had studied a retirement home to write *Mothers in the House of Love*. As a radical politician, she was deeply concerned with social conditions and the terrible poverty of the region. But her focus on vengeance and the solution she offered reproduced a discourse of enlightened modernity against backward customs that continue to denigrate Upper Egyptians, men and women. The hero and heroine of the program were a young couple, a latter-day Romeo and Juliet, whose modern education and enlightened ideas led them to reject the feud (a "backward" tradition still nurtured by older women) and to attempt to break the hold of the feudal lords (and their wives) by supporting the peasants' efforts to set up a collectively owned factory.

Al-'Assal's feminism, like her progressive politics, is part of a public discourse of reform and uplift whose contours can be traced to colonial and anticolonial nationalist efforts to transform Egypt into a modern place. Tempered by ethnography and broad sympathy in al-'Assal's case, this general attitude of knowing what is good for "society" (seen as an object to be manipulated by one's expertise) underlies the work of many of the writers of television serials, just as it shapes the myriad projects of reform, from schooling to public health plans, in which villagers find themselves involved. In places like Egypt and India, television is the main instrument for the transmission of both expertise and these public narratives of the state and the urban middle classes.[31]

Such discourses of enlightenment have their dark side. Had Umm Ahmad been able to attend her local literacy classes, she would have learned to read and write using textbooks filled with didactic stories about the value of small families, neighborly cooperation, and national responsibility. Until she gets her book bag, she is subjected to this pedagogic discourse mostly by watching television, which she does.[32] How does this discourse help her place herself? As someone who could carry a book bag? As someone whose life is different from the ones portrayed? Or as someone whose life is hopelessly inferior?

Television makes obvious the fact that the same cultural texts have different imports in different contexts. When Zaynab interprets a scene like the marriage of a sixty-year-old as a matter of cultural difference—linked to region, way of life, and morality—this is because she is so disadvantaged in terms of class and education that she fails to grasp the intentions of the more privileged creator of the program. For al-'Assal—working as an oppositional politician within the national context of a postcolonial state and arguing with fellow intellectuals, critics, and politicians in Cairo and across the Arab world while trying to reform the public—

this episode was meant to represent a revolutionary and enlightened feminist option. Only a mobile ethnography can do justice to the ways these different worlds intersect. And this intersection must be part of any thick description of television.

I hope this extended reflection on the encounter between some village women and a television serial has illustrated the way stories about book bags, marrying at sixty, and television can speak, as Geertz suggested, to big words and mega-concepts. Taking television seriously forces us to think about "culture" not so much as a system of meaning or even a way of life but as something whose elements are produced, censored, paid for, and broadcast across a nation, even across national boundaries. The hegemonic or ideological—and thus power-related—nature of mass-mediated cultural texts in the service of national, class, or commercial projects is undeniable. This, in turn, should lead us to think about the ways that aspects of what we used to think of as local culture, such as moral values about the proper age of marriage or the propriety of women's education, are themselves not neutral features to be interpreted but the sometimes contested result of other, more local, projects of power that are worth analyzing.[33]

### From Cultures to Cosmopolitans

More interesting, perhaps, is the way ethnographies of television—because its cultural texts are produced elsewhere and inserted into local households, communities, and nations—confirm for us the need to rethink the notion of culture in the singular, as a shared set of meanings distinct from those held by other communities sometimes called "cultures." This observation has become something of a commonplace in anthropology. Ulf Hannerz uses the term "cultural complexity" and has developed a distributive theory of culture to capture the ways that culture is not necessarily shared.[34] Critiques of the way the culture concept has tended to homogenize communities and create false boundaries (perhaps articulated most eloquently by James Clifford) appear in introductions to major interdisciplinary readers and in arguments like Arjun Appadurai's that "natives"—people incarcerated in place and in modes of thought—are fictions of the anthropological imagination.[35] In my own argument for "writing against culture," I too registered discomfort with the internal homogenization produced by the culture concept.[36] I explored ways to write against the typifying of communities that results from thinking of them as "cultures," and I tried to highlight the contestatory nature of discourses within communities.[37]

This is not to deny that the notion of having a culture, or being a culture, has become politically crucial to many communities previously labeled "cultures" by anthropologists—Solomon Islanders invoking *kastom*, diaspora Indians supporting fundamentalist religious organizations that glorify Hindu culture, Catalonians and Jordanians setting up national or regional folklore museums as part of what could be called the heritage industry. As Marshall Sahlins, following Norbert Elias and others, has noted about the origins of the culture concept, it is related to relative disadvantage. It developed in Germany, "a relatively underdeveloped region [as opposed to the imperial and colonial powers of Western Europe], and as an expression of that comparative backwardness, or of its nationalist demands."[38] The similarities to the conditions in regions where today the idea of culture is gaining currency are obvious. Appadurai has called this phenomenon "culturalism," in which identities are mobilized in the context of nation-states, mass mediation, migration, and globalization.[39] It is no accident that in the Upper Egyptian village I know, it was Zaynab, the woman with the most experience with foreigners, who knew what kinds of gifts I would appreciate: objects from a distinct local "culture." This "culturing" process is related to encounters with others, many of whom arrive already primed with notions of culture.

However, these reactive processes are balanced by many others that unsettle the boundaries of cultures. Much has been written on travel and migration, which has certainly been a growing part of Upper Egyptian reality—Zaynab's husband, for example, joining generations of Upper Egyptians in the city of Cairo, long dotted with clubs devoted to migrants from particular villages. Much, too, could be written about colonialism and other forms of political and economic interpenetration. In this region of Upper Egypt, for example, local life is shaped by the economics of the international sugar industry since, from the late nineteenth century, sugarcane has been the major crop.

But television is an extraordinary technology for breaching boundaries and intensifying and multiplying encounters among lifeworlds, sensibilities, and ideas. Television brings into Zaynab's home, her conversations, and her imagination a range of visions and experiences that originated outside her community (in such places as Cairo, Alexandria, Hollywood, Bombay, and even Tokyo). At the same time it places her in a particular relation to them. And with UNESCO's 1993 estimate of more than six million television sets in Egypt, Zaynab's exposure is hardly unusual.[40]

What is critical is that television's meanings are produced somewhere—for most viewers, somewhere else—and consumed locally in a variety of localities. Even if it ultimately helps create something of a "national habitus," or hints of a transnational habitus, television is most interesting because of the way it provides material which is then inserted into, interpreted with, and mixed up with local but themselves socially differentiated knowledges, discourses, and meaning systems.[41] Television, in short, renders more and more problematic a concept of cultures as localized communities of people suspended in shared webs of meaning.

Thinking about Zaynab watching Egyptian dramatic serials and films, interviews with criminals, broadcasts of Parliament in session, American soap operas, imported nature programs that take her to the Caribbean or the Serengeti Plain, and advertisements for candy, ceramic toilets, chicken-stock cubes, and Coca-Cola leads me to begin thinking about her and others in this village not as members of some kind of unified Egyptian, or Upper Egyptian, peasant culture—one in which it is improper for women over thirty to marry or older women to be out and about going to school—but in terms of the cosmopolitanism they might represent. The introduction here of the concept of cosmopolitanism might seem surprising or glib. Since it is generally associated with those who travel, those who feel at home in several parts of the world, and those who are professionals, the concept would seem to apply more readily to the progressive television writer al-'Assal.[42] Although her political and social concerns are passionately focused on Egypt, her political vocabulary is international; she is well aware of foreign literature, film, and media; she has grown children who work in Finland and France; and she expresses frustration that the work of many fine Egyptian women writers is not translated into foreign languages. She reads television texts in terms of their political perspectives, criticizing fellow writers for being conservative or caving in to government expectations. She worries about television's social impact, disapproving of an American soap opera like *The Bold and the Beautiful* for the immorality it normalizes.

However, what village women like Zaynab, her daughter Sumaya, and her neighbor Fayruz can help us understand is how wealth, education, and particular experiences in everyday life combine with television to mark out other varieties of cosmopolitanism. These are the kinds of cosmopolitanisms one finds in many rural areas around the postcolonial world and that confound the concept of "cultures."

Poverty, for example, impedes full access to the consumer culture and commodification of signs that are so conspicuously a part of a postmodern cosmopolitan's life. Yet Zaynab's life is not untouched by these features of cosmopolitanism. Television advertisements in Egypt insistently traffic in such signs, their jingles—written by advertising firms with names like Americana—enticing people to buy brand-name shampoos and yogurt. Unlike her children, Zaynab remains fairly unmoved by these advertisements. One promoting a national brand of luncheon meat suggests the complicated reasons why. This commercial, which aired regularly in the early 1990s, shows the large factory where the meat is processed. From displays of carcasses hung from butcher hooks the commercial moves to a shot of the workers, technicians in lab coats busy at gleaming stainless-steel machines. The advertisement is selling modernity—with its scientific procedures and hygiene. But to gain consumers beyond those already attracted by convenience foods, it has to overcome the aversions of women like Zaynab (who raise chickens, ducks, and pigeons at home) to eating anything "from outside." (When well-meaning German tourists give her children packages of prepared cheeses and meats, Zaynab snatches them and throws them disgustedly to the sheep.) In any case, these meat products are expensive and mostly unavailable locally, except in a few up-market grocery stores across the river in Luxor—stores Zaynab would not go to.

This is not to say that Zaynab's imagination is not broad or that she does not have great knowledge of other worlds, gleaned not just from television but from foreign friends. The hamlet she lives in, with its Euro-American folklorists, journalists, political scientists, tourists, and aging divorcées, is only an extreme version of the kinds of communities in which many villagers in Egypt and elsewhere live. Migrating husbands and imported fans and television sets (brought back from wealthy labor-importing countries) are also familiar figures and objects—the products of unequal economies, nations, and states. The postcolonial state is there, too—in a national curriculum disseminated by newly literate teachers in overcrowded classrooms with barely any resources; in literacy textbooks promulgating family planning messages; and in television serials promoting modernist ideals forged in the anticolonial nationalist movements of the first half of the century.

Yet Zaynab's life is anchored by economic constraints in her house, family, and village; the aspiration to educate her children is the only modernist national ideal within her reach, and, like most village parents, she sacrifices much for it. Zaynab has spent time in Cairo, getting medical treatment for her son. While there, she stayed in the Canadian folklorist's apartment—which was decorated with Egyptian antiques, folk art, and Bedouin rugs, but also boasted a transcriber, cassette player, and lots of books. Zaynab's subaltern relationship to this metropolitan world, related to her poverty and lack of education, is symbolized best by what she wore in Cairo. Despite her versatile knowledge, she wore the only clothes she had—clothes that announced her regional and rural origins.

This is in contrast to the form of cosmopolitanism that characterizes her wealthy neighbor, Fayruz. The first time I heard about this young woman was from her mother, the wife of the largest landowner in the village. During our first visit in 1990, I had talked to the mother about *The White Flag*, a television serial about the struggles of a retired diplomat to save his historic villa from destruction by a nouveau riche developer. She told me how some Egyptian tourists had knocked on her daughter's door and begged to watch the program there. Her daughter Fayruz, she proudly said, had cooked them dinner. She implied that Fayruz possessed both the sophistication to feel comfortable with these urban types and the "traditional" generosity to invite them to a meal.

Fayruz lives around the corner from Zaynab in a house that looks quite different. In front sits a small shop, its shelves stocked with the usual contents of a local store anywhere in rural Egypt—laundry soaps, cans of tomato sauce, halvah, cooking oil, cigarettes, and candies. The shop is also the center for an immense wholesale grocery business, which, combined with their agricultural efforts and a monopoly on government-ration distribution, has helped her husband and his brother consolidate their father's wealth.

Down the driveway is an odd structure that says worlds about Fayruz's social location. A mud-brick house adjoins a concrete-and-brick house, complete with balcony. This is the type of "villa" people with money now aspire to build. When I first met Fayruz, she lived in the spacious and tidy mud-brick house. Like all village women, she baked bread in her outdoor oven. But her house looked cleaner, because she did not need to keep livestock to boost the household income. When I returned in 1996, she had moved into the adjoining structure, with its stone floor tiles and bright blue ceramic-tiled bathroom, complete with toilet and bathtub. She showed me around the house so I could see all the furniture—beds, wardrobes, couches, armchairs, and side tables. (In contrast, Zaynab owns only a couple of locally made benches, a low table for eating, one large wooden bed, and a number of other beds made from palm reeds pruned from her four trees.) The new "modern" house had been prepared for Fayruz's younger, educated brother-in-law. But when he finally found a bride, a girl from a wealthy local family, she refused to live in the village—even in what locals might have considered a sophisticated "palace." She insisted on living in an apartment across the river in Luxor.

Compared to the distinctions that can be marked by goods in a city like Cairo, where the wealthy, educated cosmopolitan elite can have the best imported appliances and furniture and where distinctions of taste can be subtly marked (decorating at least one room with Arabesque furniture was common among the most "cultured" in the 1970s and 1980s; in the 1990s, folk arts are more popular), the distinctions in a provincial area like Luxor are cruder. Fayruz's household had furniture, a telephone, and a color television set. These set its members apart as people with money and a "modern," worldly—not rural and backward—orientation. In contrast, her father (from an older generation and, like Zaynab, more locally oriented), though perfectly willing to invest in tractors and harvesters for his agricultural enterprise, would not consider moving from his mud-brick house or buying a bigger television set.[43]

When Fayruz unlocked her wardrobe and started pulling out dresses to show me, I understood even better how her wealth enabled a different form of cosmopolitanism than Zaynab's, while her lack of education and her location in the provinces still distinguished her from urban professional cosmopolitans like al-'Assal. Fayruz showed me amazing dresses of chiffon and silk, with sequins and gold buttons, all long and with long sleeves (only the urban upper classes and movie stars would wear anything more revealing)—some with surprisingly curved bodices and extravagant flounces. I was surprised, because around the village she wore the usual black head covering and an overdress only slightly more sophisticated than most women's.

This ornate wardrobe full of extraordinary dresses out of a lavish television serial reveals a great deal about urbanity, class distinction, and the national context in which these figure for a provincial. When Fayruz went to Cairo to get medical treatment for her migraines, she stayed, unlike Zaynab, in a shabby part of town where few foreigners would live. She and her husband called on business contacts her brother-in-law had developed while attending the business school run (as part of its parallel educational system) by the venerable mosque-university al-Azhar. Whereas Zaynab, despite her contact with foreign cosmopolitans, had worn her village clothes, Fayruz, whose knowledge of other worlds came from television and Upper Egyptians with urban experience or aspirations, plucked her eyebrows, wore makeup, and put on some of the more modest dresses she had in her wardrobe. She also replaced her black head cloth with the *higab*—the head covering associated with modest Islamic dress—thereby erasing her village identity. This adoption of the higab is not surprising. For rural Egyptians, as for urban lower- and middle-class women since the 1980s, to become "modern" and urbane has meant taking on a more identifiably Islamic look and sound.[44]

We can read in these differences a contrast of cosmopolitanisms: between the resolutely national frame of an up-and-coming provincial and the sharp juxtapositions produced for a poor woman by the intersection of neocolonial travel by folklorists, anthropologists, and tourists; postcolonial nationalist modernization projects; and transnational flows of television programs. Fayruz, with her chiffon dresses and higab, can more easily imagine herself in the Egyptian serialized melodramas than can Zaynab, who distinguishes the moralities of marriage at sixty. Yet because she has neither the education nor the real urban experience of serial writers like al-'Assal (a staunch opponent of the new veiling), Fayruz asserts her sophistication by placing herself in the middle-class moral world symbolized by veiling. This is a world deliberately excluded from television.[45]

Fayruz's imaginative participation in the nation, with its power centers in the cities, will be intensified if she continues with her literacy classes. But it should be noted that she is attending more out of wounded pride (and loneliness) than any desire for female emancipation. When her brother-in-law's new bride refused to stay in the household with her, the bride apparently put on airs because of her education. Telling me these stories, Fayruz had fumed, "Is she better than me?" "Look at who my father is," she would add. Yet the bride's claims to superiority rested in part on her school diploma. In the national context, where standards are set by the urban and where television glorifies the educated and cultured, Fayruz realized she could not rely only on her wealth and family name for status.

For yet a third type of village cosmopolitanism, let us consider Zaynab's twenty-year-old daughter, Sumaya. She has the education Fayruz lacks without the wealth that enables Fayruz to live in a "modern" house and have a wardrobe full of dresses that cannot be worn in the village. Because of her education (she has completed agricultural secondary school), she too wears a version of the higab when she goes to school or dresses up, replacing the locally tailored gowns she ordinarily wears with a bright polyester store-bought outfit and high heels. She saves up to buy face creams she has seen advertised on television, and she knows how to bake cakes because of her home-economics classes. She occasionally reads the newspaper and plans to have a small family, as national propaganda urges. Sumaya's first gift to me, so different from her mother's, bespoke her generation's form of cosmopolitanism. Shyly, she presented me with a color postcard framed with green and blue twisted yarn. The postcard—outdated, printed in Italy, and of the type widely circulated across Egypt—portrayed a European bride and groom gazing into each other's eyes. The frame was her own handiwork, a design no doubt learned at school using materials only the teachers could provide. A gift her mother could not appreciate, it was a homegrown amalgam of elements originating in various communities and places, expressing her romantic fantasies (encouraged by television) and signifying her modern, state-initiated vocational education.

What the situations, cultural knowledges, code-switching abilities, and imaginative possibilities of these three village women mean for the interpretation of culture(s) after television—and everything that has made television possible and widely present in villages around the globe—is not only that (post)colonial processes of cultural hybridization have undermined the utility of more static and homogenizing conceptions of culture or cultures.[46] Nor is it just that these multiple situations, knowledges, and abilities confirm the importance of, as Bruce Robbins so nicely puts it, attending to "discrepant cosmopolitanisms."[47] It is that the hybridizations and cosmopolitanisms are worth specifying (Fayruz's, Zaynab's, Sumaya's, and al-'Assal's each being different), and that the effects of media on what Appadurai calls "the work of the imagination" and "self-fabrication" are worth tracing to particular configurations of power, education, and wealth in particular places—like an agricultural village in the heart of the tourist industry in a disadvantaged region in Egypt in the 1990s.[48]


### Anthropology for Whom?

If, as I have shown, thick descriptions of television can be made to speak to "big words," we are still left with the question of which words to choose and whether, in the end, it is only to colleagues concerned with those big words that we want to speak. The dilemma goes back at least as far as Max Weber, who, of course, noted that our questions about the flow of life were set by our value orientations. As Ien Ang puts it now, in advocating radical contextualization as the method for critical television studies, it is difficult to know where to stop or where to focus.[49] In this post-Orientalist, postcolonial-critique-of-anthropology, post-crisis-of-the-authority-of-science age, Geertz's formulation of the anthropologist's vocation as placing in the consultable record the answers others have given to our deepest questions seems less complete than it used to.[50] Closer to home, and apropos of the development of critical audience studies, Ang's call to recognize that we offer only partial and positioned truths takes us not much further.[51]

My own inclination has been to approach television as just one aspect of late-twentieth-century lives, just as I approached the poetry of the Awlad 'Ali Bedouin as an aspect of their everyday lives rather than as the object of a study of poetics. One of the benefits of working on television as a way into these lives—as opposed, for example, to focusing on poetry, religion, kinship, or political economy—is that it offers particular possibilities for worldly intervention.[52] It does so both in the way it enables us to represent to outsiders people in places like Egypt and, more appealing, in the way it enables us to work as intellectuals within the national frame that is such a crucial context today for most people, including the women and men in this Upper Egyptian village.

In *Writing Women's Worlds*, I suggested that we could write critical ethnographies that went "against the grain" of global inequalities, even as we had to remain modest in our claims to radicalism and realistic about the impacts of these ethnographies. Television, I believe, is particularly useful for writing against the grain because it forces us to represent people in distant villages as part of the same cultural worlds we inhabit—worlds of mass media, consumption, and dispersed communities of the imagination. To write about television in Egypt, or Indonesia, or Brazil is to write about the articulation of the transnational, the national, the local, and the personal. Television is not the only way to do this, of course; Anna Tsing's reflections on marginality in a remote region of Indonesia and her attention to people like Uma Adang—a singular woman who brilliantly hybridized national, local, and foreign discourses to establish herself as a shaman—were developed without talking about television.[53] But television makes it especially difficult to write as if culture and cultures, despite their "infirmities," were the most powerful ways to make sense of the world.[54]

Working on television also enables more local interventions—at the national level, with intellectuals who are our peers and counterparts. These are people I can admire or disagree with, and who themselves can read, criticize, and debate my work. If through my thick descriptions of television in particular places I can begin to tease apart the structures of power within which subaltern groups live their lives and the ways television is a new part of that—in households, in communities, and in imaginations—I perhaps can also then enter into debate with concerned writers like al-'Assal, often nationalists and modernists, regarding how to think about their audiences and political projects.

I would like to do this because I respect their social concern, but I also know that from the vantage of Upper Egyptian villagers like Zaynab and Umm Ahmad, the answers they offer to social problems facing ordinary people often appear unrealistic or patronizing. Television intersects with and extends the discourses of experts. It is directed at stereotyped audiences, the same generalized objects targeted by social reformers. Is there a way thick descriptions of such communities could complicate urban intellectuals' understanding of Egyptian villagers? Or lead them to take more seriously the complexity of the forms of cosmopolitanism found across Egypt? Is there a way to begin to question modernist dogmas about literacy, education, and companionate marriage as panaceas? To al-'Assal's credit, one of her aims in writing the serial on Upper Egypt was to show, as she put it, "that the real vengeance would be to lash out [through development] against the circumstances that have led them to be attached to the vendetta in the first place." But by continuing to subsume much more complex stories of rural life under the familiar modernizing trope of a negative "tradition" and "backwardness," she, like most Egyptian intellectuals, risks reaffirming the marginality of such women as Zaynab.

The dramas such writers produce are not without their effects, if more in the cities and among government officials, businessmen, and intellectuals than in the villages they hope to reform. One wonders, for example, how television serials with modernist messages may affect the latest developments in Zaynab's hamlet. The Luxor City Council and the Supreme Council for Antiquities have recently publicized plans to relocate the villagers and raze their hamlet as part of the plan to remove the population living adjacent to, or on top of, Pharaonic ruins.[55] Justi-fied in terms of the need to preserve the Pharaonic monuments and to stem trafficking in antiquities (another persistent complaint has been that tourists are pestered by locals),[56] this plan is also in line with the terms of an earlier World Bank proposal for the development of tourism in Luxor, and other plans going back to the 1940s. Of course, the buses that rumble up and down the new roads and idle in large parking lots, spewing exhaust, must surely damage the monuments as much as the village households, and it is well known that tourists' breath and perspiration have nearly destroyed the tombs. But in the wake of "terrorist" attacks on tourists, a big investment has been made to spruce up the ancient temple closest to the villagers. The hamlet is bathed at night by the floodlights on the ramparts and everyone talks about the day the president came.

Having heard rumors about the relocation, the distraught villagers protest to one another, "They can't move us. We have title to the land." Nevertheless, the plan calls for moving them out into the desert—away from their fields, away from the water, and away from their palm trees, as they note. Some of the houses have been designed in cooperation with the people of Gurna, the major village to be removed; others are the despised boxy concrete houses found wherever the govern-ment has built new settlements.

Whether or not the plan will come to anything only time will tell. But the question for television writers is whether they may be inadvertently providing sup-port for those who confidently brush aside the needs of such villagers. They would do this if they were to dramatize the joys of becoming modern—of living in mod-ern houses built for nuclear families and designed for hygiene (with no room to guard valuable water buffalo inside)—or if they were to celebrate the heroic patrio-tism of an amateur Egyptologist pitted against a local tomb robber and his foreign cronies. (This was the theme of a serial that aired in 1997 just as news was breaking that 250 houses in Gurna had been bulldozed.) Such plots would complement the regular programs promoting Egypt's magnificent tourist treasures in making clear what the national priorities are.

Or can television writers offer this community more possibilities for imitating the Alexandrian protagonists of *The White Flag*, the popular serial that the Egyptian tourists had knocked on Fayruz's door to watch? The final episode of that program showed people standing together, hand in hand, to block the bulldozers. Of course, they did this to save a historic villa that represented art and culture and nationalist politics. What about saving a house made by hand out of mud brick, where pigeons fly in and out of the windows and where five or ten children might be born to an uneducated and hardworking farmer?

# Notes

This essay is dedicated to Clifford Geertz, whose ideas have been important to me since I first encountered them as an undergraduate and whose support of my work at a critical moment meant so much to me. I have been stimulated by the work of anthropologists in the emerging field of media studies, in particular those in the Culture and Media Program of the New York University Anthropology Department. In 1996, Dilip Gaonkar and Ben Lee invited me to participate in a working group of the Center for Transnational Study. The papers they sent me to read inspired some of the thinking in this paper. Faye Ginsburg, Brian Larkin, Tim Mitchell, and Sherry Ortner gave me enormously helpful comments on an earlier draft. The research for the paper was enhanced by many who shared their knowledge and friendship. I am especially indebted to Fathiyya al-'Assal, Omnia El-Shakry, Siona Jenkins, Hasna Mekdashi, Reem Saad, David Sims, Boutros Wadi', Liz Wickett, and the women I have called Zaynab, Fayruz, Umm Ahmad, and Sumaya. Finally, I want to thank the National Endowment for the Humanities, the Social Science Research Council, and New York University (Research Challenge Fund and Presidential Fellowships) for support that made the research and writing of this paper possible.

1. Clifford Geertz, "Deep Play: Notes on the Balinese Cockfight," in *The Interpretation of Cultures* (New York, 1973), 412–14.
2. Timothy Mitchell, "The Invention and Reinvention of the Egyptian Peasant," *International Journal of Middle East Studies* 22, no. 2 (1990): 129–50.
3. I use pseudonyms here to preserve some anonymity for the village women. The folklorist in question, however, is Elizabeth Wickett, whose dissertation is entitled "'For Our Destinies': The Funerary Laments of Upper Egypt" (Ph.D. diss., University of Pennsylvania, 1993).
4. Clifford Geertz, "Thick Description: Toward an Interpretive Theory of Culture," in *Interpretation of Cultures*, 3–30.
5. Clifford Geertz, *Works and Lives* (Stanford, 1988).
6. Jean Baudrillard, *Selected Writings*, ed. Mark Poster (Stanford, 1988).
7. Sherry Ortner, "Resistance and the Problem of Ethnographic Refusal," *Comparative Studies in Society and History* 37, no. 1 (1995): 173–93. For a classic celebration of television viewers' resistance, see John Fiske, *Television Culture* (London, 1987).

8. Janice Radway, *Reading the Romance: Women, Patriarchy, and Popular Literature* (Chapel Hill, N.C., 1984).

9. Roger Silverstone, *Television and Everyday Life* (London, 1994), 133.

10. Ien Ang, *Living Room Wars: Rethinking Media Audiences for a Postmodern World* (London, 1996), 182 n. 1.

11. Debra Spitulnik, "Anthropology and Mass Media," *Annual Review of Anthropology* 22 (1993): 293–315; quote from 307.

12. Faye Ginsburg, "Culture/Media: A (Mild) Polemic,"*Anthropology Today* 10, no. 2 (1994): 5–15; quote from 13.

13. Brian Larkin, "The Social Space of Media" (panel organized for the annual meeting of the American Anthropological Association, San Francisco, 1996).

14. Lisa B. Rofel, "*Yearnings*: Televisual Love and Melodramatic Politics in Contemporary China," *American Ethnologist* 21, no. 4 (1994): 700–722; quote from 703.

15. Purnima Mankekar, "National Texts and Gendered Lives: An Ethnography of Television Viewers in a North Indian City," *American Ethnologist* 20, no. 3 (1993): 543–63; quote from 553.

16. I am not alone in exploring this question. Among the growing number of anthropologists working on the ethnography of television and film are Walter Armbrust, *Mass Culture and Modernism in Egypt* (Cambridge, 1996); Victor Caldarola, *Reception as a Cultural Experience: Mass Media and Muslim Orthodoxy in Outer Indonesia* (New Brunswick, N.J., 1994); Arlene Davila, "*El Kiosko Budweiser*: The Making of a 'National' TV Show in Puerto Rico" (unpublished ms.); Minou Fuglesang, *Veils and Videos* (Stockholm, 1994); Faye Ginsburg, "Aboriginal Media and the Australian Imaginary," *Public Culture* 5, no. 3 (1993): 557–78; Brian Larkin, "Parallel Modernities: Islam and the Social Practice of Media in Northern Nigeria" (Ph.D. diss. in progress, New York University); Daniel Miller, *Modernity: An Ethnographic Approach* (London, 1995); Mayfair Yang, "State Discourse or a Plebeian Public Sphere? Film Discussion Groups in China," *Visual Anthropology Review* 10, no. 1 (1994): 47–60; and Richard Wilk, "Colonial Time and TV Time," *Visual Anthropology Review* 10, no. 1 (1994): 94–102, and "'It's Destroying a Whole Generation': Television and Moral Discourse in Belize," *Visual Anthropology* 5 (1993): 229–44. Those doing ethnographies of production include faculty and students in the Culture and Media Program at New York University such as Barry Dornfeld, *Producing Public Television* (forthcoming); Teja Ganti, whose dissertation in progress focuses on the Bombay film industry; and Nancy Sullivan, "Film and Television Production in Papua New Guinea," *Public Culture* 5, no. 3 (1993): 533–56. Also see Ruth Mandel, "Soap Opera in Central Asia: Privatization and Development" (paper presented at the annual meeting of the American Anthropological Association, San Francisco, 1996), and Andrew Painter, "On the Anthropology of Television: A Perspective from Japan," *Visual Anthropology Review* 10, no. 1 (1994): 70–84.

17. Important audience studies include James Lull, *Inside Family Viewing* (London, 1990); David Morley, *Family Television* (London, 1986); and the collection edited by Ellen Seiter et al., *Remote Control* (London, 1989). Cross-cultural studies include Robert C. Allen, ed., *To Be Continued . . .* (New York, 1995), and Tamar Liebes and Elihu Katz, *The Export of Meaning: Cross-Cultural Readings of "Dallas"* (New York, 1990).

18. Lila Abu-Lughod, "The Objects of Soap Opera: Egyptian Television and the Cultural Politics of Modernity," in *Worlds Apart: Modernity Through the Prism of the Local*, ed. Daniel Miller (London, 1995), 190–210. Debra Spitulnik's suggestion, drawn from functional linguistics, that one should examine the way "forms both presuppose and

create the contexts for their interpretation" would make this notion of the framing of television messages more subtle. See Spitulnik, "Anthropology and Mass Media," 297.

19. Silverstone, *Television and Everyday Life*, 132.
20. For a discussion of the importance of the national as the relevant context for media study, see my "Editorial Comment: On Screening Politics in a World of Nations," *Public Culture* 5, no. 3 (1993): 465–67. For an intriguing argument that the national context may no longer be as crucial as the transnational for analyzing our contemporary cultural and political worlds, see Arjun Appadurai, *Modernity at Large: Cultural Dimensions of Globalization* (Minneapolis, 1996).
21. I am grateful to Brian Larkin (personal communication) for this phrase.
22. Geertz, "Thick Description," 16.
23. Ibid., 23.      24. Ibid., 21.
25. Michel Foucault, "Afterword: The Subject and Power," in Hubert Dreyfus and Paul Rabinow, *Michel Foucault: Beyond Structuralism and Hermeneutics* (Chicago, 1982), 208–26; quote from 210.
26. I have borrowed this felicitous concept from George Marcus, "Ethnography in/of the World System: The Emergence of Multi-Sited Ethnography," *Annual Review of Anthropology* 24 (1995): 95–117. In fact, my own larger research project involves an ethnography not just of Upper Egyptian villagers and urban television professionals but of urban working-class women who are as disadvantaged as Upper Egyptians but with different experiences of and relationships to the city.
27. All quotations from Fathiyya al-'Assal derive from an interview conducted by the author on 26 June 1993.
28. For more on Egyptian feminist views of marriage, see Lila Abu-Lughod, "The Marriage of Feminism and Islamism: Selective Repudiation as a Dynamic of Postcolonial Cultural Politics," in *Remaking Women: Feminism and Modernity in the Middle East*, ed. Lila Abu-Lughod (forthcoming), and Beth Baron, "The Making and Breaking of Marital Bonds in Modern Egypt," in *Women in Middle Eastern History*, ed. Nikki Keddie and Beth Baron (New Haven, 1991), 275–91.
29. See Margot Badran, *Feminists, Islam, and Nation* (Princeton, 1995); Beth Baron, *The Women's Awakening in Egypt* (New Haven, 1994); and Mervat Hatem, "Economic and Political Liberalization in Egypt and the Demise of State Feminism," *International Journal of Middle East Studies* 24, no. 2 (1992): 231–51.
30. Martina Reiker, "The Sa'id and the City: Subaltern Spaces in the Making of Modern Egyptian History" (Ph.D. diss., Temple University, 1997).
31. For India, see Veena Das, "On Soap Opera: What Kind of Anthropological Object Is It?" in Miller, *Worlds Apart*, 169–89, and Purnima Mankekar, "Reconstituting 'Indian Womanhood': An Ethnography of Television Viewers in a North Indian City" (Ph.D. diss., University of Washington, 1993).
32. For a discussion of the effects of this discourse on rural villagers, see my "Put in Their Place: Sa'idi Encounters with State Culture," in *Rural Egypt at the End of the Twentieth Century*, ed. Nicholas Hopkins and Kirsten Westergaard (forthcoming).
33. This point is made in materialist critiques of the culture concept. For good examples, see Talal Asad, *Genealogies of Religion* (Baltimore, 1993), and Pierre Bourdieu, *Outline of a Theory of Practice*, trans. Richard Nice (Cambridge, 1977).
34. Ulf Hannerz, *Cultural Complexity* (New York, 1992).
35. Arjun Appadurai, "Putting Hierarchy in Its Place," *Cultural Anthropology* 3, no. 1 (1988): 36–49; James Clifford, *The Predicament of Culture* (Cambridge, Mass., 1988); Nicholas

Dirks, Sherry Ortner, and Geoffrey Eley, eds., *Culture/Power/History* (Princeton, 1993); and James Ferguson and Akhil Gupta, eds., "Space, Identity, and the Politics of Difference," *Cultural Anthropology* 7, no. 1 (1992).

36. Lila Abu-Lughod, "Writing Against Culture," in *Recapturing Anthropology*, ed. Richard Fox (Santa Fe, 1991), 137–62, and *Writing Women's Worlds: Bedouin Stories* (Berkeley, 1993).

37. Sloppy misreadings have interpreted this as implying that there *are* no cultural differences. See, for example, Sylvia Yanagisako and Carol Delaney's introduction to *Naturalizing Power* (Boston, 1995).

38. Marshall Sahlins, *How "Natives" Think: About Captain Cook, for Example* (Chicago, 1995), 12–13.

39. Appadurai, *Modernity at Large*, 16, 146–47.

40. Hussein Amin, "Egypt and the Arab World in the Satellite Age," in *New Patterns in Global Television*, ed. John Sinclair, Elizabeth Jacka, and Stuart Cunningham (Oxford, 1996), 101–25; this statistic from 104.

41. The notion of a "national habitus" comes from Orvar Lofgren, cited in Robert Foster, "Making National Cultures in the Global Ecumene," *Annual Review of Anthropology* 20 (1991): 235–60; quote from 237. See also Abu-Lughod, "Objects of Soap Opera," for a suggestion about how viewing television might create a sense of national affiliation despite the failures of nationalist messages to reach socially peripheral viewers.

42. The discussion of cosmopolitanism has become wide-ranging. In anthropology, Paul Rabinow's "Representations Are Social Facts" (in *Writing Culture*, ed. James Clifford and George Marcus [Berkeley, 1986]) was a starting point. Key texts are Appadurai, *Modernity at Large*; James Clifford, "Travelling Cultures," in *Cultural Studies*, ed. Lawrence Grossberg, Cary Nelson, and Paula Treichler (New York, 1992); and Hannerz, *Cultural Complexity*.

43. He has agreed, however, to build his youngest son an extravagant "modern" villa—perhaps to mollify the youth whom he had forced into an arranged marriage, leaving behind a trail of gossip and the broken-hearted girl his son had promised to wed.

44. See Lila Abu-Lughod, "The Romance of Resistance," *American Ethnologist* 17, no. 1 (1990): 41–55; Lila Abu-Lughod, "Movie Stars and Islamic Moralism in Egypt," *Social Text* 42 (Spring 1995): 53–67; and Leila Ahmed, *Women and Gender in Islam* (New Haven, 1992).

45. See Lila Abu-Lughod, "Finding a Place for Islam," *Public Culture* 5, no. 3 (1993): 493–513.

46. A particularly eloquent theorist of the processes of hybridization and translation is Homi Bhabha, *The Location of Cultures* (London, 1994).

47. Bruce Robbins, in *Secular Vocations* (London 1993), 194–95, argues persuasively that the efforts of James Clifford and Arjun Appadurai to make us recognize cosmopolitanism as a feature of people and communities previously thought of as resolutely local and particular (cultures, in the old sense) enable us now to use the term more inclusively and to look for "discrepant cosmopolitanisms."

48. Appadurai, *Modernity at Large*.

49. Ang, *Living Room Wars*, 66–81.

50. Geertz, "Thick Description," 30.

51. Ang draws on the work of James Clifford, Donna Haraway, and myself to support this argument. See her *Living Room Wars*, 79–80.

52. This worldliness is what Ang says distinguishes "critical" cultural studies; ibid., 45–46, 79.

53. Anna Tsing, *In the Realm of the Diamond Queen* (Princeton, 1993).
54. Clifford Geertz, *After the Fact: Two Countries, Four Decades, One Anthropologist* (Cambridge, Mass., 1995), 43.
55. Much of this information comes from Siona Jenkins, "Lifting Roots and Moving Home," *Al-Wekalah* (March 1996): 36–37.
56. Tim Mitchell, "Worlds Apart: An Egyptian Village and the International Tourism Industry," *Middle East Report* 196 (Sept.–Oct. 1995): 8–11, 23.

# SHERRY B. ORTNER

## Thick Resistance: Death and the Cultural Construction of Agency in Himalayan Mountaineering

*If Everest climbing and anthropology are united to the extent that they are both pretty useless, they are set apart by the very different kinds of risk-taking that each encourages.*
—Mike Thompson, mountaineer/anthropologist[1]

IN MAY OF 1996, EIGHT PEOPLE IN THREE different parties died in a storm on Mount Everest. It was not the worst Himalayan mountaineering disaster in history, but it received enormous public attention, perhaps the most since the occasion in the 1920s when George Leigh Mallory disappeared with another climber into the mists near the summit of Everest and never returned. It was Mallory who had said that he wanted to climb Everest "because it is there."

The public drama of the 1996 Everest fatalities was the result of a number of late-twentieth-century developments. The advance in communications technology, for example, provided several parties on the mountain with the capacity for live communication via computer or telephone, to any part of the world at any time, directly from the mountain itself. One of the macabre effects of this was that one of the dying climbers, Rob Hall, who was stranded high on the mountain, spoke to his wife in New Zealand several times before he died. The rise in the last decade or so of so-called adventure travel (wherein relatively inexperienced individuals pay large sums of money to participate in dangerous sports that were normally the preserve of highly dedicated aficionados in the past) also contributed to the greater public impact of these events. Two of the parties that suffered fatalities in 1996 were such commercially organized groups, whose clients had paid about sixty-five thousand dollars each to be guided by a professional to the top of Mount Everest.

The 1996 disaster was also unusual in that no Sherpas died during the climbing.[2] Sherpas are members of an ethnic group who live in the environs of Mount Everest and some of the other highest Himalayan peaks and who have provided climbing support for Himalayan mountaineering expeditions since the first decade of the twentieth century. They are the (usually) silent partners to the international mountaineers, carrying supplies, establishing routes, fixing ropes, cooking, setting up camps, sometimes saving the climbers' lives, and sometimes themselves dying in the process. This paper is part of a larger project exploring the changing relationship between the international climbers (hereafter the *sahibs*, usually pronounced as one syllable, "sahb") and the Sherpas over the course of the twentieth century.[3] More broadly, it is part of an ongoing attempt to work out new ways of thinking about the mutually defining nature of culture, power, and history.[4]

### Geertz, Culture, and Power

Starting in the late 1950s, Clifford Geertz began refiguring the enterprise of anthropology around the idea of "meaning." Although he never formally defines meaning, and although he uses it in a wide range of contexts, one of its central—ah—meanings is as a set of culturally constructed and historically specific guides, frames, or models of and for human feeling, intention, and action. Meaning is what both defines life and gives it its purpose.

Geertz poses a meaning-oriented approach to human activities against a variety of positivistic and relatively mechanistic perspectives, most commonly some kind of explanation of social phenomena according to their functions or effects. Again and again he sets up his argument for an interpretive approach that depends on teasing out meanings against a kind of commonsense functionalism that posits links between phenomena on the basis of standard assumptions (or even sophisticated assumptions) about human behavior and social process without bothering to ask about underlying cultural beliefs, values, and intentions:

To discuss the role of ancestor worship in regulating political succession, of sacrificial feasts in defining kinship obligations, of spirit worship in scheduling agricultural practices, of divination in reinforcing social control, or of initiation rites in propelling personality maturation, are in no sense unimportant endeavors. . . . But to attempt them with but the most general, common-sense view of what ancestor worship, animal sacrifice, spirit worship, divination, or initiation rites are as religious patterns [that is, as particular kinds of cultural forms or meanings] seems to me not particularly promising.[5]

Geertz's battle against various forms of functionalist and mechanistic perspectives (regardless of their theorists of origin—Emile Durkheim, Karl Marx, Sigmund Freud, and so on) was important, not only because cultural interpretation makes for more subtle or complex analyses (although that is certainly the case), but also because it challenges a view of society as a machine, or as an organism, a view in which complex human intentions and complex cultural formations are reduced to their effects on that social machine or social organism. Yet in setting up his argument as a binary opposition between "good" nonreductionistic cultural analysis and "bad" mechanistic functional analysis, Geertz set a certain trap for himself: all the issues of power, domination, and social asymmetry fall on the "bad" mechanistic side. Again and again, then, Geertz winds up seeming to oppose issues of meaning and issues of power. This is visible in the quote above, and Geertz repeats the move thirty years later with even more force:

No matter how much one trains one's attention on the supposedly hard facts of social existence, who owns the means of production, who has the guns, the dossiers, or the newspapers, the supposedly soft facts of that existence, what do people imagine human life to be all about, how do they think one ought to live, what grounds belief, legitimizes punishment, sustains hope, or accounts for loss, crowd in to disturb simple pictures of might, desire, calculation, and interest.[6]

It is not of course that Geertz ignores politics or power, and it is important to recognize what he did and did not do. For this we must turn particularly to one of his most stunning pieces of empirical work, *Negara: The Theater State in Nineteenth-Century Bali*.[7] *Negara* is an analysis of the cultural construction of "the state" and of the forms of rule and legitimacy in another place and time. It is a tour de force of ethnographic and historical research, social/political/economic analysis, and cultural interpretation. It is written specifically against any kind of political-economic reductionism:

It is not difficult, indeed it is fatally easy, to fit the Balinese state as here described to one or another of these familiar models, or to all of them at once. No one remains dominant politically for very long who cannot in some way promise violence to recalcitrants, pry support from producers, portray his actions as collective sentiment, or justify his decisions as ratified practice. Yet to reduce the negara to such tired commonplaces, the worn coin of European ideological debate, is to allow most of what is most interesting about it to escape our view.[8]

Geertz establishes beyond a doubt that power is organized differently, and sometimes profoundly differently, in other times and places, and also that political systems are not simply systems of control but also systems of meaning. Yet in the end he overstates his case. The less exotic dimensions of power that are acknowledged as operating are so subordinated to the cultural argument as to be virtually dismissed.

In contrast, in the past two decades, there has been a tremendous push in other quarters to make power and domination central to cultural theory.[9] Coming from several directions—critical studies (feminist, ethnic, minority, and postcolonial studies), various post- and neo-Marxisms, and the highly influential work of Michel Foucault, issues of power have swept the theoretical landscape.[10] Within this general shift, one of the most significant developments from the point of view of traditional anthropology has been the emergence of colonial and postcolonial theory, launched in large part by the publication of Edward Said's *Orientalism*, which itself draws particularly on the work of Foucault.[11]

The Foucault move was to insist on looking at cultural forms and practices not in terms of their "meanings" (which, in this poststructuralist moment, had become a suspect term in any event) but in terms of their "effects," both on those to whom they are addressed and on the worlds in which they circulate. Thus, for example, a variety of practices that purport to bring to light a sexuality that has been repressed—Christian confession or psychoanalysis, among others—are examined for the ways in which they construct certain subject positions for actors and contribute to the proliferation of ever subtler regimes of modern power and knowledge.[12] Similarly, Said argued that Western scholarship about "the Orient" must be understood as a Foucauldian discourse, an "enormously systematic discipline" that both emerges from and constitutes the colonial project(s) of power, the project "by which European culture was able to manage—and even produce— the Orient politically, sociologically, militarily, ideologically, scientifically, and imaginatively."[13]

The Foucault/Said shift, along with all the other shifts in cultural theorizing toward the power of power, effectively knocks out, or drastically narrows, questions of meaning and "culture" in the Geertzian sense. The main point of this paper will be to argue for, and to try to demonstrate, the continuing importance of meaning and culture in this sense, but the power shift in cultural theorizing has been vitally important and I do not wish to undercut it. Whatever its theoretical and conceptual shortcomings, it has put a range of issues on the table that cannot be ignored. One of these is the idea of Orientalism itself, and in the first part of the paper I will be concerned to show the ways in which Orientalism structures Western mountaineers' perceptions, representations, and treatment of the Sherpas in relation to the extraordinary level of mortal risk in Himalayan mountaineering. In the second half of the paper, however, I will return to the importance of a Geertzian perspective, particularly as it allows us to understand the cultural construction of power's other side(s): agency and "resistance."

## Death and Orientalism

*The Meanings of Climbing.* Though my concern in this section is with Orientalism as a discourse that produces certain effects, I cannot avoid beginning with the ways in which the deployment of Orientalist discourse at particular moments and in particular encounters depends on what might be thought of as failures of meaning.

Himalayan mountaineering took shape in the last decades of the nineteenth century, on the fringes of the British empire in India. From the beginning, mountaineering expeditions took porters to carry their goods and otherwise assist in the chores of the expedition—cooking, cleaning, setting up and taking down camps. As the goods were carried higher and higher on the mountains, the porters needed to learn at least some of the technical skills of mountaineering as well. Almost from the beginning, men from an ethnic group called Sherpa distinguished themselves as being especially good at high-altitude work and soon came to dominate porter work in Himalayan mountaineering—so much so, in fact, that the term *Sherpa* simply became synonymous with high-altitude porter.[14]

Between the sahibs and the Sherpas there was always a power differential (which will be discussed further on) but also a profound difference in the meanings each attributed to mountaineering. For the sahibs, climbing was clearly a form of "deep play." Geertz had borrowed the idea of deep play from Jeremy Bentham, who used it to think about games in which the stakes are so high that it does not appear worthwhile to play the game—yet people play anyway. Geertz's point is that people engage in certain forms of deep play all the time, not because they fail to recognize the poor odds or the nonutility of the game, but because such play pays off in terms of the production of meaning, of insight into important dimensions of life and experience.[15]

Mountaineering fits this picture almost perfectly. In the quite voluminous firsthand mountaineering literature, mountaineers often discourse in fascinating ways on the kinds of meaning and insight they derive from the sport: about the moral fiber of the inner self, about the nature of bonding and friendship, about the peace and calm of high, cold places against the noise and bustle of modern society. All of this makes the risk of accident and death worthwhile; indeed it seems precisely the risk of serious or fatal accident that produces the payoff of meaning.[16] As one author recently suggested, with tongue only slightly in cheek:

If [dying is] done properly (during an ascent, descent, or bivouac), erasure from the list of the quick confers glory all 'round: on the dead for proving their will to climb, on the mountain for the new respect it demands, and on the survivors for their courage to continue in the face of disaster. Unlike any other sport, mountaineering demands that its players die.[17]

Yet none of this is true for the Sherpas, who are on the expeditions with a very different set of intentions. There is in fact a double disjunction here—between the sahibs' and the Sherpas' motives, and between the sahibs' and the Sherpas' power. It is this double disjunction that gives rise to the Orientalism that has characterized the sahibs' construction of the Sherpas over the course of the twentieth century. By Orientalism here I mean not only a kind of racist "othering," but also at the same time a yearning for solidarity and even identity with the other that (perhaps) makes Orientalism different from classic racism. This yearning cannot be pursued in the present paper, but it is an important dimension of the sahib-Sherpa relationship and it lurks behind the discussion.

In any event, virtually all the evidence indicates that the Sherpas' *primary* motive for climbing has always been money. Fame, or "name," has also been important, but largely for its further money-making effects. This is not to say that Sherpas are insensitive to the beauty of the mountains, or to the personal friendships they may develop on expeditions, or to certain pleasures of competition, and so forth. Moreover, it is the case that other kinds of motives have recently begun to play a larger role in the Sherpas' relationship to mountaineering, including a sense of "challenge" that is similar to the sahibs', and issues of cultural identity that will be discussed in another context. Nonetheless, for most of the twentieth century, for most Sherpa individuals, the primary motivation for climbing has been money and material benefit. Climbing has always paid more, and produced more in the way of other forms of income (equipment to sell, trips abroad), than any other form of "unskilled" (that is, non-literacy-based) labor available anywhere in the region.[18]

Given these different perspectives, death plays an entirely different role in the economy of meaning of mountaineering for the Sherpas from the one it plays for the sahibs. For the sahibs, the risk of death is what makes the sport glorious; for the Sherpas there is nothing noble about the risk at all; there is only a kind of threat that must be managed, negotiated. For the sahibs, ordinary life pales before the intensity of mountaineering; for the Sherpas, mountaineering is simply the best-paying way to support ordinary life. This means that when death occurs on expeditions, as it does with great regularity, there will be a highly problematic gap between sahib and Sherpa reactions. Before we get to that, however, a few words need to be said about the level of risk involved.

*Risk.* High-altitude mountaineering is one of the most dangerous sports on earth. The most frequent kind of death is sudden and shocking—a slip or drop off a sheer face, a fall into a crevasse, or—the biggest killer in terms of numbers—burial in an avalanche.[19] But there is also slow death from "altitude sickness," an innocuous-sounding phrase that refers to the sequelae of inadequate oxygen intake, such as strokes, cerebral edema, pulmonary edema, and other bodily breakdowns.

It is difficult to get precise statistics on death rates in Himalayan mountaineering; a variety of numbers are bandied about.[20] "One out of ten Himalayan climbers does not return."[21] "The death rate on expeditions to the Everest area runs about one in eight."[22] "For every ten climbers who enter the ice fall [on Everest], one does not emerge."[23] For every two climbers to reach the summit [of Everest], another has died in the attempt."[24] Elizabeth Hawley, an extremely knowledgeable journalist who has lived in Kathmandu for many years, told a reporter in 1966, "Some 4,000 people have tried to climb Everest, 660 have succeeded, and 142 have died."[25] This puts the ratio at about one death for every five successes. Concerning Sherpas alone, "From 1950 through the middle of 1989, 84 Sherpas died on mountaineering expeditions."[26] On Everest alone, "of the 115 climbers who have died, 43 have been Sherpas."[27]

The imprecision and incomparability of these figures—not to mention the impersonalness of statistics in general—should not lead one to glide over them too quickly. If one looks at the question from the actor's point of view, the sense of sudden, close, and relentless death becomes almost overpowering. There is probably not a single Himalayan climber who has not lost at least one close friend—and usually many more—in a mountaineering accident, and who has not been on at least one expedition that suffered a fatal accident or other death. The great British climber Chris Bonington totaled up what he called his "catalogue of deaths": of eight people he climbed with on one particular expedition, four are now dead; of ten people he climbed with on another expedition, four are now dead; and so forth, to a total of fifteen out of twenty-nine people.[28]

Much the same can be said for the Sherpas. Of the more than thirty climbing Sherpas I interviewed about their expedition experiences, there was not a single one who had not lost at least one (and usually more) close friend, covillager, or— unlike most sahibs—kinsman in a mountaineering accident, and not a single one who had never been on an expedition with a fatal accident. Indeed, for some climbing Sherpas, nearly every expedition they had worked for had had a fatal accident. And it is probably fair to say that there is no Sherpa at all—man, woman, or child, climber or nonclimber—who does not personally know a fellow Sherpa who was killed in mountaineering.

It should come as no surprise then (at least to nonmountaineers) that, under some conditions at least, any given Sherpa might become terrified, panicked, or simply utterly demoralized during a climb. This occurs most often after there has been a death on the expedition, but it may also occur under visibly very dangerous conditions, or when an individual has had a near miss or has become exhausted. Yet the question of showing (extreme) fear or of breaking down in an utterly de-moralized way opens the Sherpas to various forms of classic Saidian Orientalism: if they show terror or other forms of strong emotion at the time of an accident, the sahibs view this with contempt and sometimes respond with force; if they show no fear or other strong feelings at such times, their apparent lack of reaction is viewed as a strange, and almost inhuman, form of "Oriental fatalism."

*Sherpa Breakdown and Sahib Contempt.* Sherpas have broken down out of terror on many expeditions. In a few cases a sahib has allowed them their feelings as normal and human. The members of the 1952 Swiss Everest expedition deserve special mention on this point, as they wrote about some Sherpas who refused to continue under extreme conditions:

The cold and the wind are now so cruel to bear that two Sherpas, again, Ang Norbu and Mingma Dorji, fearing frostbite, stop, refuse to continue and declare that they are going down. How to stop them? And besides, do we have the right? In adventures of this sort, man must remain free and the only judge of what he can, of what he is willing to, do.[29]

The Swiss sahib's respect, either for the Sherpas' feelings or for their judgment as to the extremity of the danger, cost them a lot: this failed 1952 expedition had received the first permission to climb Everest via the route through Nepal that allowed the British to triumph the following year.

Normally, however, the sahibs have responded to Sherpa shows of fear with contempt or worse. On the 1922 Everest expedition, for example, seven Sherpas (and no sahibs) were killed in an avalanche. Although the sahibs themselves were quite upset about the Sherpas' deaths, they nonetheless interpreted the surviving Sherpas' reactions through Orientalist lenses. Thus, for example, John Noel wrote that the surviving Sherpas "had completely lost their nerve and were crying and shaking like babies."[30] On the 1931 German expedition to Kangchenjunga, one of the top Sherpas was killed, and the other porters became extremely upset; only three would climb above the place where he fell.[31] Later, two of those who continued "broke down and cried," largely it seems because, after so many others left, they were seriously overworked. Yet the leader, Paul Bauer, wrote: "They needed some connection with the world they left behind to strengthen their hold on reality and prevent superstitious feelings arising."[32]

On the 1938 German expedition to Nanga Parbat, led again by Herr Bauer, the expedition came across the dead bodies of a Sherpa and a sahib from a 1934 climb. The sahibs tried to prevent the Sherpas from seeing the bodies, but "instinct is too powerful with these children of nature," and after that only one porter would work above Camp IV.[33] And Klaus Becker Larsen, who tried to solo Everest in 1951, wrote: "When confronted by real hardships and dangers [the Sherpas] have their tails down like the majority of primitive people with whom the conception of honour has not yet arisen."[34]

When Sherpas refuse to climb out of fear and demoralization, and yet, for whatever reasons, the sahibs absolutely require that they continue, the sahibs have often resorted to force to keep them moving. Thus, in the case of the 1931 Kangchenjunga expedition noted earlier, the Germans felt they had no choice but to force two of the Sherpas to continue. The leader's own contempt is both manifest in his actions and projected onto his "loyal servant":

[After the fatal accident]. . . . Dorji became hysterical, put down his load and undid the rope to go back. We took him firmly by the collar and forced both him and Pasang to go on with us up to the terrace. My loyal servant Kami curled his lips contemptuously when he saw them being dragged up by the rope.[35]

A more recent, and highly publicized, example of the use of force occurred during the 1978 Austrian Everest expedition, on which Reinhold Messner became the first person to reach the top of Everest without supplementary oxygen. Messner reached the south col (just under eight thousand meters) with two Sherpas, but there was a terrible storm and the Sherpas became exhausted. One continued to help but the other, Mingma, crawled into his sleeping bag and—in a fairly standard practice among Sherpas when they are faced with impossible circumstances—became unresponsive. What happened next is not clear, but according to Sherpa accounts Messner flew into a rage, beating and kicking Mingma to get him to keep moving. From Messner's point of view, he saved the Sherpas' lives. The Sherpas saw it quite differently, however, and went to the press after the expedition, describing Messner's behavior as grossly unacceptable and saying that they doubted his claim (though it is now generally accepted) to have summitted solo and without oxygen.[36]

*Sherpa Impassivity and "Oriental Fatalism."* On the other hand, there are many reports of extreme danger or near-accidents when the Sherpas have shown little fear. This behavior is generally met with approval and respect by the sahibs; it fits with their own notions of bravery, and it is what they want or have been led to expect from the Sherpas. There is, however, one situation in which it is clear that the sahibs expect, and indeed want, the Sherpas to have or show strong emotions: when there is an actual death (as opposed to a near miss or simply very dangerous conditions) on an expedition. Yet often the Sherpas do not show any visible reaction at all. This in turn has generated, throughout the twentieth century, the notion in the mountaineering literature that the Sherpas are less emotionally affected by (violent) death than are the sahibs, an expression of one or another variant of their Oriental fatalism.

On the 1922 Everest expedition, as noted earlier, seven porters were killed in an avalanche. Although Noel had observed the Sherpas to be "crying like babies" right after the accident, General Bruce also noted that they "dismissed their troubles very rapidly and very lightly, holding simply that the men's time had come, and so there was no more to be said about it."[37]

Before going on, I must say that this understanding of the Sherpas' reactions is simply wrong. I have never heard a Sherpa shrug off an accidental or violent or sudden death with the notion that the person's time had come, or that it was ordained on high, or that it did not matter because the person would be reincarnated. In my own experience, Sherpas are very shaken by such events, both in terms of the loss itself, and as signs of something seriously amiss. There is a certain logic to assuming that people who believe in reincarnation (perhaps like people who believe in heaven) might take death more lightly than those who do not, but it is nonetheless—one could say interestingly—not the case.

A more recent example of the Oriental fatalism line comes from the 1975 British Southwest Face Everest expedition, when a young deaf and mute porter fell into a stream and drowned. Doug Scott and Chris Bonington were extremely upset about the accident (Bonington's own son had drowned some years before) but "on our return to camp, the ever pragmatic Mick Burke pointed out that the Sherpas were not unduly troubled because they could shrug it off with a thought that his time had come and he had gone to a better life."[38]

Similarly, during Messner's 1978 ascent of Everest, there was an avalanche in the icefall (a very dangerous section of the climb). No one was hurt and the Sherpas were seemingly unfazed by it. The Austrians attributed the Sherpas' lack of reaction to their Buddhist beliefs and then segued into the usual Oriental fatalism line: "It's easy for the Sherpas. They simply believe everything is ordained from above," someone says. "If one of them dies, then it must be meant to happen."[39]

Again, climbing Sherpas are usually deeply affected by deaths on expeditions.[40] They may finish the particular climb on which the death occurred out of a sense of commitment or professionalism. The sahibs may think they are not reacting. In fact, however, after the expedition individuals will often stop climbing for several years, or even permanently. On the 1974 French Everest expedition, for example, there was an avalanche that killed the French leader and six Sherpas. Pasang Nuru was one of the surviving Sherpas:

They were opening the route between Camps II and III. There were many avalanches and the Sherpas asked the leader to change the route. But he didn't agree, he didn't want to change the route, and he came up [to Camp II]. He stayed one night, and that night an avalanche killed six Sherpas and the leader. . . . [Pasang Nuru's] older brother was killed. When he went to look for his brother he found one of the members and two of the Sherpas alive with no shoes, and he helped them down. . . . After that he stopped climbing for three years; he just did trekking.[41]

And the cook on the Annapurna Women's Expedition, Yeshi Tenzing, had been buried in that same avalanche: "Yeshi survived but wisely decided to give up the hazardous business of being a climbing Sherpa and took up the lower-paying but safer job of cook boy."[42]

Pertemba, who worked with Chris Bonington on many expeditions, also stopped for several years after a series of climbing deaths of people to whom he was close:

The only major problem of the [Southwest Face 1975 Bonington] expedition was that they lost one summitter. . . . They had a memorial service in Base Camp. Also, after the expedition he went to the UK and visited the climber's family. . . . He didn't climb for three years after that [and only resumed because old climbing friends put pressure on him]. He had lost a lot of climbing friends.[43]

A final example of the way Sherpas are affected by deaths on expeditions is the case of veteran climber Domai Tsering, who was the *sardar* (Sherpa foreman) on the fateful Japanese ski expedition on which six Sherpas died. Domai Tsering was my landlord in 1979 in Khumjung, when he told me the story:

[Most of the Sherpas on the expedition were his relatives] because he was the *sardar*. Three of the six who died were related to him, one was his own younger brother. His mother, his wife, himself, had much *dukpa*, suffering. Also many of his good friends died. After the deaths the Sherpas wanted to stop the expedition, but he and the Japanese told them to continue. [But] that was the end of it, he never went again.[44]

These kinds of reactions, however, are invisible to the sahibs, who persist in the idea that the Sherpas are largely unaffected by death because of their Buddhist beliefs.

In sum, Orientalism is real and, as Said has argued, extraordinarily impervious to disruption. With respect to death in Himalayan mountaineering, it operates as an almost perfectly Foucauldian/Saidian mechanism: it "subjects" the Sherpas, in the double sense of constructing their (subordinate) identity and of causing them to submit to whatever disciplines/educations the sahibs choose to enact. It creates for them an impossible position: if they show their fears in the face of death, they are children; if they do not show—or perhaps do not even allow themselves to experience—their fears, they have failed to develop the higher moral sensibilities of the West.

Yet as real as Orientalism is, it is only part of the story. There is life beyond even the most totalizing discourse, and there are ways of rearranging the world beneath and beyond the discursive frames of the sahibs.[45] It is time to return to meaning and agency.

### Thick Resistance: The Cultural Construction of Agency

Sherpas on expeditions have been observed performing one or another of their (Tibetan Buddhist) religious practices, from the very beginning of Himalayan mountaineering up to the present. Minimally, they chant mantras at almost any time—in the camp, on the climb, in situations of both great danger and routine activity. Maximally, as we shall see, they stage large-scale collective offering rituals to the gods in base camp and draw the sahibs into joining them in the rituals.

Religion is the quintessential Geertzian domain of culture and meaning. While Geertz uses the notion of meaning in a range of ways, it is arguable that his use of it in the context of religion colors his entire sense of what *meaning* means: it is a set of broad conceptions—about what the world is like, how it is put together, how human social beings should conduct themselves within it—and a complex of practices ("rituals") whose effect is to imbue those conceptions with authority and truth. Religious meanings are representations of the big picture of life in a given time and place and a set of practices through which people come to believe deeply in those representations.

Meaning treated in this way seems to carry us a long distance from the vision of Said or Foucault. Certainly, as I discussed earlier, Geertz sets up an opposition between meaning-driven approaches and power-driven approaches; for all intents and purposes he sets aside the latter as shallow and unilluminating. At the same time it can be argued that the power theorists' emphasis on cultural/discursive/ideological effects, and general lack of interest in meanings and intentions in the Geertzian sense, constructs the same split from the other side. The point can be made with respect to power's other face, resistance, as well. If questions of power tend to be split off from questions of meaning, so too do discussions of resistance, which appear in many studies—as I have argued at some length elsewhere—to be culturally "thin," insufficiently grounded in local views of the meaning of morality, justice, subjecthood, and agency.[46]

A few quick words about the last term: I view *agency* as a piece of both the power problematic and the meaning problematic. In the context of questions of power, agency is that which is made or denied, expanded or contracted, in the exercise of power. It is the (sense of) authority to act, or of lack of authority and lack of empowerment. It is that dimension of power that is located in the actor's subjective sense of authorization, control, effectiveness in the world. Within the framework of questions of meaning, on the other hand, agency represents the pressures of desires and understandings and intentions on cultural constructions. Much of the meaning uncovered in a cultural interpretation assumes, explicitly or implicitly, an actor engaged in a project, a game, a drama, an actor with not just a "point of view" but a more active projection of the self toward some desired end.[47] In the first context, agency (which can be shorthanded as empowerment) is both a source and an effect of power, in the second (where it underwrites "the actor's point of view"), it is both a source and an effect of "culture." The pivotal position of agency across the two theoretical arenas will open up a number of possibilities as the discussion proceeds.

Turning then to the Sherpas, I want to try to show, through a kind of tacking back and forth between Geertz and Foucault/Said, how the cultural construction of power is always, simultaneously, the cultural construction of forms of agency and effectiveness in dealing with powerful others.[48] I will do this through a consideration, first, of the ways in which power and the means of dealing with it are configured in Sherpa religion and, then, of a series of practices of Sherpas on expeditions, as they attempt to achieve some measure of control over both the sahibs and death.

*"The Way of Power."* As I have discussed elsewhere, a large part of Sherpa religion is predicated on a particular set of relationships between powerful but remote gods, ordinary humans, and various kinds of harmful or destructive beings, "demons."[49] Without the help and blessings of the gods, humans are vulnerable to the encroachment of demons who will wreak havoc in human affairs. People cannot hold off (much less defeat) the demons themselves; they must have the help of the gods in this never-ending struggle.

The gods clearly model a certain form of power in Sherpa social life. They are remote to begin with; they are also easily offended, and when offended threaten to withdraw even further. The basic forms of religious action—*kurim*, rites of offerings to the gods in order to gain their protection—are designed to engage the gods in alliance with humans and thereby harness their power. Gods are invited into the human realm in ritual and treated as honored guests, presented with lavish offerings of food, drink, incense and the like. They are then subjected to a mixture of polite requests and subtle manipulations designed to draw them into a role of active protection on behalf of the worshipers.

This little schema—learning how to deal with powerful beings so that they become allies against bad others—is enacted as ritual over and over again in Sherpa life, from the daily morning offerings in the household to vast annual rites in the temples. The idea that one needs a powerful protector to deal with other powerful beings (in this case to defend against the encroachments of demons) is repeated in the relationship between the humans and the gods themselves. Thus, people need duly empowered religious specialists—lamas—to gain sufficient purchase on the gods.[50]

This package of practices and beliefs constitutes the formal structure of Sherpa religion. It is *meaning* almost in the sense of information (not of course to be despised on that account). In turn, however, it encodes a more general set of assumptions about power: that certain kinds of power are evil and capricious and are not subject to negotiation; that other kinds of power are in principle benevolent but in practice remote (and indeed somewhat unreliable); that power of the latter sort can be negotiated with and transformed into relations of support and protection; that such negotiations require a very delicate blend of gentle solicitation and more manipulative or coercive measures; and so forth.

Pushing the latent meaning here one step further, there is in Sherpa religion a basic statement about agency—about the ability of persons to accomplish things in the world. On the one hand there is a position of humility—people are weak, cannot do difficult things on their own, need help and protection. Hubris in this system, as countless folktales insist, is imagining that one can accomplish major projects on one's own. On the other hand there is also an insistence that key forms of power are negotiable, that the actor can and must do things to engage with such power and transform it into protection, alliance, and sometimes—although I cannot pursue this point here—friendship.

Thus, although the Sherpas operate with several different notions of power, one of the most salient is a rather Foucauldian conception, in which power is relatively fluid and transformable through practice. While one could say that the gods "have power over" humans, this seemingly simple relationship is actually subject to transformation in several respects. On the one hand, in more esoteric religious theory, the gods' power is itself an effect of human belief and practice. In this view, which is the sophisticated "high religion" version of the idea that the gods would "withdraw" in the absence of faith and ritual, the gods' power is not some absolute property that they possess, but is itself produced and nourished through "religion work." And, as discussed a moment ago, the point works in the other direction as well: the gods' power is not lodged in some absolute differential between gods and humans but rather is something that can be harnessed by humanity, allied with human purposes, drawn upon for human needs. This view of power is one that gives a great deal of agency to the nominally unpowerful; the name of the game is neither bowing before power nor "resisting" it, but figuring out how to both acknowledge its force and shape it to one's own purposes.

It is not for nothing, then, that the tradition of Tibetan Buddhism, of which Sherpa religion is a relatively faithful enactment, has been called "The Way of Power."[51] It is both an extended meditation upon the meaning, uses, and appropriations of power in human affairs and a set of practices for engaging actively and productively with or against power. Far from constructing anything resembling

"Oriental fatalism," in other words, Sherpa religion constructs a certain kind of quite effective agency. In the next few sections of the discussion, I turn to the ways in which these conceptions have been deployed in practice.

*The Blessings of the Lamas.* In the early decades of the twentieth century, just as the Sherpas were first getting involved in mountaineering, they were also founding the first celibate monasteries in their home region of Solu-Khumbu.[52] The monasteries in turn embarked on a campaign to upgrade Sherpa popular religion, cleaning up certain rituals, adding new ones, and generally urging Sherpas as individuals to act more in accord with orthodox Buddhist precepts in their daily lives.[53] Some of the specific monastic changes will play a role in this paper. More generally, however, the foundings of the monasteries in the early decades of the twentieth century, and continuing monastic activism, generated a heightening of religious commitment and religious identity for most Sherpas, which they brought with them to the mountaineering labor experience.

But there was a problem. Especially in the early years of both monasticism and mountaineering, it appears that the high lamas were not very supportive of the young Sherpas' involvement in expedition work. The lamas' reasons were multiple—they were concerned about both sahibs and Sherpas disturbing the mountain gods and thereby making trouble for the whole community; they also felt pity (as we shall see) for the young Sherpas who had to make their living in this dangerous way; and perhaps they saw in mountaineering and other new forms of work a first glimpse of a competing worldview and way of life. In any event, while they could not make the young Sherpas stop climbing, they did (and do) have a great deal of generalized authority in the community. They also are believed to have the power to send sorcery and black magic against their enemies. The first order of business for the climbing Sherpas, then, was to get the lamas on their side.

The earliest Everest expeditions approached the mountain from the north (Tibetan) side, and had to pass by the monastery at Rumbu ("Rongbuk"). The head lama was the Zatul Rimpoche, the instigator of the founding of the early Sherpa monasteries, and thus in a sense the spiritual head of Sherpa religion. (The picture of him that I used on the cover of *High Religion* was taken by a member of the 1922 Everest expedition.)[54] The lama had a number of reservations about the climbing enterprise. He was unhappy about dealing with foreigners, writing in his diary that he "was feeling very sick" about meeting with the "heretics" of the expedition.[55] And he was unhappy about the dangers and risks to which they were exposing the Sherpas. After seven Sherpas died in the avalanche on the 1922 expedition, the leader, General Bruce, sent money to the lama for funeral rites for the men. The lama wrote, "I was filled with great compassion for their lot who underwent such suffering on unnecessary work."[56]

Zatul Rimpoche's views and feelings were later graphically represented in a mural at the monastery. When the next Everest expedition came through in 1924, John Noel was shown a fresco that had been painted by the monks:

This extraordinary picture shows the angered Deity of the mountain surrounded by weird, wildly dancing demons, white lions, barking dogs and hairy men, and at the foot, speared through and through, lies the naked body of the white man who dared to violate [Everest].[57]

Other lamas voiced similar kinds of concern or disapproval. Tenzing Norgay, who along with Edmund Hillary was the first to stand on top of Mount Everest, wrote in his autobiography that when he was young, "the lamas told many stories of the terror of the snows—of gods and demons and creatures far worse than yetis [abominable snowmen], who guarded the heights and would bring doom to any man who ventured there."[58] Individual climbing Sherpas who are worried about their fates will seek divinations from lamas, and they too are often told that a given year, or a given expedition, is dangerous for them and they should not go.[59] Thomas Laird quotes a lama in the 1980s who was still saying that when the mountains are violated the gods will flee and then all human endeavors will go badly.[60]

For the Sherpas, who were obviously going to continue to climb, then, it was important to gain the lamas' support in dealing with potentially angry gods. While, as noted earlier, it is possible to gain the protection of the gods directly, through one's own prayers and petitions, it is much more effective to go through the lamas, who not only request or petition the gods for help, but also actually have the training and the ritual empowerment to control them. One factor that may have worked in the Sherpas' favor on this matter was what we may think of as the benevolent side of the sahibs' Orientalism. It seems clear that, from the earliest expeditions on, the sahibs were fascinated by their visits to the monasteries—to Rumbu on the northern (Tibetan) route to Everest and later to Tengboche on the southern (Nepal) side.[61] I am guessing, based on my own experience of visiting monasteries with Sherpa friends, that the Sherpas made it clear to the sahibs that large donations were in order, that quite large donations were in fact made, and that these had at least some effects on the lamas' attitudes.

It may seem crass to suggest that money played a role in bringing the lamas around. I do not mean to imply by this that they did not care about the welfare of the Sherpas, and indeed for that matter even of the sahibs (who are, after all, "sentient beings" too). Yet, as discussed earlier, it is perfectly appropriate to seek to turn power to one's interests through the medium of material gifts—that is what offering rituals are all about. Everyone in a sense simply did what, culturally speaking, they were supposed to do.[62]

Whether or not it was the sahibs' money that did the trick, we know that the lamas gradually came around. Despite the Zatul Rimpoche's reservations about dealing with foreigners, he nonetheless repeatedly offered them warm hospitality. The visit to Rumbu became such a fixture of the early expeditions, and the Zatul Rimpoche became such a figure of respect, that after his death he was eulogized in the *Himalayan Journal*. The author describes him as "this good and distinguished friend of many expeditions."[63]

The Tengboche reincarnate lama has been similarly drawn into an enduring relationship with mountaineering. I was present in his rooms in Baudha, outside of Kathmandu, in 1990, when the *sardar* of an upcoming expedition came in and, having made the proper donations, had a huge handful of charms and a large bag of rice blessed collectively for all the Sherpas on the expedition. (We shall see what happens to some of that rice later.) The lama has also standardized the process of receiving sahib donations; he is aware that the sahibs need receipts for tax purposes and keeps a stack of them at hand.

*Controlling the Gods and the Sahibs.* From the Sherpa point of view, mountaineering is high risk multiply compounded. On the one hand it is physically dangerous, and one needs the gods' protection for one's safety; on the other hand one is up closer to the gods' domain and more likely to cause offense. The need for religious caution on the one hand, and religious activism on the other, is heightened.

But the problem with enacting the relevant religious practices on Himalayan climbing expeditions has always been that the Sherpas are not free agents. For one thing, the sahibs often require the Sherpas to do things that would offend the gods (including sometimes the sheer fact of climbing the mountain). For another, sahibs themselves often do offensive things out of ignorance. The issue for the Sherpas then is not simply enacting correct and effective religious behavior to get some measure of protection against the risks; it is a matter of drawing the sahibs as much as possible into the Sherpas' specific concerns. One of the biggest points of contention over possible offense to the gods to emerge over the course of the century has been the butchering of animals on expeditions.[64]

For twentieth-century Sherpas, killing is both sinful to the person who kills and, in the mountaineering context, offensive to the gods of the mountains. By all accounts, throughout most of the twentieth century, and certainly including all of my own experience with Sherpas on this issue, Sherpas have universally and viscerally hated to kill things, get very upset when they have to do it, and go to great lengths to avoid it. Although not in fact vegetarians, they normally have access to butcher-caste Nepalis to do the killing. On the expeditions, however, they are at the bottom of the hierarchy; the climbing sahibs often want fresh meat, and unless the Sherpas can impose their anxieties on the sahibs in this matter, they will have to do the killing.

The notion that it is important not to kill animals on expeditions is only partly "traditional." The issue of killing had been made a focus of the monastic reforms that were going on simultaneously with the development of mountaineering. Although there is in fact a general Buddhist injunction against killing, it is not clear how strictly the Sherpas had adhered to it in the past. We know, for example, that some Sherpas were practicing animal sacrifice in the late nineteenth and early twentieth centuries, in a ritual practice borrowed from the Hindu Nepalis.[65] When the Zatul Rimpoche came from Rumbu in 1919 to dedicate the newly built Tengboche monastery, he told Sherpas that they should not be worshiping a Nepali god (whom they called by a Sherpa name, "Nupki Gyelwu") and should not be killing animals as blood sacrifice. The monks of the newly founded monasteries made the issue of not killing animals a major point in upgrading Sherpa Buddhism. This injunction clearly struck a chord. Nupki Gyelwu worship was discontinued, and by at least the 1930s the Sherpas showed the kind of deep aversion to killing that I observed later in my fieldwork:

The Sherpas have a curious dislike of slaughtering a sheep. They love meat . . . but they jeb at the actual killing of the animal. If no one else will oblige they cast lots amongst themselves, while the loser is usually so upset that he bungles the job and makes two or three half-hearted blows with the kukri instead of one, before severing the beast's head.[66]

A key moment in both impressing the monastic point of view about killing on the early-twentieth-century expedition Sherpas, and demonstrating the value of mobilizing powerful religious figures to control the sahibs, came on the 1922 Everest expedition. The Zatul Rimpoche, who, as we have seen, was none too happy about the whole situation, asked the members of the expedition not to kill within twenty miles of the monastery or on the mountain itself. General Bruce, the leader of the expedition, complied.[67] His compliance is famous, because it is taken to be one of the reasons the next (1924) expedition received permission to climb.[68] At the same time, the Zatul Rimpoche's ability to control these powerful but unruly sahibs was no doubt not lost on the Sherpas.

The Sherpas did not always succeed in getting the sahibs under control in this matter. In the following story, they were partly successful, but then things broke down, producing the feared results:

Mingma Tenzing told a story of leading a Dutch expedition on Makalu [in the seventies]. The Sherpas made the Dutch promise to keep a very clean expedition—no killing animals, no burning garbage [bad smells offend the gods]. And the expedition was totally success-ful—no avalanches, no accidents—success. So when they all got back to base camp the sahibs decided to have a celebration, and they sent down to a nearby village to kill a buffalo. And that night there was a terrible rock and boulder avalanche which would have killed them all—it came all the way down to base camp, only splitting at the last minute and missing them on both sides.[69]

In that same era, the Sherpas were more successful with another expedition:

Sonam Girmi arrived at French Pass to direct the movement of supplies just in time to save the hen from becoming a dinner. Without emotion, but with obvious concern, Sonam told us it would be inappropriate to kill anything on a mountain one is about to climb. His voice was patient; the proper action was clear to him, but long experience had taught him that the sahibs are often unaware of such simple precautions. The chicken went to Tukche with the mailrunner, and rice and cabbage was served for dinner.[70]

Controlling the sahibs in these situations could never be guaranteed, espe-cially—as Sherpa religion would predict—without the backing and authority of a figure like the Zatul Rimpoche. The sahibs' uncontrollability, while maintaining control over the Sherpas, is precisely part of what is meant by saying that they "have power." It may not be an accident that the Sherpas began to have more success with the no-killing rule in the seventies, when the counterculture was in full force in the United States and Europe; there were various shifts in that era toward a more egalitarian relationship with the sahibs that cannot be explored in this paper. But if the question of killing on the mountain was never fully resolved, there is another practice in which the Sherpas had more visible success:

*The Evolution of the Big Base Camp* Puja. If one side of gaining and maintaining religious protection is a matter of avoiding offense to the gods, the other side is, as noted earlier, a matter of actively petitioning their support and pleasing them with offerings. At the very least, one can hum or chant prayers and mantras, and most Sherpas do this both as a daily ritual and in times of fear and danger.[71] The sound of Sherpas humming or chanting their mantras is virtually a standard feature of expeditions, both in camp and on the move. In addition, Sherpas make small offerings to the gods as individuals, or in small groups, to start the day, and carry with them rice blessed by lamas (or, in a pinch, rice over which they themselves recite a blessing) to sprinkle to the gods in times of serious danger:

The next day we moved up to Camp 2. Nima Tenzing had with him a polythene bag full of holy rice which, whilst chanting prayers, he scattered over potentially dangerous-looking crevasses, slopes and seracs. . . . When Nima arrived at Camp 2, he took one look at the tier upon tier of seracs and threw the remainder of the rice in a sweeping gesture at the entire North West face of Kangchenjunga.[72]

Or, in another example, a climber was knocked down and partly pinned down by a falling block of ice and was dug out: "As he left he passed one of the Sherpas, a young kid who looked under twenty, standing over the hole created by the shifting block, chanting a mantra and tossing sacred rice blessed by a lama."[73]

There is a patronizing tone to these anecdotes; it is likely that the sahibs think of practices like this as "superstitious." The fact remains, however, that the Sherpas have not only gained the space for such minor—but to them important—practices; the record shows that they have actually systematically expanded that space over time. In particular, starting (again, perhaps significantly) in about the mid-1970s, the Sherpas began to organize their offering rituals on a larger and more public scale at the base camp and to recruit the sahibs to participate. Ever larger and more serious base camp offering rituals, or *pujas*, are reported in the expedition literature.[74]

At first the Sherpas may have been uncertain about their own (religious) authority to perform *pujas*. Although lay individuals can pray on their own, public rituals are supposed to be led by duly empowered lamas. The religious establishment's claims on this point are very serious—rituals conducted by people not properly empowered are at best empty and ineffectual—just "singing and dancing," as the Sherpas say—or at worst dangerous, angering the gods, who might cause the practitioner to go crazy. Thus, at the first big base camp *puja* I have found in the literature, some Sherpas were reading the prayers seriously, while others were fooling around and laughing.[75]

But a serious approach to Base Camp *puja*s took hold fairly quickly after that, and these large and elaborate events are now a fairly standard part of any major expedition. Sometimes the Sherpas demand quite a bit of cooperation from the sahibs, and—if it is not too inconvenient for them—they usually comply:

[Lopsang, the *sardar*] explained that before we could climb the mountain safely, we had to have a ceremony in which we would raise flags and make offerings of food and drink in honor of the mountain gods. Because this was an inauspicious time in the Tibetan calendar for the making of prayer flags, we would have to wait until September for the flags to be made at the Kathmandu prayer flag factory. Then it would be at least twelve days before the mail runner could return with them. . . . Fortunately, the timing of the ceremony fitted in reasonably well with the timetable I had planned for the climb.[76]

And, while sometimes the sahibs are humoring the Sherpas, at other times there is even a sense of sharing in the benefits of the rituals, if only at the Durkheimian level of promoting social solidarity among all the members of the expedition:

A few of the Sherpas spent an afternoon building a six-foot stone altar on the edge of our camp, standing a pole in the center to serve as a central stringing point for our lines of prayer flags.
A few mornings before we planned to take our first steps on the mountain, we climbed out of bed early and gathered at the altar for the Pujah, a Buddhist blessing ceremony. . . . We didn't comprehend the religious significance the Sherpas did from the ceremony, but it gave us all a chance to feel joined in a team effort.[77]

The fact that Base Camp *puja*s have been established by now for almost a quarter of a century in turn seems to have had relatively long-term effects on the Sherpas' sense of their relationships with their gods. As with the high lamas who were brought around from an initial posture of resistance, so the Tengboche lama is recently quoted as saying, "Before, the gods didn't like climbing, but everything has changed."[78]

In the big Base Camp *puja*s, the Sherpas have found a form for making the various modes of power with which they are dealing work synergistically. They engage the sahibs in the important religious work of pleasing the gods, not just by having the sahibs attend (as in the episode described earlier), but also by asking them to make contributions of food and drink to the offerings (reportedly, up to and including bottles of scotch), which the sahibs seem quite happy to do. What the sahibs perhaps don't realize is that the point of the *puja* is precisely to engage the gods in protecting the Sherpas from the risks created by the sahibs.

Despite everyone's best efforts, however . . .

## Death Happens

It will be recalled that the Sherpas often seem impassive in the face of death on expeditions, and that this triggers various Orientalist responses from the sahibs. I have also noted a move into higher Buddhist practices that was taking place for the Sherpas at the same time as the move into mountaineering. While it is risky to draw too simple a connection between the two developments, the Sherpas themselves clearly sought to pull religion into mountaineering whenever they could. Before death, religion provides ways of transforming power into protection; once a death has occurred, religion has other important things to offer, including ways of handling strong feelings so that one can get on with life.

Even at the level of popular religion, with which all Sherpas are familiar, there is an injunction against exhibiting strong emotions around death, for which there are several rationales. One is that the deceased has not fully departed yet (and this is especially true in the case of violent accidents), and hearing the crying of the living will make it difficult for the deceased to sever attachments and move on. It is also sometimes said that too much crying at funerals will cause blood to rain down, or cause a veil of blood to cover the eyes of the deceased so that he or she cannot find "the road," the way to a (good) rebirth. The issues here are somewhat gendered; in ordinary life women often display intense grieving while (generally) men do not; women at funerals are often reminded by the lamas to stop crying, as hearing such crying keeps the deceased attached to his or her previous life or causes blood to rain down.

These injunctions were amplified by the monks in the newly founded monasteries. Monks in particular are enjoined to smooth out their feelings, as feelings get in the way of both general ritual work and personal spiritual progress. One of the particular benefits of religious training is that it gives one techniques for handling, smoothing out, and letting go of strong personal emotions. If there is anything "oriental" about the Sherpas' apparent nonreactions to sudden death on expeditions, it is closer to the religious emphasis on this kind of inner discipline (and the idea that men are better than women at achieving this kind of discipline) than it is to the idea of fate or reincarnation.

The religious emphasis on inner discipline is also profoundly linked to the issues of the cultural (here, religious) construction of power and agency that are central to this paper. It is by disciplining themselves through meditation and other practices that the lamas gain the powers that allow them to control the gods. The religious model discussed earlier, in which relatively weak laypeople need lamas to control the gods, is founded in turn on this idea that power grows from religious self-discipline, which trained religious practitioners have learned and laypeople have not.

Yet, while this model establishes a series of power differentials, it also embodies a model for overcoming them. Laymen can of course take training and become lamas, but the more general idea that (some) power grows at least in part from self-discipline is meant to apply to all persons and all social relations. When protection fails, and death happens, it is this side of the Tibetan Buddhist construction of power and agency that is brought into play.

In order to see this, let us consider the following incident: I was staying in Khumjung village in 1979 when word came back that a young climbing Sherpa named Ang Phu, of that village, had just been killed on Everest. Ang Phu, whom I did not know personally, had by all accounts been an enormously well-liked young man, and the news sent shock waves through the village. There was much weeping and anger; there was much speculation about what had happened, seizing upon every scrap of information (and misinformation). People could talk and think about nothing else for days.

The day after we heard the news, I went up to Tengboche monastery (a few hours' walk from Khumjung) for a previously scheduled lunch date with the Rimpoche, the head lama. I and several Sherpas were having lunch in the lama's chambers when one of the Rimpoche's servants came in to say that Ang Phu's family had arrived and needed to see him immediately. The group, consisting of the father, who was a village lama (married, as opposed to a monk), a (male) cousin (who counts as a virtual brother), and two sisters, was shown in. I will quote from my fieldnotes, with only minor grammatical changes, to give a sense of the intensity of the event and also my own confusion about it:

Ang Phu's father, cousin, and two sisters came in, the father quite hysterical. He did his prostrations to the lama crying and choking and saying they tell him his son isn't coming back, begging the Rimpoche for a blessing (*molom*). The Rimpoche, however, was quite cool. He told the man to collect himself saying, "You're a *choa* (religious practitioner), you should know better, instead of crying you should read *cho* (sacred text) and calm your family." He then closed his eyes and chanted quietly to himself for two or three minutes (which *was* soothing) and then called for his divination book (*tsi*) and worked out some texts for the father to read.

[People did indeed begin to calm down and pull themselves together. But] I was quite shocked by the lack of *nyingje*—compassion, sympathy, pity—manifested by the lama. At one point he even seemed to crack a joke and laugh. But later another man who had been present said approvingly, this is how high lamas are. If their own mother and father die they simply meditate for five minutes and that's the end of their grief. Too much crying will cause it to rain blood. . . . In response to my saying that the lama showed no *nyingje*, he said that that *was nyingje*.[79]

As the note indicates, I was rather stunned by what I had witnessed. I was upset by the depth of the shock and grief of Ang Phu's family and also by the lama's seeming coldness. The coldness seemed to link up with earlier ideas I had had about the "selfishness" and impersonalness of higher Buddhism,[80] and I was thus bothered as well by the other man's endorsement of the lama's behavior. The event has disturbed me for years, and I have come back to this fieldnote entry many times, putting it into and then taking it out of a variety of other arguments. Here we are in another corner of classic Geertz territory: (the text of) the heavily charged encounter that demands interpretation—*what is being said*? And why was this, for most of the Sherpas present, a "good" and productive encounter?

I think now, in light of the discussions in this paper, that what the lama was doing was *empowering* Ang Phu's family, particularly the father. Virtually every move the lama made can be read as offering some form of power, some sense of agency and control, to people from whom it had been stripped. The lama's own coolness and composure was projected as both a model *of* his own, the correct, inner state ("that's how lamas are") and a model *for* its enactment.[81] Behind the modeling of the correct organization and display of feelings is his authority; he is not merely saying, in effect, "you *could* be this way and feel better," but "you *should* be this way." Further, he reminds the father that he is a *choa*, which itself carries a double charge of empowerment: that the man is *obligated* by his role and training to remember his lessons in inner discipline and public performance, but also that he does have these resources to draw on and the status and (em)power(ment) of being a trained lama, however "small," in the hierarchy. In exactly the same way, and with the same double charge, he reminds the man that he is a father, with both the empowering resources and moral responsibilities of that position. And finally of course there is the practical transfer of religious resources: he gives the man a set of texts to read that will begin the after-death process, that will allow the family to help the deceased move away from attachments to this world, and toward the best possible rebirth that ritual efforts can bring about. He gives the family (as indeed the whole religious system gives the family) the means and the power to do something. This then is the *meaning* (or one of the meanings) of the lama's behavior.

Whether it had the intended *effects*, however, is a different question, posed here not so much in the sense of (re)constituting certain asymmetrical relations and subject positions (although that still lurks in the background) as in the ordinary-language sense of producing the desired results. Some Sherpas may find themselves neither comforted nor empowered by what might be called the monastic or "high religion" model of disciplining the (traumatized) self. Thus, for example, it has become increasingly common for Sherpas who hear of a (Sherpa) death on an expedition to go up to base camp and grieve very openly and demonstratively for their lost relative; to bring a lama to do funeral rites at the camp; or to drag home husbands, brothers, and sons who have survived.[82] Suicides in relation to mountaineering deaths are also not unheard of: The wife of Dawa Tenzing, one of the famous early *sardar*s, is reported to have committed suicide in 1956 upon hearing (mistakenly) that her husband and (correctly) that her son were killed in an avalanche.[83] And in the specific case that we have been discussing, the lama's behavior and its underlying meanings did not speak equally effectively to everyone in the room. As I learned a few days later,

Ang Phu's cousin, who had come to visit the Rimpoche with the father, went up to Everest Base Camp [and went on a rampage]: he kicked over the dinner table and ruined all the food, screamed that he was going to kill the sahibs, and more. Then he jumped into the river near Pangboche and had to be pulled out.[84]

Yet to recognize that the lama's performance did not have the same effect on everyone is not to negate the fundamentally Geertzian point that that performance had certain intended meanings: the modeling and transferring of (would-be) empowerment and agency to people overwhelmed with loss and grief.

### Conclusions: Ironies of Theory

I have argued that Geertz's commitment to "meaning" was radical at the time he first articulated it, and of continuing vital importance; that his most costly move (in retrospect) was seeming to pose issues of meaning in opposition to issues of power; and that later, power-centered theories (especially of the Foucauldian/Saidian sort) worked from the same opposition but flipped it over and excluded issues of meaning. Thus we are now in the ironic situation that the theoretical position generally taken as the more radical is that which excludes an interest in the "meanings"—the desires and intentions, the beliefs and values—of the very subjects on whose behalf the workings of power are exposed.[85]

The general argument of the paper, then, has been a plea for the continuing need in social theory for a rich and complex conception of culture and meaning in the Geertzian sense. But this is not in any way to dismiss the important insights generated by the Foucauldian/Saidian insistence that symbolic orders ("cultures," "discourses") are (part and parcel of) systems of domination and must be studied for their dominating/subjugating effects, both in terms of the (re)construction of subordinate/superordinate subject positions and in terms of the (re)production of regimes of power/knowledge. The first part of this paper was an enactment of a piece of this project, an illustration of sahib Orientalism in Himalayan mountaineering, which has authorized repeatedly risking and costing the lives of people defined as not caring about life.

Yet to show the operations of Orientalism, as Said himself said early on, is to say nothing about the "brute reality" of the "lives, histories, and customs" of those at whom it is directed.[86] If one cares about those lives, and if one imagines, however naively, that there is a possibility of gaining access to them despite the blinders of one's own culture, then one must still make the Geertzian move into "culture" and meaning. In the second half of the paper, then, I tried to show the ways in which Sherpa religion constructs cultural notions of power and agency and the ways in which their construction of power and agency allows them to manage lamas, gods, sahibs, and deep personal grief in ways that are (for many) effective. Neither submitting to power nor "resisting" it in any simple sense, the Sherpas work through it and turn it to their purposes.

There is actually a double layering of theoretical value in Geertz that I have been mining for this discussion. Most obviously, Geertz's methods allow us to read the "texts" of Sherpa culture—in this case religious rituals—for their underlying assumptions—in this case the ways in which Sherpas think about power and agency. But Geertz's framework more generally assumes an "actor" whose subjectivity is both the source and the product of such cultural constructions. It also assumes that understanding "the actor's point of view" is central to the interpretive practice of "thick description." On these and other grounds then, Geertz's theory is particularly open to (nonreductive) questions of "agency"—of how actors formulate needs and desires, plans and schemes, modes of working in and on the world. Just as the work of Foucault is both a cultural/historical interpretation of the changing Western discourse on power *and* a theorization of the workings of power as such, so the work of Geertz provides a model for understanding the cultural construction of "agency" in particular times and places *and* provides one of the more promising points of departure for theorizing agency as such.

## Notes

Thanks to Peter H. Hansen, Tim Taylor, and Lila Abu-Lughod for extremely helpful comments. The fieldwork (1990) most immediately related to the discussions in this paper was supported by funds from various offices at the University of Michigan, for which I am very grateful. Deepest thanks to Clifford Geertz for having been a generous adviser (who also knew when to leave a student alone) and for having remained a good friend and the kind of *zhindak* (boss, patron, protector) the Sherpas would appreciate.

1. Mike Thompson, "Risk," *Mountain* 73 (1980): 44–46, 45.
2. A Sherpa on one of the expeditions died of altitude sickness earlier.
3. *Sahib* is a Hindi term meaning "boss" or "master," or (in address) "sir." Until about the 1970s, the Sherpas used it to both refer to and address the international climbers. The fact that they stopped is part of another piece of this story. But I will continue to use it here as it signals the lingering colonial influence, and the continuing inequality, of the climber-Sherpa relationship, despite the Sherpas' best efforts.
4. See Nicholas B. Dirks, Geoff Eley, and Sherry B. Ortner, eds., introduction to *Culture/Power/History: A Reader in Contemporary Social Theory* (Princeton, 1994).
5. Clifford Geertz, "Religion as a Cultural System," in *The Interpretation of Cultures* (1966; reprint, New York, 1973), 125.
6. Clifford Geertz, *After the Fact: Two Countries, Four Decades, One Anthropologist* (Cambridge, 1995), 43.
7. Clifford Geertz, *Negara: The Theater State in Nineteenth-Century Bali* (Princeton, 1980).
8. Ibid., 123.
9. For an overview of these and other developments within the context of anthropology, see Sherry B. Ortner, "Theory in Anthropology Since the Sixties," *Comparative Studies in Society and History* 26, no. 1 (1984): 126–66.
10. Dirks, Eley, and Ortner, *Culture/Power/History*.
11. Edward M. Said, *Orientalism* (New York, 1979).

12. E.g., Michel Foucault, *History of Sexuality*, vol. 1, trans. Michael Hurley (New York, 1978).

13. Said, *Orientalism*, 3.

14. Sherry B. Ortner, *Life and Death on Mount Everest* (Princeton University Press, forthcoming).

15. Clifford Geertz, "Deep Play: Notes on the Balinese Cockfight," in *Interpretation of Cultures*.

16. Thompson ("Risk," 45) talks about how risk is central to what he calls "the aesthetics of high standard mountaineering." See also Richard G. Mitchell, *Mountain Experience: The Psychology and Sociology of Adventure* (Chicago, 1983), 156–58; Mitchell tries to distinguish between difficulty and danger as motivators in mountaineering and argues that most mountaineers seek the former but not the latter. I was not entirely persuaded by his discussion.

17. Bruce Barcott, "Cliffhangers: The Fatal Descent of the Mountain-Climbing Memoir," *Harper's*, August 1996, 65.

18. Thompson ("Risk," 45) questions the idea that the Sherpas have been in it largely for the money. I disagree with him on this point but must reserve discussion for another context.

19. As I was working on the first draft of this paper in 1995, the death on K2 of Alison Hargreaves, the first woman to climb Mt. Everest without oxygen, was reported on the radio; as I was working on the second draft in 1996, I heard about the Everest disaster with which I opened the paper.

20. Doug Scott, in "Himalayan Climbing: Part Two of a Personal Review," *Mountain* 101 (1985): 32, complained about the lack of good information on Himalayan climbing accidents: "Magazine editors have a responsibility to publish details and statistics of accidents as well as success[es] so we would all know what to expect."

21. Arlene Blum, *Annapurna: A Woman's Place* (San Francisco, 1980), 20.

22. Jon Fleming and Ronald Faux, *Soldiers on Everest: The Joint Army Mountaineering Association–Royal Nepalese Army Mount Everest Expedition, 1976* (London, 1977), 40.

23. Stacy Allison with Peter Carlin, *Beyond the Limits: A Woman's Triumph on Everest* (Boston, 1993), 206.

24. Patrick Morrow, *Beyond Everest: Quest for the Seven Summits* (Camden East, Can., 1986), 63.

25. Quoted in Claudia Glenn Dowling, "Death on the Mountain," *Life*, August 1996, 42.

26. James F. Fisher, *Sherpas: Reflections on Change in Himalayan Nepal* (Berkeley, 1990), 146.

27. Jim Carrier, "Gatekeepers of the Himalaya," *National Geographic*, 6 December 1992, 82.

28. Chris Bonington, *The Everest Years: A Climber's Life* (New York, 1987), 246.

29. Gabriel Chevalley, René Dittert, and Raymond Lambert, *Avant-premières à l'Everest* (n.p., 1953), 162, my translation. A brief note on Sherpa names (one could write a whole essay on the subject): Sherpas usually (but not always) have two "first" names (like *Mingma Dorji*), of which the first (here, *Mingma*) is usually the day of the week on which the person was born (*Mingma* means Tuesday) and the second is a more personal name. In addition, some Sherpa children have *Ang*, which means *child*, attached to their names, and it may stick with them when they grow up (like *Ang Norbu*, in the case of this quote). Sherpas do not traditionally have family or "last" names, although in urban or international settings they will normally use *Sherpa* as a last name, except for members of the Lama clan, who use *Lama*. And finally, the sahibs often—and not entirely surprisingly—confuse the situation further in their writings, so that it is impossible to know

whether the Mingma on expedition A is the same as the Mingma on expedition B, not to mention whether he is the same as a certain Ang Mingma or Mingma Norbu on expedition C. The usage I follow for Sherpa names, then, is to use the full set of names provided in any given text, or by the individual in question.

30. Captain John Noel, *The Story of Everest* (New York, 1927), 157.

31. Paul Bauer, *Kangchenjunga Challenge* (London, 1955), 137, 155; Kenneth Mason, *Abode of Snow: A History of Himalayan Exploration and Mountaineering* (London, 1955), 199. I make no effort to sort the sahibs by ethnicity, as this would mainly reproduce stereotypes.

32. Bauer, *Kangchenjunga Challenge*, 157.

33. Paul Bauer, "Nanga Parbat," *Himalayan Journal* 11 (1939): 103.

34. Klaus Becker Larsen quoted in Walt Unsworth, *Everest: A Mountaineering History* (Boston, 1981), 253.

35. Bauer, *Kangchenjunga Challenge*, 156.

36. Reinhold Messner, *Everest: Expedition to the Ultimate*, trans. Audrey Salkeld (New York, 1979); Ronald Faux, *High Ambition: A Biography of Reinhold Messner* (London, 1982); Unsworth, *Everest: A Mountaineering History*, 470; *San Francisco Chronicle*, 16 June 1978, 25.

37. Brigadier-General Charles Granville Bruce, *The Assault on Mount Everest, 1922* (New York, 1923), 76.

38. Chris Bonington, *Everest the Hard Way* (New York, 1976), 78.

39. Messner, *Everest: Expedition to the Ultimate*, 86.

40. There is of course some variation in Sherpa's reactions. Many may react more strongly to the deaths of other Sherpas than to the deaths of sahibs, but Sherpas in general are also famous for forging close personal relations with at least some sahibs on expeditions and some may react as strongly to the death of a sahib they have come to feel close to as to the death of a Sherpa.

41. Ortner, fieldnotes, August 1990. At the time of this interview with him, he was climbing again but still wanting to stop.

42. Blum, *Annapurna*, 83.

43. Ortner, fieldnotes, August 1990.

44. Ortner, fieldnotes, Fall 1979.

45. For similar arguments about the Tibetans vis-à-vis British Orientalism, see Peter H. Hansen, "The Dancing Lamas of Everest: Cinema, Orientalism, and Anglo-Tibetan Relations in the 1920s," *American Historical Review* 101, no. 3 (1996): 712–47.

46. Sherry B. Ortner, "Resistance and the Problem of Ethnographic Refusal," *Comparative Studies in Society and History* 37, no. 1 (1995): 173–93.

47. These points are worked out more fully in my article "Making Gender: Toward a Feminist, Minority, Postcolonial, Subaltern, etc., Theory of Pratice," in Sherry B. Ortner, *Making Gender: The Politics and Erotics of Culture* (Boston, 1996).

48. Foucault of course said this too but never developed the point.

49. Sherry B. Ortner, *Sherpas Through Their Rituals* (Cambridge, 1978).

50. See also Vincanne Adams, *Tigers of the Snow and Other Virtual Sherpas: An Ethnography of Himalayan Encounters* (Princeton, 1996), on the centrality of this structure.

51. John Blofeld, *The Way of Power: A Practical Guide to the Tantric Mysticism of Tibet* (London, 1970).

52. Sherry B. Ortner, *High Religion: A Cultural and Political History of Sherpa Buddhism* (Princeton, 1989).

53. Ortner, *Life and Death*.
54. Ortner, *High Religion*.
55. Alexander W. Macdonald, "The Lama and the General," *Kailash: A Journal of Himalayan Studies* 1, no. 3 (1973): 230.
56. Ibid., 231; see also Hansen, "Dancing Lamas," for a more detailed discussion of this encounter.
57. Noel, *Story of Everest*, 160. It is difficult to know, without seeing it, whether the mural meant what Noel thought it meant. In standard Tibetan Buddhist iconography, there is often a naked, human-looking figure being trampled under the foot of a god in his ferocious (*takbu*) aspect, but the naked figure in such cases is normally said to represent a demon being subdued by the god. (Why demons are represented in human form in these contexts is another question.) But Noel's interpretation is not implausible either.
58. Tenzing Norgay, *Tiger of the Snows* (New York, 1955), 24; Tenzing was a very religious man, but seems to have held little affection for the monastic establishment and the high lamas. He was sent to Tengboche monastery as a boy, but a monk hit him on the head and he ran away (18). After the Everest triumph, he was approached by monks for a large donation to their monastery, but he refused and turned over some of his earnings to some sort of community fund instead (99).
59. See M. S. Kohli, *Nine atop Everest: Story of the Indian Ascent* (Bombay, 1969), 102; Rick Ridgeway, *The Boldest Dream: The Story of the Twelve Who Climbed Mount Everest* (London, 1979); I also recorded many cases of Sherpas seeking divinations before expeditions. Lama divinations are always somewhat negotiable. As with medical advice in Western culture, if the recipient is dubious about the outcome, other divinations may be sought, or a lama may be asked to redo the original divination with other suppositions. These kinds of negotiations are another aspect of the Sherpas' agency and lack of fatalism in relation to their religion.
60. Thomas Laird, "Mountains as Gods, Mountains as Goals," *Co-Evolution Quarterly* 31 (Fall 1981): 127.
61. See Hansen, "Dancing Lamas."
62. See especially the chapter on offering rituals in Ortner, *Sherpas Through Their Rituals*.
63. Hugh Ruttledge, "In Memoriam: The Late Head Lama of Rongbuk Monastery," *Himalayan Journal* 17 (1952): 159.
64. Another, though more occasional, issue has been the question of stepping on summits. Sherpas have refused to step up themselves (see Kohli, *Nine atop Everest*, 188) and have occasionally tried to get sahibs to hold back, too; see, for example, Jim Curran, *K2: Triumph and Tragedy* (Boston, 1987), 84; Elaine Brook, "Sherpas: The Other Mountaineers," *Mountain* 101 (1985): 37.
65. Kathryn March, "Of People and Naks: The Meaning of High-Altitude Herding among Contemporary Solu Sherpas," *Contributions to Nepalese Studies* 4, no. 2 (1977): 83–97; Ortner, *Life and Death*.
66. H. W. Tilman, *The Seven Mountain-Travel Books* (1938; reprint, Seattle, 1983), 473; see also Tom Weir, *East of Kathmandu* (London, 1955), 104–5. I must own up to my own story, from my first fieldwork in 1966, which is quite resonant with Tilman's. The occasion was my first birthday in the field, and Bobby Paul (my husband at the time, and still a good friend and professional colleague) and I decided to celebrate. We bought a chicken and asked our assistant, Norbu (not his real name), to ask a poor Chhetri man who lived in the village to kill it for dinner—*not*, mind you, to kill it himself. Norbu procrastinated about leaving the house for several hours, and then disappeared for several more hours. He finally returned after dark with the poor dead thing, sullenly

plucked it and chopped it up, bones and all, with a blunt *kukhuri*, so that it was full of bone slivers, and cooked it briefly. My birthday "celebration" consisted of tough bits of treacherous chicken, eaten late at night in a by-then very cold house. We never asked Norbu to have anything killed again.

67. Bruce, *Assault on Mount Everest*.
68. Ian Cameron, *Mountain of the Gods* (New York, 1984), 188; Ruttledge, "In Memoriam," 159. The no-killing rule was actually part of the Dalai Lama's permission for the climb. See Hansen, "Dancing Lamas."
69. Ortner, fieldnotes, August 1990.
70. Andrew Harvard and Todd Thompson, *Mountain of Storms: The American Expeditions to Dhaulagiri, 1969 and 1973* (New York, 1974), 96.
71. Mantras are different from prayers; they are not addressed to gods for a response, but are meant to work automatically, generating both merit and protection directly.
72. Peter Boardman, *Sacred Summits: A Climber's Year* (Seattle, 1982), 116.
73. Dick Bass and Frank Wells with Rick Ridgeway, *Seven Summits* (New York, 1986), 116.
74. *Puja* is the Nepali/Hindi term for any kind of religious ritual. It is now in general use among urban, if not village, Sherpas (replacing the Tibetan/Buddhist *kurim*). It is often written the British colonial way, with an *h* at the end.
75. Bonington, *Everest the Hard Way*, 76.
76. Blum, *Annapurna*, 89–90; see also Bass and Wells, *Seven Summits*, 118.
77. Allison, *Beyond the Limits*, 206. The good effects of the "pujah" on the "team effort" were very short lived. According to Allison, the expedition broke down later into very nasty and self-serving individual behaviors.
78. Carrier, "Gatekeepers of the Himalaya," 84.
79. Ortner, fieldnotes, Fall 1979.
80. Ortner, *Sherpas Through Their Rituals*.
81. The "model of/model for" distinction is from Geertz, "Religion as a Cultural System."
82. Al Burgess and Jim Palmer, *Everest: The Ultimate Challenge* (New York, 1983), 87; Morrow, *Beyond Everest*, 71; Yuichiro Miura with Eric Perlman, *The Man Who Skied Down Everest* (San Francisco, 1978), 117.
83. Messner, *Everest: Expedition to the Ultimate*, 54.
84. Ortner, fieldnotes, Fall 1979.
85. This was precisely the opposition and irony that was operating in the Gananath Obeyesekere-Marshall Sahlins debate. See Ortner, "Making Gender."
86. Said, *Orientalism*, 5.

# Contributors

SHERRY B. ORTNER is Professor of Anthropology at Columbia University. She is currently completing her third book on the Sherpas of Nepal, *Life and Death on Mount Everest: Sherpas and Himalayan Mountaineering* (Princeton University Press). She has also begun a project on the American middle class.

STEPHEN GREENBLATT is Professor of English at Harvard University. He is the author of books on early modern literature and culture, including *Shakespearean Negotiations*, and the general editor of *The Norton Shakespeare*. With Catherine Gallagher, he is currently writing a study of New Historicism.

RENATO I. ROSALDO JR. is Lucie Stern Professor in the Social Sciences at Stanford University. He is the author of *Ilongot Headhunting, 1883–1974* and *Culture and Truth: The Remaking of Social Analysis*, among other books, and is currently doing research on cultural citizenship among Native Americans, Mexicans, and Chicanos in San Jose, California.

WILLIAM H. SEWELL JR. is Max Palevsky Professor of Political Science and History at the University of Chicago. His most recent book is *A Rhetoric of Bourgeois Revolution: The Abbé Sieyes and "What Is the Third Estate?"* He is currently at work on a book on history and social theory.

NATALIE ZEMON DAVIS is Henry Charles Lea Professor of History Emeritus from Princeton University and is currently associated with the University of Toronto. Her most recent book is *Women on the Margins: Three Seventeenth-Century Lives* (Harvard University Press, 1995).

GEORGE E. MARCUS is Professor and Chair of Anthropology at Rice University. Among his many publications are *Writing Culture*, co-edited with James Clifford (University of California Press, 1986), and "A Timely Reading of *Naven*: Gregory Bateson as Oracular Essayist," which appeared in *Representations* 12. Since 1992, he has been the editor of the fin de siècle annual *Late Editions*, published by the University of Chicago Press until the year 2000.

LILA ABU-LUGHOD is Associate Professor of Anthropology and Middle East Studies at New York University. She is the author of *Writing Women's Worlds* (University of California Press, 1993) and the editor of *Remaking Women: Feminism and Modernity in the Middle East*, forthcoming from Princeton University Press. She is currently writing a book on the cultural politics of Egyptian television drama.

# Index

Television: anthropology's role in understanding, 111–14, 122, 128–29; concept of culture and, 123; thick description of, 113–14, 115, 122, 128; in Upper Egyptian village, 114–15, 117, 120–21, 123–25, 129–31

Thick description, 22; Geertz on, 4, 14–16, 17–19, 21, 26, 28, 114; of television, 113–14, 115, 122, 128

Weber, Max, 56–57, 77, 128
Wittgenstein, Ludwig, 33

Zatul Rimpoche, 149, 150, 152

| | |
|---|---|
| Compositor: | Wilsted & Taylor Publishing Services |
| Indexer: | Andrew L. Christenson |
| Text: | 11/13 Baskerville |
| Display: | Baskerville Bold |
| Printer: | Malloy Lithographing, Inc. |
| Binder: | Malloy Lithographing, Inc. |